An Introduction To
The Gospels

An
Introduction
To The
Gospels

Mitchell G. Reddish

Abingdon Press
Nashville

AN INTRODUCTION TO THE GOSPELS

Copyright © 1997 by Abingdon Press

This book is printed on acid-free, recycled paper.

Library of Congress Cataloging-in-Publication Data

Reddish, Mitchell Glenn, 1953–
    An introduction to the Gospels/Mitchell G. Reddish.
        p.   cm.
    Includes bibliographical references and index.
    ISBN 0-687-00448-9 (pbk.: alk. paper)
    1. Bible. N.T. Gospels—Introductions.   I. Title.
BS2555.2.R364   1997
226'.061—dc21

97-5098
CIP

book design by J. S. Laughbaum

97 98 99 00 01 02 03 04 05 06 — 10 9 8 7 6 5 4 3 2 1

MANUFACTURED IN THE UNITED STATES OF AMERICA

To the Big Chill group
a true community of faith
in appreciation for
your support, camaraderie, and hilarity

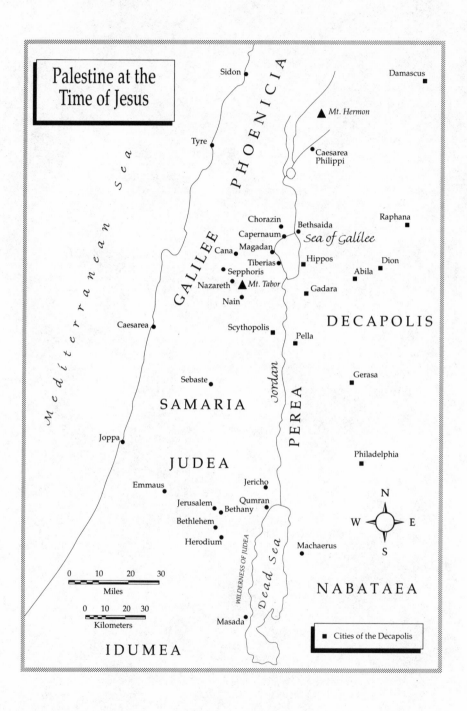

Palestine at the Time of Jesus

Sidon

Damascus

PHOENICIA

▲ Mt. Hermon

Tyre

Caesarea
Philippi

Mediterranean Sea

Chorazin

Raphana

Bethsaida

GALILEE

Capernaum

Sea of Galilee

Magadan

Cana

Hippos

Dion

Tiberias

Abila

Sepphoris

Nazareth ▲ Mt. Tabor

Gadara

Nain

DECAPOLIS

Caesarea

Scythopolis

Pella

Jordan

Gerasa

Sebaste

PEREA

SAMARIA

Joppa

JUDEA

Philadelphia

Emmaus

Jericho

Jerusalem Qumran

Bethany

Bethlehem

Herodium

WILDERNESS OF JUDEA

Machaerus

Dead Sea

| 0 | 10 | 20 | 30 |

Miles

| 0 | 10 | 20 | 30 |

Kilometers

N

W ✦ E

S

■ Cities of the Decapolis

Masada

NABATAEA

IDUMEA

Contents

❖

Preface 9

Chapter 1. The Formation of the Four Gospels 13
  From Oral Traditions to Written Records. 13
  What Is a Gospel?. 18
  The Synoptic Problem 26
  John and the Synoptics 32
  Who Wrote the Gospels?. 34

Chapter 2. The World of the Gospels 44
  The Political World 44
  The Social World. 53
  The Religious World 63

Chapter 3. The Gospel of Mark 73
  Social Setting 73
  Telling the Story 76
  Major Themes in the Gospel of Mark 83
  Outline of the Gospel of Mark. 88
  Reading Guide to the Gospel of Mark. 89

Chapter 4. The Gospel of Matthew 107
  Social Setting 107
  Features of Matthew's Gospel 111
  Major Themes in the Gospel of Matthew 115
  Outline of the Gospel of Matthew. 120
  Reading Guide to the Gospel of Matthew. 121

Chapter 5. The Gospel of Luke 144
  Social Setting 144
  Literary and Stylistic Characteristics. 146

Major Themes in the Gospel of Luke 151
Outline of the Gospel of Luke 156
Reading Guide to the Gospel of Luke 156

Chapter 6. The Gospel of John 180
Social and Historical Origins 180
Literary and Stylistic Characteristics 184
Major Themes in the Gospel of John 189
Outline of the Gospel of John 193
Reading Guide to the Gospel of John 194

Chapter 7. The Other Gospels 214
Beyond the Canonical Gospels 214
The Process of Canonization 230
The Gospels and the Historical Jesus 236

Notes 241

Selected Bibliography 246

Index 251

Preface

❖

The four Gospels—Matthew, Mark, Luke, and John—are usually considered the heart of the New Testament. As someone once commented to me, "The Gospels are the most important part. Everything else in the New Testament is just commentary on the Gospels." Although I would not agree with the latter part of this statement, I would concur that the Gospels are central. Repeatedly, Christians and non-Christians have turned to these works to learn more about the life and teachings of Jesus of Nazareth. For some readers, these works contain the "old, old story" that they have heard from childhood and that continues to shape their lives. Sometimes this familiarity with the Gospel stories is a hindrance rather than a help in clearly hearing the message of the Gospels. Ears have become dulled from "overhearing" the Gospels. For other readers, the Gospels are uncharted territory, containing stories and sayings with which they are unacquainted. For readers from both groups, assistance is often needed to enable them to read and understand these first-century texts.

This book was written to help provide that assistance. It is designed to provide readers with a solid, reliable introduction to the major issues in Gospel studies as well as to give them a concise guide to the contents of the Gospels. As its title indicates, it is an *introduction*. That means first of all that it is not intended to serve as a substitute for the Gospels themselves, but to lead the reader into these texts. The reader should carefully read each of the Gospels in conjunction with the appropriate chapters in this book. To call this study an introduction also means that the book assumes that the reader has had little or no previous academic study of the Gospels. Because the work is written for the nonspecialist, I have tried to keep endnotes to a minimum. Obviously, I am much more indebted to the work of other scholars than is indicated by the few notes to each chapter.

This study begins by discussing the origin, development, and interrelationships of the four Gospels. The second chapter acquaints the reader with the social, political, and religious context out of which the Gospels arose. Chapters 3–6 are the heart of this study. These four chapters deal individually with each of the four New Testament Gospels. These chapters explore the basic introductory issues of each Gospel: date and location of writing, the audience to which the work was addressed, literary characteristics of the Gospel, and distinctive themes in the work. Unfortunately, too often "Introductions to the Gospels" end after discussing these issues and fail to provide sufficient help for a person interested in actually reading the Gospels. This work attempts to alleviate that problem by providing for each Gospel a "Reading Guide," a section-by-section discussion of the contents of that particular Gospel. This Reading Guide is intended to focus the readers' attention on the text of the Gospel and aid them in interpreting the text. Readers are strongly encouraged to read each Gospel in its entirety prior to reading the chapters on each Gospel. In addition, readers should keep a copy of the Gospel open in front of them to read as they work through the Reading Guide.

The final chapter of this study moves beyond the confines of the New Testament canon and examines some of the gospels that are not included in the church's Bible. Most of these works will likely be unfamiliar to the reader. They are a fascinating assortment of diverse traditions about Jesus that circulated in the early centuries of the Christian church. These works are important windows into the formative years of Christianity and occasionally offer us additional insights about the New Testament Gospels.

The basic methodological approach of this study is a literary inquiry into the Gospels. As scholarship has emphasized in the last few decades, the authors of the Gospels were creative writers, each telling his (or her) own distinctive story about Jesus of Nazareth. I have tried to listen to each of these stories and to enter into the story world of each Gospel. In recent years several new approaches to biblical studies (such as narrative criticism, reader-response criticism, rhetorical criticism, and social-scientific criticism) have contributed to our understanding of the literature of the Bible. This work has benefited from insights from these approaches as well.

Several persons deserve my deepest thanks for their assistance in this project: Clyde Fant, my colleague at Stetson University, who graciously and carefully read this manuscript and made numerous corrections and suggestions; my other colleagues in the Department of Religious Studies at Stetson University, who have encouraged and supported my work; Edgar McKnight and Alan Culpepper, who made helpful suggestions in the initial stages of this project; and especially my family—Barbara, Tim, Beth, and Michael—who have been generous and patient in allowing me the time to work on this manuscript.

Mitchell G. Reddish

Chapter 1

❖

The Formation of the Four Gospels

Since the four Gospels—Matthew, Mark, Luke, and John—begin the New Testament, readers often assume that these works were the earliest written products of the Christian church. This assumption is often coupled with the beliefs that the authors of the four Gospels were eyewitnesses of the events they narrate and that the composition of the Gospels was a relatively simple process of preserving in writing what they had seen and heard firsthand. Such assumptions about the Gospels, however, are inaccurate. All the letters of Paul in the New Testament were written prior to any of the Gospels being completed. The authors of the Gospels, or at least the persons responsible for the final form of the Gospels, were almost certainly not eyewitnesses; and the Gospels themselves are the end products of traditions that were transmitted and preserved in various forms, both oral and written.

From Oral Traditions to Written Records

Jesus of Nazareth left behind no written records. He was not an author, but a teacher and preacher. His method of communication was exclusively oral. Furthermore, there is no indication that Jesus expected or desired that his message would be preserved in writing and passed along for generations. He was addressing a first-century audience, dealing with their concerns and situations. The reason his stories and sayings are available to modern readers is that some of his followers considered them important enough to remember and pass on.

These Jesus traditions were almost certainly preserved at first only in oral form. This statement may seem surprising, even incredulous, to readers today. We live in a highly literate society in which the printed media are extremely important. Books, newspapers, magazines, and journals are found in almost every household. Computers, a relatively recent communication tool, present visual representations of words on computer monitors. For many of us, even a trip to the grocery store necessitates a written shopping list, lest we forget the items we need to purchase. First-century Palestine, however, was primarily an oral culture. The ability to read and write was a privilege of the upper class of Palestinian society, as was true of the Mediterranean world in general. Jesus and the crowds to whom he spoke were primarily peasants. They were not a part of the educated elite. The Gospels give scant information about Jesus' education and literacy. The Gospel of Luke contains the story of Jesus as a precocious twelve-year-old engaged in dialogue with the teachers in the Temple. Luke reports, "And all who heard him were amazed at his understanding and his answers" (2:47). If this story is historically accurate, it still tells us nothing about Jesus' formal education. Likewise, the additional statement that "Jesus increased in wisdom and in years, and in divine and human favor" (Luke 2:52) is no evidence for Jesus' ability to read or write. A person can be wise, yet remain uneducated and illiterate.

Later in the Gospel of Luke, Jesus during his ministry in Galilee is described as reading from the scroll of Isaiah in the synagogue at Nazareth, "where he had been brought up" (4:16-30). If this passage is historically authentic, then we certainly have here evidence of Jesus' ability to read. Many scholars, however, have raised questions about the historical reliability of what is described in this passage. Luke 4:16-30 seems to be an expansion of Mark 6:1-6. The Markan text tells of Jesus teaching in the synagogue in his hometown and the ensuing astonishment of his listeners. Mark does not mention, though, that Jesus read in the synagogue. One must, therefore, use the Lukan passage with caution as evidence of Jesus' literacy.

On the other hand, a passage in the Gospel of John seems to imply that Jesus was educated. In reporting one of Jesus' teaching episodes during his ministry, the Gospel reports that people were astonished at his teaching, saying, "How does this man have such learning, when he has never been taught?" (7:15). The phrase translated in the NRSV as "have such learning" literally means "know what is written" or "know letters." In the context of first-century Judaism, the people's question concerns Jesus' familiarity with and knowledge of the Jewish law. They are puzzled about how one could have such a deep understanding of the scripture, yet lack formal scribal training in the law (cf. Mark 1:22).

The only passage in the New Testament that speaks about Jesus writing anything is also in John. The story of the woman who is caught in adultery, John 7:53–8:11 (the passage is textually suspect), states that twice during the confrontation with the religious leaders who brought the woman to Jesus, he "bent down and wrote with his finger on the ground" (8:6, 8). What he wrote is not known. Once again, one cannot draw any certain conclusions from this text about Jesus' educational or literacy level. Reviewing all the evidence, the safest conclusion about Jesus is that he possibly, perhaps even probably, had rudimentary skills in reading and writing. Any claims beyond that are mere speculation.

The New Testament likewise provides us little information about the educational background of Jesus' followers. The book of Acts records the amazement of the Jewish leaders in Jerusalem at the boldness of the disciples Peter and John in their teaching and preaching. They considered the two to be "uneducated and ordinary men" (Acts 4:13). Like the description of Jesus in John 7:15, this statement probably means that they lacked formal scribal training in the Jewish scriptures. Aside from this episode, the New Testament provides no information about the educational sophistication of Jesus' disciples. As will be discussed later, none of the Gospels was likely written by a disciple of Jesus, so these literary documents are no evidence of the disciples' literary skills. What the Gospels do tell us about the earliest followers of Jesus is that they were almost all working-class persons—fishermen, tax collectors, housewives. In ancient Palestine formal education for children was rare. Shaye Cohen claims that "in all likelihood elementary education was the responsibility of the family" and "generally in the ancient world elementary education did not go beyond paternal instruction in a craft."[1] Thus most people in the ancient world never became skilled at reading and writing, although quite a few probably had rudimentary skills necessary for business transactions.[2]

The basic oral nature of ancient Mediterranean societies, then, explains why the earliest traditions about Jesus would have been oral traditions. Stories about Jesus and collections of his teachings would have been passed along from one person to the next and from one community to another. These oral traditions would have been used in many different ways in the early Christian communities. When Jesus' followers were preaching to outsiders, they would have told stories about Jesus. When they were teaching new converts about their faith, they would have recounted Jesus' sayings and teachings. When controversies arose among the early Christians, someone would have remembered an incident in the life of Jesus or one of his teachings that would help guide the church. In each of these settings, as well as others, the early Christian community preserved, shaped, and passed on events and teachings from the life of Jesus.

Oral traditions are more fluid, that is, less fixed, than written traditions. As stories are told and retold they are intentionally and unintentionally shaped and reshaped by the tellers. Different settings for the tradition require changes in the form and content of the tradition. For example, a student who attends a campus lecture will describe that lecture in an informal conversation with her friends differently from the way that she would report on the lecture to her classmates in a formal setting. If the student were to describe the lecture to another group of friends a week later, the description would be different still. Thus both in new situations and over time, oral traditions change. Such variations in traditions can be seen in the Gospels where different versions of sayings and events occur (for example, compare the different versions of Jesus' teachings on divorce in Matt 5:31-32; 19:9; Mark 10:11-12; and Luke 16:18). Some of these variations arose during the oral stages of the tradition, while other changes arose during the written stages of the material.

As the traditions about Jesus were passed on, not only did changes in the material occur, but selectivity naturally took place. The sayings and stories with which the immediate hearers identified or which addressed their concerns or needs were the traditions that were preserved. Many of the teachings and activities of Jesus were lost as they fell into disuse and were forgotten. Note the comment of the author of the Gospel of John: "But there are also many other things that Jesus did; if every one of them were written down, I suppose that the world itself could not contain the books that would be written" (21:25). The book of Acts contains an example of a saying of Jesus that is not found in any Gospel but was remembered by the early Christian community: "It is more blessed to give than to receive" (Acts 20:35).

Eventually, the early Christian community began to preserve in written form some of the Jesus traditions. By the end of the first century, all four Gospels presently in the canon had been written. Other collections of sayings of Jesus were likely in existence as well. These additional collections included such works as the Q document and the *Gospel of Thomas*, both of which will be discussed later. If at first the church had been content with oral traditions, why did it begin to produce written records?

Several factors seem to have contributed to the move from oral to written traditions. First, the earliest followers of Jesus apparently expected him to return to earth very soon after his death and resurrection to bring to fulfillment the coming reign of God. Even the apostle Paul expected Jesus' return shortly, likely within his own lifetime. As long as the early Christians operated under that expectation, little need existed for preserving the traditions of Jesus for the long term. Why worry about preserving material for future generations when the end was expected during the current generation? As the years passed and the expected imminent return of Jesus did not occur, the early church realized the need for a more permanent preservation of the traditions.

A second factor contributing to the need for written records was the death of the earliest followers of Jesus. As long as eyewitnesses of the life of Jesus were alive, they served somewhat as a verification of the authenticity of stories about Jesus. If questions arose about what Jesus said or did, someone could ask one of his disciples. When they began to die, however, another authoritative source was needed. Written records helped fill this need.

The missionary needs of the early church was a third factor that likely led to the development of written records about Jesus. As the early Christians moved out beyond Palestine and scattered throughout the Mediterranean world spreading their message about Jesus and making converts to the Christian faith, they needed resources to use to teach the new converts about Christian beliefs and practices. The collected Jesus traditions would have been a valuable educational resource for the church.

The growth of the Christian movement contributed to a fourth reason for the written collections of Jesus traditions. Alternate understandings of Jesus and the Christian faith began to arise and compete with each other. What were the acceptable views about Jesus and his teachings? Which traditions about Jesus or interpretations of Jesus were valid? The four canonical Gospels helped answer these questions, although they did not always provide the same answers. These four Gospels represent four different interpretations of the life of Jesus. They helped shape the early Christians' view of Jesus and eventually were seen as the orthodox or correct understanding of Jesus.

These factors, along with others, resulted in the formation of written records about Jesus. One should not assume, however, that an orderly progression occurred from oral traditions to written records. On the contrary, even after written Gospels appeared, they struggled for recognition and authority alongside the oral traditions. For example, Papias, an early bishop in the church in Asia Minor (ca. 60–130 CE), is quoted by the fourth-century church historian Eusebius as saying, "For I did not suppose that information from books would help me so much as the word of a living and surviving voice."[3] Even after the written Gospels appeared, then, some church leaders preferred the oral traditions over the written records about Jesus.

Thus the development of the New Testament Gospels was the result of a long and circuitous process. Initially oral traditions were shaped, altered, passed along, reshaped, and used in a variety of ways and situations. Written collections of sayings and/or stories eventually appeared, competing in some instances with oral traditions, but finally gaining dominance over oral records. In the New Testament, the final form of these Jesus traditions was the Gospels.

What Is a Gospel?

For the person familiar with the New Testament, the answer to the question "What is a Gospel?" might seem obvious: a Gospel is one of the four writings in the New Testament that describe the life and teachings of Jesus of Nazareth. That answer is true, but it is not sufficient because it does not tell us what kind of writings the Gospels are. Furthermore, it limits the term *gospel* to the New Testament writings alone. The Greek word *euangelion*, translated as "gospel," means "good news." This word was used among the ancient Greeks for the announcement of military victories or other instances of good fortune. Inscriptions from the Roman imperial period apply the word *euangelion* to the life and activities of the emperor. The Priene inscription of 9 BCE, for example, declares that the birthday of Caesar Augustus was for the world "the beginning of his good messages [or 'good news']."[4]

For the early Christians the story of Jesus was the "good news" that they proclaimed to the world. In the New Testament, particularly in the writings of Paul, *euangelion* is used to describe the message about Jesus that was the content of the church's preaching and teaching. The Gospel of Mark, for example, opens with the statement, "The beginning of the good news (*euangelion*) of Jesus Christ." When written works describing the life and teachings of Jesus began to appear, the word *euangelion* was a fitting designation for these works. In this way the word *gospel* came to be used to describe certain writings that circulated in the Christian communities.

An examination of the various works labeled "gospels" in the early church reveals that the term was applied to works with widely differing forms and contents. Some "gospels," like the four in the New Testament, are primarily narrative works, containing stories about Jesus and his teachings. Other "gospels," such as the *Gospel of Thomas*, are collections of sayings attributed to Jesus, with little or no narrative material connecting the sayings. Are all of these works appropriately designated "gospels"?

On that question scholars disagree. Some scholars argue that the canonical Gospels should define the characteristics of the gospel genre. Those who follow this approach often conclude that gospels are narratives that provide information about the life, teachings, and activities of Jesus of Nazareth. One recent definition of the genre of the canonical Gospels, for instance, states, "A Gospel is a narrative, fashioned out of selected traditions, that focuses on the activity and speech of Jesus as a way to reveal his character and develops a dramatic plot that culminates in the stories of his passion and resurrection."[5] This definition virtually eliminates any of the noncanonical gospels from being considered as authentic gospels. Some are excluded because they are not narratives but collections of sayings or dialogues (such as the *Gospel of Thomas* and the *Gospel of Mary*); others are excluded because even though they contain narrative materials they focus only on one aspect of the life of Jesus rather than on his entire life and death. Examples of the latter type would be the *Infancy Gospel of Thomas* and the *Protevangelium of James*. In chapter 7 of this book we will raise again the question of the appropriateness of the term *gospel* for these works that are not a part of the canon and discuss the contents of some of them. Because the focus of our study, however, is the canonical Gospels, we will concentrate on the use of the word *gospel* as it applies to them.

Precritical reading of the Gospels viewed them as historical writings about Jesus or as biographies of Jesus. Such readers assumed that the material in the Gospels was historically accurate and that the task of the Gospel writers had been to transmit faithfully the historical details about the life and teachings of Jesus. According to this view, the writers exercised very little creative control over the works they produced. With the rise of new approaches to the study of the Gospels in the twentieth century, scholars began to reach new conclusions about the Gospels. Using the approach of source criticism, scholars demonstrated that the Gospels were not created *ex nihilo* (out of nothing) but were dependent upon earlier source materials. Form criticism revealed that behind the written Gospels stood oral traditions that circulated in set forms or patterns and that became the basis for much of the Gospels. Redaction critics discovered that the Gospel writers were not merely collectors and transmitters of traditions they had received, but were also creative editors (redactors), who arranged, altered, and shaped the traditions in order to present a particular understanding of Jesus and his teachings. In other words, scholars began to recognize that the Gospels were not simply historical accounts, but were a special type of literature.

But to what type of literature do the Gospels belong? If they are not history, at least not in the modern sense of the term, then what are they? During most of this century the dominant answer has been that the Gospels are in a class by themselves; they represent a new literary genre. According to this view, the author of the Gospel of Mark, the first Gospel to be written, produced a new kind of literature, unlike any writing that had been published before. Mark basically expanded and preserved in writing the *kerygma*, the preaching, of the early church. The core element of the kerygma of the church was the proclamation of the death and resurrection of Jesus. Mark took these stories and added to them oral traditions about the life and teachings of Jesus, resulting in a literary genre unparalleled in the ancient world.

Recently more and more scholars have become dissatisfied with this understanding of the Gospel genre. They argue that although the Gospels are not exactly like other writings of the ancient world, they do bear enough resemblances to certain types of ancient literature to call into question the claim that the Gospels are a unique type of literature. What then are the predecessors of the Gospels? What are their literary role models?

Scholars have focused on ancient biographies as the best parallels to the canonical Gospels. Examples of pre-Christian Greco-Roman biographies include Xenophon's *Memorabilia* and Isocrates' *Evagoras*. Later examples include Suetonius' *Lives of the Twelve Caesars* and Philostratus' *Life of Apollonius of Tyana*. Charles Talbert, whose research has facilitated the quest for finding the genre of the Gospels, has defined ancient biography as "prose narration about a person's life, presenting supposedly historical facts which are selected to reveal the character or essence of the individual, often with the purpose of affecting the behavior of the reader."[6] In biographies the activities, accomplishments, and teachings of an individual often were presented to dispel erroneous understandings of the person and to present a model that was to be followed by the readers. David Aune, another proponent of the view that the Gospels are biographies, notes that Greco-Roman biographies are of several types and that the Gospels are not exactly parallel to any of the Greco-Roman biographies. He argues that the Gospels represent an adaptation of ancient Greco-Roman biographies.[7] The Gospel writers, then, roughly followed a literary convention that would have been familiar to first-century readers. The earliest readers of the Gospels likely would have viewed the works as biographical, as accounts of the life of Jesus.

One must be cautious, however, in too quickly identifying the Gospels as biographies. Modern biographies are different from ancient biographies. Modern biographers are usually interested in portraying the psychological development of an individual and the factors that influenced and shaped a person's character and development. Such were not concerns of ancient biographers. Furthermore, even though ancient biographers wrote with historical intentions, ancient understandings of history and the methods and sources available to them for determining historical accuracy were different from that of modern writers. A certain amount of fiction and exaggeration was allowed and even expected in ancient biographies. Since ancient biographers and historians had little access to the speeches and sayings of their subjects, an accepted technique was to create speeches that were deemed appropriate to the occasion. For example, Thucydides, a Greek historian of the fifth century BCE, describes how he used speeches. Thucydides was one of the more scrupulous historians according to modern historiographical standards, but even he states that at times he resorted to creating speeches that were suited to the speaker and the situation. Thucydides wrote:

> With reference to the speeches in this history, some were delivered before the war began, others while it was going on; some I heard myself, others I got from various quarters; it was in all cases difficult to carry them word for word in one's memory, so my habit has been to make the speakers say what was in my opinion demanded of them by the various occasions, of course adhering as closely as possible to the general sense of what they really said.[8]

Other ancient writers were even more prone to use fiction in their works in various ways. What this means for us as modern readers of ancient biographies, including the Gospels, is that we should not expect the same concern for historical reliability and the same standards of historiography to be present in these ancient works as are found in modern scholarly writings. Thus even though the Gospel writers may have written what they supposed to be historically accurate, there is no guarantee that the events or details described by the evangelists are in actuality historically correct. Perhaps an example from one of the Gospels would help clarify this point. In the Gospel of Luke, the author describes the birth of Jesus as occurring in connection with a census that was taken "while Quirinius was governor of Syria" (2:2). Elsewhere Luke implies that Jesus was born during the reign of Herod the Great or, at the latest, within a year after his death.[9] Herod died in 4 BCE; Quirinius was not governor or legate of Syria until 6 CE Obviously Jesus could not have been born during the reign of Herod (which the Gospel of Matthew explicitly says) and during the rule of Quirinius. Luke presented this information as historical fact. Luke likely supposed that the information was historically accurate. Luke's *intention* to present historical information, however, was thwarted by faulty data.

Another characteristic of ancient biographies must be kept in mind when we read the Gospels. Ancient biographies were often written in order to praise or laud an individual. Stories were selected and edited to present a particular view or interpretation of the person, at times for the purpose of presenting a model for others to follow or for correcting erroneous views or misunderstandings about the person. With the Gospels a similar situation occurred. The Gospel writers were not interested in simply writing down all the traditions about Jesus they could find. Rather their task was to present to their readers a specific interpretation of who Jesus was. Their works are not "objective" historical accounts (no account is ever bias-free), but rather are narratives shaped to reveal particular understandings of Jesus. The Gospels are theological works as much as or more than they are historical works. The evangelists selected from the traditions available to them the stories and teachings of Jesus that were compatible with their understandings of him. They often reshaped and retold these traditions in order to highlight or downplay certain aspects of the life and teachings of Jesus. The Gospels then can best be understood as theologically interpreted history.

The difference between an objective, historical account of the life of Jesus and what one finds in the Gospels has often been described as the difference between a photograph and a painting. Suppose one wanted to capture a likeness of a person. One could use camera and film to take a photograph of that person. Assuming that one's photography skills are acceptable and the film and camera perform satisfactorily, one should end up with a good photographic representation of the subject. Anyone who sees the photograph should be able to recognize the person from it. On the other hand, one could choose to invite an artist to paint a portrait of the person. The artist could spend some time getting to know the person and then decide to paint an impressionistic portrait. Perhaps the artist discovers that the person is very insightful and decides to paint the person with very large eyes. Maybe the person is a good listener, always attentive to people and their needs. The artist then may decide to portray the person with prominent ears to symbolize this. When completed, the artist's portrait of the person may not look at all like the photograph that was taken. The artist has exercised artistic license to present a particular understanding of the person. The artist has used paint and canvas to interpret who the person is. Is the artist's portrait any less true than the photograph? No, assuming that the artist has correctly understood and portrayed the "true" personality and identity of the person. In many ways the portrait is a better "likeness" of the person than the photograph is.

We need to view the Gospels as portraits rather than as photographs. In some cases what they present may not correspond to what actually happened, just as a portrait may not always look like a photograph. The Gospel writers, like portrait artists, were interested in sharing with their readers their understanding of the significance of the life and teachings of Jesus. As we shall see, the "portraits" of Jesus in the four Gospels are each different. No two Gospel writers tell the story of Jesus in the same way; each interpreted Jesus differently.

Because the Gospels are narratives or stories about Jesus, often the appropriate questions to ask of the text are literary rather than historical questions. Materials may be arranged or structured in a certain way not because the events actually happened in that order, but because the author chose to arrange them in that way for literary reasons. When we read the Gospels, we need to ask questions about narrative plot, that is, how the events in the story are connected. The plot is what provides order to the story. It keeps the story moving and provides an explanation for why events happen. We should also examine the characters in the story. Who are the major and minor characters? How does the author present these characters? What roles do they play? Are they sympathetic or antagonistic? What do they contribute to the story? When we read the Gospels as narratives rather than history, we should pay attention also to the settings in the story. Where and when do events happen in the story? Of what significance are these settings? For example, why do the resurrection appearances of Jesus in Matthew occur in Galilee while in Luke they occur in or around Jerusalem? In addition to what the authors tell us—that is, the contents of their story—we also need to take note of how the authors tell their story. What rhetorical or literary devices do they use to shape their presentations of the material? Such techniques might include repetition of words or phrases, the use of irony, symbolism, foreshadowing, echoing, intercalation ("sandwiching" one story within another), and juxtaposition.

Because we view the Gospels, then, as the products of creative authors or storytellers, we learn to listen to the distinctive stories that each author is telling. We must resist the temptation to weave all four Gospels together into one unified story. To do so would be to do a grave disservice to the Gospel writers. Mark does not tell the same story that Matthew does. Matthew does not narrate the same story that Luke does. John tells an even different story yet. For those who are familiar with the Gospels, perhaps through years of hearing or reading the Gospels in the context of worship or church study, the task of hearing the distinctive voice of each Gospel writer is especially difficult. One begins to fill in Mark's shorter account with scenes from Matthew or Luke. Or one interprets stories in Luke with the aid of information from John. Disparate or contradictory information from various Gospels is often harmonized, blended together into a "homogenized" Gospel. This process takes place often unintentionally in the mind of the reader because he or she is so familiar with the stories of the Gospels.

An illustration of how easily this blending of accounts occurs is the popularized retelling of the story of the birth of Jesus. In recounting the Christmas story, people usually include Joseph and Mary and their trip to Bethlehem, the angels, the three Magi, shepherds, a stable, a manger, the innkeeper, the animals in the stable, Herod and his attempt to kill the baby Jesus, and several other details. If asked to indicate whether these items are found in Matthew or Luke, most people would likely be puzzled. They assume all the material is contained in both Gospels. (Some of the information, in fact, is not found in any Gospel but comes from later church tradition. The enumeration of three wise men and the presence of animals at the birth of Jesus are examples of such elaboration.) What has happened is that people have melded together the Lukan and Matthean nativity stories into one account. By so doing, they have obliterated the distinctives of each narrative.

The desire to blend the various Gospels into one story is understandable. The inconsistencies, variations, and contradictions among the four Gospels can create theological and historical difficulties, especially for persons who view the Gospels as completely accurate historical documents. These differences are not problems noticed only recently by critical scholars. When the four Gospels were brought together during the second century, church leaders began to notice these variations. The critics of the church noticed them, also, and used these contradictions and inconsistencies to argue against the validity of the Christian faith.

Faced with this problem, what options did the church have? It could have decided that only one Gospel was the correct version. The other three would then be dismissed as nonauthoritative. This was the route taken by Marcion, a Christian of the second century, who rejected all the Gospels except the Gospel of Luke, which he heavily edited. Fortunately, the church refused to follow Marcion. Another option the church had was to weave one Gospel from all four. Tatian, also in the second century, accomplished this task with the production of the *Diatessaron*, a continuous narrative of the life of Jesus. (The title "Diatessaron" literally means "through [the] four [Gospels]".)[10] Although popular for a while, particularly in Syria, Tatian's work eventually fell into disuse.

Rather than follow the path of Marcion or Tatian, the Christian church ultimately opted to keep all four Gospels—Matthew, Mark, Luke, and John—as a part of its sacred texts, in spite of, or perhaps even because of, their differences and contradictions. The church wisely realized that to accept either of the other two options would mean that the church would lose more than it would gain. The church valued the distinctiveness of the four Gospels. Each had something different to say about Jesus. From the church's viewpoint, no one Gospel completely interpreted the mission and message of Jesus. The church valued the multifaceted witness to Jesus presented through the four Gospels.

The intentional preservation of four different Gospels by the early church imposes some interpretive restraints on us as we read the Gospels. First, we must resist the temptation to harmonize, to force all the Gospels into one chronological, historical, or theological mold. If the early church could live with the inconsistencies, then so should the modern reader.

Second, we must allow each Gospel to tell its own story of Jesus. The Gospel writers were creative, individual writers. We must listen to each story for its own presentation of Jesus of Nazareth.

The approach to the Gospels that we take in this book follows that path. We will view the Gospels primarily as narratives about Jesus, told with a theological purpose. We will listen for the distinctive story that each Gospel writer tells. We will not be so much concerned about historical questions as we will about literary and theological questions. To return to our earlier analogy, we will be examining four different portraits of Jesus, rather than looking for one photograph. Some readers may be hesitant to approach the Gospels in this way, feeling that the historical questions are the most important ones to answer. Keep in mind, however, that even for the church, the importance of the Gospels has not been so much the "facts" they present about Jesus but their interpretation of his significance. It is this interpretation that we are looking for. We will be asking, "How do the four Gospels present the story of Jesus?"

The Synoptic Problem

Through the centuries readers of the four Gospels have noticed that when placed alongside one another, three of the Gospels—Matthew, Mark, and Luke—are similar, whereas the other Gospel, John, is vastly different. Matthew, Mark, and Luke follow basically the same order in their presentation of Jesus; they tell many of the same stories; they contain similar sayings of Jesus, at times word for word. Because of these similarities in content and arrangement, the first three Gospels in the New Testament are often called the synoptic Gospels. ("Synoptic" means "to view together," that is, to have the same point of view.)

Closer examination of the synoptic Gospels yields several conclusions. First, not only are similarities present among all three Gospels, but in some cases the similarities are limited to only two Gospels. Matthew and Mark may contain information not found in Luke or they may convey the information in a different way than Luke does. Or Luke and Mark may contain similar material that is missing or different from Matthew. Often Matthew and Luke contain similar traditions that are absent from Mark.

Furthermore, Matthew often presents material that is not found in either Mark or Luke. Likewise Luke contains material that is unique to that Gospel.

How do we account for these similarities and at the same time explain the differences? Were all the Gospel writers dependent upon a common source or sources? That explanation would account for the material common to all three but would not explain the differences among the Gospels. Did they copy from one another? If so, which Gospel was the common source? Why do Matthew and Luke at times disagree with Mark's presentation? What about material unique to one of the Gospels? Where did it come from? The difficulty expressed by these questions comprises what scholars call the synoptic problem.

Due to the close similarity of certain passages in the synoptic Gospels (verbatim in some instances), almost all scholars are convinced that the best explanation is one of literary dependence. Oral traditions are more fluid, that is, less fixed, than written traditions. For that reason common dependence on oral traditions would not explain the high degree of similarity among the Gospels. Assuming literary dependence of one Gospel on another, the question then is, which Gospel was used as a source for the others? Raymond F. Collins has demonstrated how wide an array of possible answers to this question could be proposed. He illustrates eighteen different possibilities:[11]

A dependence of a second Gospel on a first, and of a third on the second:

Mt	Mt	Mk	Mk	Lk	Lk
↓	↓	↓	↓	↓	↓
Mk	Lk	Mt	Lk	Mt	Mk
↓	↓	↓	↓	↓	↓
Lk	Mk	Lk	Mt	Mk	Mt

A dependence of two Gospels on a first:

Mt	Mk	Lk
↙ ↘	↙ ↘	↙ ↘
Mk Lk	Mt Lk	Mt Mk

A dependence of one Gospel on both of the others:

A dependence of a second Gospel on the first, with the third depending on both the second and the first:

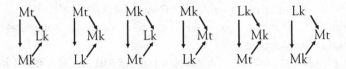

In the fifth century Augustine argued that Matthew was the first Gospel written, that Mark borrowed from and condensed Matthew, and that Luke then used both Matthew and Mark. This view continued to hold sway for several centuries. In 1789 the German scholar J. J. Griesbach agreed with Augustine that Matthew was written first but he argued that Luke was written second, based on Matthew, and that Mark borrowed from Matthew and Luke. In recent years the Griesbach hypothesis (sometimes called the "Two-Gospel Hypothesis") has gained support from a minority of New Testament scholars, most notably W. R. Farmer.[12] Supporters of the Griesbach hypothesis argue that this proposal explains the agreements among all three Gospels, explains why Matthew and Luke are often in agreement against Mark (Luke used Matthew; in these places Mark opted not to follow them) and also explains the agreements between Mark and Matthew and between Mark and Luke (Mark used both of them).

Although the Griesbach hypothesis is appealing due to its simplicity, most scholars do not accept this solution to the synoptic problem. The Griesbach hypothesis does provide explanations for some problems, but at the same time, it appears to create even more serious problems. For example, if Mark is dependent on Matthew, why would Mark opt to omit from his account such major sections of Matthew as the birth narratives, the Sermon on the Mount, and the resurrection appearance stories? Also, if Luke is dependent on Matthew, how does one convincingly explain major differences between those two Gospels, as in the case of the totally different birth stories of Jesus? Furthermore, since very little of Mark is not contained already in Matthew and Luke, why would Mark have bothered to write his Gospel and present such little new information?

For these and other reasons, most New Testament scholars today support the idea of the priority of Mark. The first person to argue this position was Karl Lachmann in 1835. He was soon supported in this view by others such as Hermann Weisse and H. J. Holtzmann. The claim that Mark was the first Gospel written and was subsequently used by Matthew and Luke arose to help explain material common to all three Gospels. Several arguments are used to support this view.

First, both Matthew and Luke appear to follow the order of Mark's Gospel. When they do diverge from Mark's arrangement, they never do so in the same manner and they always return to Mark's order after inserting additional material. Furthermore, Matthew and Luke agree in their arrangement only in the places where they are following Mark. For example, Matthew and Luke both contain sayings similar to those in Matthew's Sermon on the Mount (not found in Mark), yet they have arranged them and placed them in their Gospels very differently.

Second, almost all of Mark's Gospel is contained in Matthew or Luke. Matthew reproduces almost 90 percent of Mark; Luke includes around 50 percent of Mark. Only three or four of Mark's pericopes (small units of material) do not appear in one of the other two Synoptics. It is easier to believe that Matthew and Luke expanded Mark than to accept that Mark would have omitted so much material contained in Matthew and Luke.

Third, when parallel passages are examined, reasons can more easily be given to explain why Matthew or Luke would have altered Mark than why Mark would have altered Matthew or Luke. Included in this argument would be grammatical, stylistic, and content changes. Compared to Matthew and Luke, the writing style of Mark is rough and its grammar is awkward and poor. Matthew and Luke smooth these out. Mark, for example, often inelegantly connects sentences by the word "and" (*kai* in Greek). Matthew and Luke omit many of these. Particular words or phrases are changed by Matthew and Luke to make them more acceptable to their readers. For example, Mark contains Latin or Aramaic words that Matthew and Luke omit (cf. Mark 5:41 with Matt 9:25 and Luke 8:54; and Mark 7:11 with Matt 15:5). In some places Matthew and/or Luke change words or phrases to make them less theologically offensive. Mark 6:5 tells that in Jesus' own hometown "he could do no deed of power there." The text of Matthew states, "He did not do many deeds of power there" (13:58), thus softening the negative description of Jesus' work.

If Mark was written first then used by Matthew and Luke, as the proponents of Markan priority argue, this would explain the agreements among all three Gospels. Yet, how does one account for the places where Matthew and Luke contain similar material that is lacking in Mark or is told differently in Mark? In order to deal with this problem, scholars have proposed that Matthew and Luke relied upon another source, which they designate Q (possibly derived from the German word *Quelle*, meaning "source," although disagreement exists over this derivation). No copies of Q are extant today. This document was likely a written collection of sayings of Jesus interspersed with a few narrative sections, such as the accounts of the preaching of John the Baptist (Luke 3:7-9, 16-17), the temptation story (Luke 4:1-13), and the story of the healing of the centurion's slave (Luke 7:1-10). It contained no birth story, baptismal narrative, or accounts of Jesus' death and resurrection. Although some scholars disagree, one popular version of the Q theory holds that this hypothetical source was written in Greek in Palestine or Syria around 50–60 CE. It likely reflects the views of an apocalyptic version of Jewish Christianity. Most scholars conclude that Luke has preserved the order and the wording of Q in most cases better than Matthew has. (For this reason the Q material is normally cited according to the Lukan form.)

How do scholars reconstruct this hypothetical document? Since Q represents a common source used by Matthew and Luke but not used by Mark, any material that is found in Matthew and Luke but is absent from Mark is likely Q material. Conclusions about Q based on this type of approach are the most reliable. However, in some cases Q likely contained some sayings that are independently attested in the Gospel of Mark. To assume that Mark and Q never overlapped would be unrealistic. Evidence that similar material was in Q and Mark is found in the presence of several doublets, that is, duplicate versions of sayings that are found twice in Matthew and/or Luke. In these cases, Matthew and Luke would have derived one version of the saying from Mark; the other version they would have taken from Q. (An example of one such doublet is Matt 13:12 and Luke 8:18, derived from Mark; and Matt 25:29 and Luke 19:26, derived from Q). Quite possibly some of the material that is unique to Matthew or Luke is derived from Q, assuming that either evangelist could have omitted some Q material that the other Gospel writer chose to include. They certainly followed this practice in their use of the Markan material.

Reconstruction of the contents of Q based on this latter approach is rather speculative, however.

What might the contents of Q have looked like? Various reconstructions have been proposed. The following outline of the contents of Q by John Kloppenborg gives a good idea of the possible contents of the Q document:[13]

(1) John's preaching of the Coming One	Q 3:7-9, 16-17
(2) The temptation of Jesus	Q 4:1-13
(3) Jesus' inaugural sermon	Q 6:20b-49
(4) John, Jesus and "this generation"	Q 7:1-10, 18-28; (16:16); 7:31-35
(5) Discipleship and mission	Q 9:57-62; 10:2-24
(6) On prayer	Q 11:2-4, 9-13
(7) Controversies with Israel	Q 11:14-52
(8) On fearless preaching	Q 12:2-12
(9) On anxiety over material needs	Q 12:(13-14, 16-21), 22-31, 33-34
(10) Preparedness for the end	Q 12:39-59
(11) Two parables of growth	Q 13:18-19, 20-21
(12) The two ways	Q 13:24-30, 34-35; 14:16-24, 26-27; 17:33; 14:33-34
(13) Various parables and sayings	Q 15:3-7; 16:13, 17-18; 17:1-6
(14) The eschatological discourse	Q 17:23-37; 19:12-27; 22:28-30

The contents of Q seem to have been primarily a collection of wisdom sayings, prophetic or eschatological pronouncements, and ethical exhortations. What happened to the Q document is unknown. Why would the early church have allowed such a collection of the sayings of Jesus to disappear? Some scholars have suggested that after the Gospels of Matthew and Luke appeared, which contained so much of Q, the need for Q was not compelling. However, that suggestion is weakened by the analogous situation of the Gospel of Mark. It continued to circulate even after Matthew and Luke incorporated almost the entirety of Mark in their works. We will never know all we would like to know about Q. Although Q remains a hypothetical document and some scholars still question whether such a collection of sayings ever existed, the Q hypothesis remains for most New Testament scholars the best solution to explaining the material common to Matthew and Luke but not in Mark.

The priority of Mark and the existence of the Q document are the major elements in the most widely accepted solution to the synoptic problem. Known as the Two-Source Theory, this proposal claims that Matthew and

Luke used both Mark and Q as sources for the writing of their works. Still unexplained, however, are the materials found only in Matthew and the materials only in Luke. These traditions are usually labeled M and L, respectively. The following diagram illustrates the Two-Source Theory as widely held in modern scholarship:

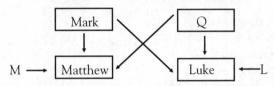

B. H. Streeter in 1924 argued that M and L were written sources. His proposal was labeled the Four-Document Theory. Most scholars today, however, are less likely to claim that M and L represent specific documents or even specific sources. Rather, M and L stand for additional information available to Matthew and Luke. This material may have been derived from written sources, oral sources, the evangelist's own contributions, or a combination of any of these.

John and the Synoptics

Anyone who reads the synoptic Gospels and then reads the Gospel of John surely must feel as if he or she has entered a different world. Although all four writings describe the life and teachings of Jesus, the Gospel of John does so in a way vastly different from that of the synoptic writers. A lot of the material that is central to the Synoptics is absent from John, including birth narratives, the baptism and temptation of Jesus, preaching about the kingdom of God, exorcisms, the use of parables, the Lord's Prayer, Peter's confession of Jesus at Caesarea Philippi, the transfiguration, the elements of bread and wine at the Last Supper, and the agony in Gethsemane. On the other hand, some of the most distinctive material in John is not in the Synoptics. Included here would be the miracle of changing water into wine, the story of Nicodemus, the story of the Samaritan woman at the well, Jesus' Jerusalem-centered ministry, the "I am" sayings of Jesus, the raising of Lazarus, the foot-washing episode at the Last Supper, and the reference to the "Beloved Disciple."

Furthermore, some material that appears in both the Gospel of John and in the Synoptics is presented in very different ways. In the Synoptics the episode usually called the cleansing of the Temple occurs during the last week of Jesus' life; in John the incident takes place at the beginning of his ministry. In the Synoptics the confession by the disciples of Jesus' identity as Messiah is slow to develop; in the Gospel of John the disciples recognize Jesus as the Messiah from the outset. In the synoptic Gospels the last supper that Jesus shares with his disciples prior to his arrest and crucifixion is presented as a Passover meal; in John the meal takes place on the evening prior to Passover.

Alongside these major differences between the Synoptics and John, several striking similarities can also be noted. C. K. Barrett has called attention to ten passages in the Gospel of John that occur in the same order as they appear in Mark.[14] Furthermore, in some of these passages there are verbal similarities. In some parallel passages John and Mark are similar in some unusual details. In the story of the feeding of the five thousand, found in all four Gospels, only Mark and John mention the monetary amount of two hundred denarii in relation to buying food for the crowd. In the story of the anointing of Jesus at Bethany, only Mark and John describe the value of the ointment that is used to anoint Jesus as being three hundred denarii. Even more interesting is the presence in Mark and John of an unusual word to describe this ointment. Both Gospels describe the ointment using the Greek word *pistikos*, usually translated "pure," although the word is so rare in ancient Greek that we are not certain of its meaning. The word *pistikos* occurs nowhere else in the New Testament and is rarely found outside the New Testament.

Barrett also notes some parallels between the Gospels of John and Luke. The sisters Mary and Martha appear in the Gospels of Luke and John only. Jesus' betrayal by Judas is attributed in both Gospels to Satan. In Luke and John the prediction of Peter's denial of Jesus is made during the Last Supper (Mark and Matthew describe it after the meal). Only Luke and John state that the *right* ear of the high priest's slave was cut off in the Garden of Gethsemane. Both Luke and John report that at Jesus' tomb on Easter morning two angels (or men) were present. (Matthew and Mark mention only one.)

Because of these similarities as well as the other stories and traditions shared by John and the Synoptics, the general consensus for a long time was that John knew and used the Synoptics, at least Mark and Luke. In 1938, however, P. Gardner-Smith published a book entitled *Saint John and the Synoptic Gospels* in which he argued that John did not know or have access to any of the synoptic Gospels. The differences between John and the Synoptics are too great to assume literary dependence. Similarities between John and the Synoptics are to be explained, rather, on the basis of similar oral tradition. The author of

John was familiar with some of the same oral traditions that lie behind the Gospels of Mark and Luke. Although C. K. Barrett and others have continued to argue strongly that John is dependent on the Gospels of Mark and Luke, the prevailing opinion of New Testament scholars today is that John is literarily independent of the synoptic Gospels. The relationship of all four Gospels may be diagrammed as follows:

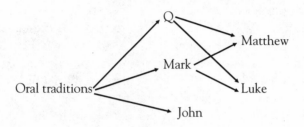

The differences between the Gospel of John and the Synoptics led Clement of Alexandria in the second century to describe the fourth Gospel as a "spiritual Gospel," while the other Gospels were seen as more historical works. At one time it was common for writers to claim that the Synoptics were history and John was more theology or interpretation. Such dichotomy cannot be maintained, however. As we have noted already, the Synoptics are not purely historical works. They are at most theologically interpreted history, a mixture of theological interpretation and history set in narrative form. The Gospel of John must be viewed in the same way. Whereas at times the Jesus of the Gospel of John may seem further removed from the "historical Jesus" than the Jesus of the Synoptics, some episodes in the Gospel of John may indeed preserve more reliable historical information than corresponding passages in the Synoptics. Both the Synoptics and John, we must remember, are primarily theological portraits of Jesus of Nazareth. We should not pit John against the Synoptics, but rather hear each of them as a unique story about Jesus.

Who Wrote the Gospels?

The titles affixed to the Gospels in most English Bibles ("The Gospel According to Mark," "The Gospel According to Matthew," etc.) are almost certainly not original to the Gospels. These were likely added later when the Gospels began to be collected and circulated together. None of the

Gospels makes any claim to authorship, thus the attempt to determine the authors of the Gospels must rely on information that can be gleaned from early comments about the Gospels as well as clues that can be detected within the Gospels themselves.

The Gospel of Mark

The earliest tradition about the authorship of Mark is found in the writings of the fourth century church historian Eusebius who quotes from Papias (ca. 60–130 CE), a bishop in Asia Minor. Papias, quoting from someone referred to only as "the elder," says:

> Mark became Peter's interpreter and wrote accurately all that he remembered, not indeed, in order, of the things said or done by the Lord. For he had not heard the Lord, nor had he followed him, but later on, as I said, followed Peter, who used to give teaching as necessity demanded but not making, as it were, an arrangement of the Lord's oracles, so that Mark did nothing wrong in thus writing down single points as he remembered them.[15]

On the basis of this statement, which is apparently the source for assertions of Markan authorship in other early writings, the popular view arose that the author of this Gospel was Mark. This Mark is usually considered to be John Mark, mentioned in Acts as a resident of Jerusalem and one-time traveling companion of Paul (Acts 12:12, 25; 13:13; 15:36-39). John Mark is also mentioned elsewhere in the New Testament in association with Paul (Col 4:10; 2 Tim 4:11; Phlm 24) and with Peter (1 Pet 5:13). As attractive as this view may be, scholars have noted problems with this traditional ascription of authorship. The statement by Papias is problematic on several counts. His statement does not make clear that what Mark wrote was our present Gospel of Mark. Furthermore, who was "Mark" that he names? Marcus was a common Roman name. Since he gives no further identification of this Mark, the logical assumption is that he was a well-known figure in the church. John Mark certainly fits that better than anyone else we know from the early church. That identification, however, is still only an unfounded assumption. Also questionable is the claim that the Gospel was based on Mark's remembrances of Peter's proclamations. Most scholars today are convinced that much of the material in the Gospel circulated previously as independent oral traditions in a variety of forms.

Some of the material used by the author of the Gospel likely came from written collections of materials.

Occasionally one encounters the suggestion that the enigmatic young man in 14:51-52 who flees the Garden of Gethsemane naked is a veiled reference to the author of the Gospel. For example, it is suggested that the young man may have been sleeping in the house where the Last Supper was eaten. He awoke and followed Jesus and the disciples to the Garden of Gethsemane. This house is then identified with the house of Mary, the mother of John Mark, in which the disciples later met (Acts 12:12). Thus the young man is John Mark, himself, the author of the Gospel. This suggestion is a marvelous example of imagination run wild and should be dismissed as a fanciful and unconvincing argument.

Evidence in the Gospel itself has led many readers of the Gospel to question the traditional view of authorship. The author of the Gospel does not seem to be too familiar with Palestinian geography. In 7:31 he describes Jesus leaving the city of Tyre and passing through Sidon on his way to the Sea of Galilee, described as being "in the midst of the region of the Decapolis" [author's translation]. This description places the city of Sidon south of Tyre and places the Sea of Galilee in the midst of the cities of the Decapolis, both of which are incorrect. Is it likely that a native of Palestine, as John Mark was, would have made such errors? Also, certain passages in the Gospel contain erroneous statements about Palestinian or Jewish practices. The story of the death of John the Baptist (6:14-29), for example, contains several historical inaccuracies. (Among the errors is the claim that Herodias was the wife of Philip. Actually she was the wife of another brother of Herod.) The statement about divorce in 10:12 reflects Roman rather than Jewish practice. The explanation in 7:3 that all the Jews "do not eat unless they thoroughly wash their hands" is an overstatement more likely to be made by an outsider than a Jewish person. These discrepancies certainly do not disprove authorship by John Mark, but they raise enough serious questions about the traditional view to lead many New Testament scholars to conclude that this answer to the authorship question is highly unlikely. Most scholars are content to identify the author as an unknown first-century Christian who was likely non-Palestinian, of possibly even non-Jewish, background. His name may have been Mark, but we have no clue as to the identity of this Mark.

The Gospel of Matthew

The traditional view of authorship of the Gospel of Matthew is that it was written by Matthew, a tax collector who became a disciple of Jesus (Matt 9:9; 10:3; Mark 3:18; Luke 6:15). As was true with the Gospel of Mark, the earliest identification of the author of the Gospel of Matthew comes from Papias, as quoted by Eusebius. In regard to Matthew, Papias is reported to have stated, "Matthew collected the oracles in the Hebrew language, and each interpreted them as best he could."[16] This statement by Papias is even more problematic than the one about Mark. Two major questions are, "What is meant by 'oracles' (*logia*)?" and "What does 'in the Hebrew language' mean?" As for the latter question, "the Hebrew language" could mean strictly Hebrew, or more likely, it refers to Aramaic, a related language that was the common language of first-century Palestine. If *logia* is understood to mean the Gospel of Matthew, a major problem arises because almost all scholars agree that this Gospel is not "translation Greek," that is, the Gospel was not originally written in another language and only later translated into Greek. Thus Papias does not seem to be referring to our present Gospel of Matthew. Some have argued that *logia*, which literally means "sayings," refers to a collection of passages from the Hebrew Bible used as a testimony to Jesus, or to a collection of sayings of Jesus that circulated in the early church. (Some have even suggested that Papias was referring to the Q document.) None of this gets us any closer to determining authorship, since if Papias is talking about the Gospel of Matthew he is wrong about the language in which it was written. Such inaccuracy certainly does not inspire confidence in his attribution of authorship to Matthew.

One of the major problems in accepting Matthean authorship for this Gospel is related to the Two-Source Theory, which claims that Matthew was dependent on Mark. This yields the totally unbelievable situation in which Matthew, a disciple of Jesus and an eyewitness of much of what he presents in his Gospel, borrows the majority of his information from Mark, one who was not a disciple or an eyewitness. (This would still be true even if one accepts the traditional view of John Mark as the author of the Gospel of Mark.) We are left then with a situation similar to the one with the Gospel of Mark: the external evidence for authorship does not hold up under scrutiny and the Gospel itself provides no identity of its author.

Why was Matthew's name associated with this Gospel if he did not write it? Several plausible suggestions have been offered. Perhaps in the Christian community in which the Gospel was produced, Matthew was highly revered, maybe even having founded the church there. This perhaps explains the author's special interest in Matthew as indicated by the change of the tax collector's name from Levi to Matthew (cf. Matt 9:9 with Mark 2:14; Luke 5:27). Maybe certain traditions or stories in the Gospel had been attributed to Matthew. Perhaps the disciple Matthew was responsible for an early collection of materials that was later used in the composition of the Gospel. (Could a remembrance of this underlie the statement of Papias?) Since authorship by a disciple would grant the work more authority, perhaps Matthew's name was attached for that reason. It has been suggested that the name of Matthew was chosen instead of another disciple due to the similarity between his name and the Greek words for disciple (*mathētēs*) and learning (*mathēsis*). The purpose of the Gospel is then fulfilled when readers become true disciples and learners like Matthew.

Since neither the Gospel itself nor early church tradition provides a reliable identification of the author, scholars have searched the Gospel of Matthew for hints about the person responsible for writing the Gospel. A minority of students of the Gospel have argued that the author was a gentile Christian. As evidence they point to the strong polemic in the Gospel against Pharisaism and Israel (3:7-10; 21:43; 23:1-36), sympathy for the spread of the gospel to the gentiles (13:38; 24:14; 28:19), and errors in the Gospel concerning the Hebrew Bible or Judaism. (One example of the latter is 21:5 where the author misreads the synonymous parallelism, common in the Hebrew Bible, of Zech 9:9, with the result that Jesus is portrayed as riding into Jerusalem on two animals at the same time!)

The majority of interpreters, however, believe that the author was a Greek-speaking Jewish Christian. They point to the extensive use of the Jewish scriptures in the Gospel, emphasis on the Jewish law, and the author's concern for the relationship between Judaism and Christianity. Some even go so far as to identify the author as an individual with formal training as a Jewish scribe, due to the methods of scriptural interpretation he uses and the supposedly veiled description of himself in 13:52. Overall, the evidence in the Gospel seems to be inclined more toward the identity of the author as being a Jewish Christian rather than a gentile Christian. That first-rate scholars studying the same material can reach completely opposite conclusions on the authorship question, however, should serve as a caution against dogmatism in this matter. Uncertainty in this issue should caution us also against basing any interpretation of the Gospel on a particular view of authorship.

The Gospel of Luke

The third Gospel in the canon is different from the other three Gospels in that it is part of a two-volume work, Luke-Acts. (Cf. the opening sections of the two books, Luke 1:1-4 and Acts 1:1-5.) The question of authorship, then, involves not only the Gospel, but also its companion work. Writings from late in the second century CE attribute authorship of these two works to Luke, a physician and traveling companion of the apostle Paul. Internal support for Lukan authorship has centered on the so-called "we-sections" of Acts, those passages describing Paul's journeys that are written in a first-person plural format, seemingly implying that the author accompanied Paul during those sections of the itinerary (16:10-17; 20:5-15; 21:1-18; 27:1-28:16). Combining these sections with information from elsewhere in Acts and from letters in the New Testament attributed to Paul, inter- preters have concluded that the most likely traveling companion of Paul's during the times indicated was Luke the physician (cf. Phlm 24; Col 4:14; 2 Tim 4:11). Additional support for this view is the claim that Luke-Acts displays an expertise in medical terminology of the first century. Few scholars would make such a claim today, however, since studies have shown that Luke-Acts in fact demonstrates no greater knowledge or use of medical terminology than was common among other writers of the first century.

Whereas a number of excellent New Testament scholars still advocate the traditional view of authorship, the majority of interpreters are more skeptical about this tradition. Ascription of authorship to Luke likely arose from the very first from the "detective work" of readers who sought clues in the New Testament to determine who Paul's traveling companion was in the "we-sections." The problem with this approach is that other plausible explanations can be offered for the use of "we" in these passages. Some scholars have argued that the first-person plural accounts are indications of another source, possibly an itinerary or diary kept by one of Paul's traveling companions, that was used by the author in the writing of Acts. A weakness of this suggestion is the similarity in style of the "we-sections" and the remainder of Acts. A better suggestion is that the use of the first-person plural in these sections describing Paul's sea voyages was a literary device, either a conscious attempt to lend credibility to the accounts by writing as an eyewitness, or an accepted style for describing sea voyages. Vernon Robbins has argued the latter point, showing that ancient writers used "we" when describing sea voyages, not as an indication that they personally participated in the trip, but as a standard literary technique.[17] Ancient readers, familiar with the genre of sea voyages, would not have necessarily assumed that the author was an actual participant in the voyage.

Along with the difficulty of understanding the purpose and origin of the "we-sections," the differences between Paul's own letters in the New Testament and what is contained in the book of Acts seriously weaken the claim that the author of Luke-Acts was a traveling companion of Paul. These differences include discrepancies in events (e.g., correlation of the visits of Paul to Jerusalem described in Gal 1–2 with the visits mentioned in Acts) and differences in the theology of Paul as presented in Acts and as found in his own writings (e.g., in Paul's letters the death of Jesus is central to Paul's theology of salvation; in Paul's speeches in Acts the death of Jesus is scarcely mentioned). Furthermore, Paul was a frequent letter writer, sending letters to churches and individuals. Yet the author of Acts seems unaware of the contents of Paul's letters or even that Paul wrote letters. For these reasons many scholars are convinced that the person who wrote Luke-Acts was very likely not Luke, the physician and traveling companion of Paul.

The superb quality of the Greek grammar and style of the work (among the best in the New Testament) and the author's familiarity with certain literary conventions of the day (e.g., the dedication paragraphs at the beginning of Luke and Acts) indicate that the author was likely a well-educated individual whose native language was Greek. The author was clearly not one of the original followers of Jesus, for he does not include himself as one of the eyewitnesses of the events he narrates and indicates that he has relied on various written sources to compose the Gospel (cf. Luke 1:1-4). Was the author a Jewish or gentile Christian? The author's familiarity with the contents and style of the Septuagint has suggested to some students of the Gospel that the author was a Hellenistic Jewish Christian. On the other hand, the universal outlook of Luke-Acts (i.e., its inclusion of gentiles in God's salvation) and the avoidance of Semitic words and phrases found in Mark have led most scholars to identify the author of this two-volume work as a gentile Christian.

The Gospel of John

During the last quarter of the second century, Irenaeus, bishop of Lyons, wrote, "John, the disciple of the Lord, who also had leaned upon His breast, did himself publish a Gospel during his residence at Ephesus in Asia."[18] This statement is apparently the basis for the popular belief that John, one of the twelve disciples, who was the son of Zebedee and brother of another disciple James, was the author of the fourth Gospel. This disciple John is identified as the person referred to in the Gospel as "the disciple whom Jesus loved" (cf. 13:23-26; 19:25-27; 20:1-10; 21:1-14, 20-24).

The closest that the Gospel itself comes to identifying its author is in 21:24-25, which states, "This is the disciple who is testifying to these things and has written them, and we know that his testimony is true. But there are also many other things that Jesus did; if every one of them were written down, I suppose that the world itself could not contain the books that would be written." The disciple who is mentioned is the "disciple whom Jesus loved," usually referred to as the Beloved Disciple, who according to this statement is the source and authority behind the Gospel. This statement seems to imply at least three stages in the composition of the Gospel: The core of the Gospel is dependent upon the memory and perhaps even written witness of the Beloved Disciple; a community of followers (the "we" of v. 24) collected, preserved, and reshaped his teachings; finally, one of his followers ("I" in v. 25) was responsible for the final version of the Gospel. This scenario is perhaps a forced or even simplistic reading of the text, but most scholars posit some type of multistage composition of the Gospel of John in which the Gospel evolved through several editions or redactions. The final chapter, chapter 21, is clearly an epilogue that was added subsequent to the completion of the remainder of the Gospel. Some scholars have argued that 1:1-18 (the prologue), chapters 11–12 and 15–17 as well as other passages were likely added by the final editor of the Gospel who also rearranged some of the material in the earlier editions of the Gospel. The issue of authorship of the fourth Gospel thus becomes a complicated one.

Even if one were to assume that the Beloved Disciple had a major role in the writing of the fourth Gospel, one is not much closer to determining authorship. Nowhere in the Gospel of John is "the disciple whom Jesus loved" ever identified by name, much less identified with the disciple John. In fact, serious difficulties with this identification can be pointed out, including the absence from the Gospel of John of the three episodes in the

Synoptics in which John was a privileged witness—the raising of Jairus' daughter (Mark 5:21-43; Matt 9:18-26; Luke 8:40-56), the so-called trans-figuration (Mark 9:2-8; Matt 17:1-8; Luke 9:28-36), and Jesus' agony in the Garden of Gethsemane (Mark 14:32-42; Matt 26:36-46; Luke 22:39-46). Also, if the Beloved Disciple were John the son of Zebedee, so prominent in the Synoptics, why does he not appear in the fourth Gospel until chapter 13? Because of these difficulties some scholars have suggested other persons as the Beloved Disciple, including Lazarus, the only person in the Gospel who is explicitly mentioned as one whom Jesus loved (11:3). Other interpreters have argued that the Beloved Disciple is not a historical figure but is a symbol of either the church or the perfect Christian disciple.

More than likely the Beloved Disciple was a historical figure, a leader in the community that preserved his teachings and ultimately produced the fourth Gospel. While the identity of this enigmatic figure remains obscure, his legacy continues in the Gospel that has been attributed by tradition to John. Whether the Beloved Disciple was the actual author of the early form(s) of the Gospel, later redacted by a follower, or whether he was only the source of many of the traditions that were eventually woven together in the Gospel is unknown.

Due to similarities in writing style, themes, and vocabulary between the Gospel of John and the letters of John in the New Testament, most scholars believe that these works were all produced by the same group of early Christians. This group, often called the "Johannine community" or the "Johannine school," was likely a group of Christians whose founder and leader had been the Beloved Disciple. This community preserved, shaped, and reworked the Jesus traditions that the Beloved Disciple passed on to them and ultimately produced the Gospel of John and the letters of John to address the theological needs of their Christian group. The book of Revelation may have come from this same community as well.

Our quest for determining authorship of the Gospels has been somewhat frustrating. We cannot with certainty, or even probability, name the person responsible for the writing of any of the canonical Gospels. We must consider the authors as anonymous. That is not a total loss, however. Whereas the early church deemed authorship important and sought to associate each of the Gospels with an apostle (Matthew and John) or someone closely associated with an apostle (Mark and Luke), apparently the authors themselves did not consider declaring their identities to be important. For them, the authority of their works resided not in authorship, but in the contents of the works themselves. The focus of each work is not the author, but the subject matter—Jesus of Nazareth.

Since we must profess ignorance about the identity of the authors, we will for the sake of convenience refer to the evangelists by the traditional names of Matthew, Mark, Luke, and John. These are all masculine names, thus we will use masculine pronouns when referring to the authors. Readers should realize, however, that the Gospel writers could very well have been women. Several prominent women were active and were leaders in the early church—Priscilla, Phoebe, Euodia, Syntyche, Lydia—and Luke records that several women were followers of Jesus and even helped support him materially (Luke 8:1-3). Any of these or the many unnamed other women of the first-century church could have been the authors of one or more of the New Testament Gospels.

Chapter 2

❖

The World of the Gospels

One major disadvantage that confronts the modern reader of the Gospels is that unlike ancient readers we are separated by a chronological and cultural gap from the world in which the Gospels were produced. Modern institutions, social customs, religious practices and beliefs, and political systems are different from those of the ancient Roman world. Customs and practices readily understandable to first-century readers are sometimes puzzling to modern readers. The events described by the Gospels cover the life span of Jesus (ca. 6 BCE–30 CE), with almost exclusive attention focused on the last one to three years. The Gospels themselves, however, were likely written between 70 and 100 CE. Thus our exploration of the world of the Gospels will encompass not only the years of Jesus but also the era of the writing of the Gospels.

The Political World

The History of Palestine

Palestine is a land that has known many conquerors. In 587 BCE Nebuchadrezzar, king of Babylon, captured Jerusalem, destroying the city and its Temple. A large segment of the inhabitants of Jerusalem and the surrounding area was taken captive to Babylon. Babylon itself fell victim to another power when Cyrus of Persia conquered the kingdom in 539 BCE Cyrus instituted a policy of allowing captured peoples, including the former inhabitants of Judah, to return to their homelands. Slowly the restoration of Judah took place as some of the exiles traveled back to Palestine and began to rebuild the area.

The Hellenistic Period. The Jewish people were still under the control of the Persians when the Macedonian king Alexander the Great began his conquest of the world in 334 BCE, in which he defeated the Persians and extended his territory all the way to India. Palestine came under Alexander's control in 332, having surrendered without opposition to Alexander's army. When Alexander died in 323 BCE his territory was taken over by his generals, although not without armed conflict among them. When one of the generals, Ptolemy, took control of Egypt, and another general, Seleucus, gained control of Syria and Mesopotamia, Palestine was caught in the middle. The Ptolemies soon gained control of this area and ruled over Palestine until 198 BCE when the Seleucid king, Antiochus III, defeated Ptolemy V at Paneas in northern Palestine (later called Caesarea Philippi). Palestine then became a part of the Seleucid dynasty.

One of the results of Alexander's conquests was Hellenization, or the spread of Greek culture. Greek cities were established in conquered territories; Greek theaters and gymnasiums were built; and temples were erected for the worship of the Greek gods. Many of the local people began to adopt Greek customs and practices, such as wearing Greek clothing and giving their children Greek names. The Greek language became the common language in a large part of the ancient world. (The universal spread of the Greek language is the reason why the New Testament, including the Gospels, was originally written in Greek.) Certainly not everyone under the control of the Hellenistic rulers learned to speak Greek; indigenous languages remained. Greek, however, became the official language. It was the language of international commerce and politics. It was the language of the educated and socially elite. This common language helped bind the Hellenistic world together. One of the results of the universalization of the Greek language during this period was the production of a version of the Hebrew scriptures in Greek. Because most Jews living outside Palestine could not read or understand Hebrew, a need existed for a translation of the Hebrew scriptures into a language that the people did understand. Begun during the third century BCE, the Septuagint became widely used throughout the Hellenistic world for several centuries.[1]

Hellenization continued after the death of Alexander through the efforts of his successors. In Palestine both the Ptolemaic and the Seleucid rulers encouraged the spread of Greek culture. Some of the Jews in Palestine, particularly among the upper class, readily embraced Hellenism, adopting Greek customs and practices. Others were more reticent, resisting the encroachment of beliefs and practices that they saw as antithetical to

Judaism. Although no one in Palestine completely escaped Hellenistic influence, some remained more committed to tradition than others.

A critical situation developed in Palestine when Antiochus IV Epiphanes took over the Seleucid reign in 175 BCE. Tensions between the pro-Hellenistic and the anti-Hellenistic factions within Jerusalem boiled over. The leader of the Hellenistic supporters, Jason, succeeded in getting Antiochus to depose the current high priest, Jason's own brother, and appoint him to the position. Jason became the victim of a similar intrigue, when three years later he was expelled by another rival for the office. In the midst of this conflict within Judaism, Antiochus IV, for reasons that are not clear, issued a decree in 167 BCE outlawing the practice of Judaism in Palestine and converted the Temple in Jerusalem into a temple to Zeus. One response to this action was an armed revolt led by a rural priestly family. Judas Maccabeus, the leader of the uprising known as the Maccabean Revolt, succeeded in regaining the Temple. In December 164 BCE the Temple was rededicated to the worship of the Jewish god, an event commemorated by the Jewish festival of Hanukkah.

Judas and his followers continued the struggle against the Syrians (the Seleucid capital was in Antioch, Syria), eventually winning political as well as religious freedom for the Jews. Judas himself did not live long enough to see political independence, but through the leadership of his brothers Jonathan and Simon independence was won. Both of these men succeeded in acquiring for themselves the position of high priest, as well. Under Simon, the last Maccabean brother, a new dynasty was born, the Hasmonean dynasty, which controlled Palestinian affairs from 142–63 BCE. Simon and his descendants increased their territorial holdings, at times with the aid of the Romans. The small Judean state was enlarged by the addition of the territories of Samaria and Galilee to the north, Idumea to the south, and some of the area on the east bank of the Jordan River.

The Roman Period. The Romans became intimately involved in Palestinian affairs in 63 BCE as the result of squabbles between two Hasmonean brothers, John Hyrcanus II and Aristobulus II. After the death of their mother, Alexandra Salome, the ruling queen, conflict erupted between the brothers as they vied for political control of Palestine. Eventually both men appealed for help to Pompey, the Roman general who was in the area. Pompey did intercede, putting Hyrcanus in charge, but also subjugating the territory to Roman control and releasing some of the area from Jewish control. Along with Hyrcanus, an Idumean ruler named Antipater eventually was given oversight of Palestine. Antipater appointed his two sons, Phasael and Herod to help govern. In 40 BCE Antigonus, one of the sons of Aristobulus II, successfully led a coup against the rulers of the Jewish state. With the aid of the Parthians, he was able to capture Hyrcanus and kill Phasael. (Antipater had been murdered earlier.) Herod fled to Rome, where he was able to acquire from the Roman Senate and the emperor Octavian the title of king of Judea. With the aid of the Roman army Herod was able finally to drive out Antigonus and his supporters and claim his kingdom in 37 BCE.

The rule of Herod the Great, as he came to be known, lasted until 4 BCE. During this time he endeared himself to the Romans and as a result was granted more territories to rule. In many ways Herod was a shrewd and ruthless ruler, willing to eliminate anyone who he felt was disloyal or a threat to his throne. For these reasons he executed, among others, his favorite wife (altogether he had ten wives), his mother-in-law, his brother-in-law, three sons, and several close friends.

One of Herod's most lasting accomplishments was his building campaign. Herod completed several major construction projects during his reign. He built an exceptional, artificial harbor and spectacular city on the Mediterranean coast, naming it Caesarea in honor of the emperor. He rebuilt the city of Samaria, renaming it Sebaste, also in honor of the emperor (Sebaste is Greek for Augusta). He built, refortified, or enlarged several fortresses and palaces, including the Herodium, Machaerus (where John the Baptist was later beheaded), and Masada. The city of Jerusalem benefited greatly from his building activity, gaining a theater, amphitheater, royal palace, towers, and other structures. His most famous building project was the Jerusalem Temple. The Temple built after the period of the Babylonian exile, completed in 516 BCE, was not magnificent enough for Herod's capital city. Thus around 20 BCE he initiated the complete rebuilding of the Jewish Temple. The majority of the work was finished in about a year and a half, but final work on it was not completed until shortly before it was destroyed by the Romans in 70 CE. The completed Temple was an impressive structure, a worthy tribute to a person of Herod's ego.

Herod was not well-liked among his Jewish citizens. In addition to disliking him for his cruel and despotic ways, the people never fully accepted Herod as one of them, as Jewish. That opinion was based partially on Herod's ancestry. His grandfather, like other Idumeans, had been converted to Judaism by coercion. John Hyrcanus, a Hasmonean ruler who brought Idumea under Jewish control, had given the people a choice: accept Judaism or be killed. Thus Herod was regarded as half-Jewish at best. But Herod's own actions, as well, contributed to their estimate of him. Herod was Jewish only as it was convenient to him. Granted he rebuilt the Jewish Temple in Jerusalem, but he also built temples to other gods in non-Jewish cities in his kingdom and promoted Hellenistic culture throughout his territory. He was not a faithful adherent to Jewish customs and even removed and replaced the Jewish high priests at his pleasure (supposedly a lifetime position). Josephus, the first-century Jewish historian, states that Herod, knowing how the populace felt toward him, issued an order when he was fatally ill that some of the leading citizens that he had arrested earlier were to be executed at his death, thus ensuring that the people would grieve and mourn at the time of his own death. Fortunately, the orders were never enforced.[2]

With the approval of Rome, at Herod's death in 4 BCE governance of his kingdom passed to three of his sons, although none was given the title of king that their father had borne. Archelaus received the title of ethnarch and was given control over Judea, Samaria, and Idumea; Herod Antipas was awarded Galilee and Perea and given the title of tetrarch; Philip obtained Batanea, Trachonitis, and Auranitis, which were basically gentile territories located northeast of the Sea of Galilee. He was awarded the title of tetrarch. (An ethnarch was lower in status than a king and a tetrarch was lower than an ethnarch.) Archelaus was as cruel and disliked as his father. After a delegation of Jewish citizens went to Rome in 6 CE to complain about Archelaus, the emperor Augustus removed him from office and banished him to Gaul. The emperor then placed the territory of Archelaus under direct Roman rule, sending a Roman governor (called a "prefect," and later "procurator") to be in charge.

Philip ruled his territory well, remaining in his position until his death in 34 CE. During his reign the ancient city of Panias was rebuilt and renamed Caesarea Philippi in honor of the emperor. At his death his territory was added to the Roman province of Syria. Only three years later, however, in 37 CE this territory was given to Agrippa I (called in the New Testament, "Herod"; see Acts 12:1-23), a grandson of Herod the Great (his father was Aristobulus IV, another of Herod's sons). The title of king was bestowed on Agrippa.

Herod Antipas, the remaining ruling son of Herod, who also is called simply Herod in the New Testament, is perhaps most familiar to readers of the Gospels as the person responsible for the death of John the Baptist. Antipas remained in office until 39 BCE, when ambitious greed led to his downfall. Envious of the title of king that had been bestowed upon Agrippa, the wife of Antipas convinced him to go to Rome to seek a similar title for himself. Instead of awarding him the title "king," the emperor Caligula exiled Antipas to Gaul. In 40 CE his former territory was added to that under the control of Agrippa. In 41 CE Judea and Samaria were also given to him to rule, thus making his kingdom approximately the same as that ruled over by his grandfather, Herod the Great. This arrangement lasted only three years, however, due to the death of Agrippa in 44 CE

Following the death of Agrippa, Palestine was placed under the control of Roman procurators. A few years later, ca. 50 CE, Agrippa's son, Agrippa II, was given control of the Jerusalem Temple, the right to appoint the high priests, and certain territories in and around Palestine to rule. He died ca. 92 or 93 CE

During the period of Roman control of Palestine, the Jewish people chafed under this foreign domination. At various times, minor outbreaks of violence would occur that would be quickly and ruthlessly squelched. In 66 CE a major revolt against the Romans occurred, sparked by the attempt of the Roman procurator Florus to plunder the Temple treasury. Initially successful in gaining control of Jerusalem and various fortresses in Palestine, the Jews were finally no match for the powerful Roman army. In 70 CE the Roman general Titus succeeded in capturing and leveling both Jerusalem and its Temple. Allegedly contrary to the wishes of Titus, his soldiers set the Temple ablaze, completely destroying it. Herod's magnificent Temple perished, with only one wall left standing, the western wall. The destruction of Jerusalem effectively ended the revolt, although Jewish rebel forces continued to control the fortresses of the Herodium, Machaerus, and Masada. The Romans took control of the Herodium shortly after the fall of Jerusalem; the besieged occupiers of Machaerus capitulated to the Romans in 72. A group of Jewish resistance fighters continued to hold out at the nearly impregnable fortress of Masada near the Dead Sea. The Romans did not move against Masada until late in 73 CE when the Roman general Flavius Silva put the mountain fortress under siege. In April of the following year, the Romans succeeded in capturing Masada, thus eliminating the remaining armed resistance to Roman rule.

The Jewish-Roman war dealt a devastating blow to Judaism and the people of Palestine. The Temple, the center of Jewish worship, and its sacrificial system were gone. Along with the demise of the Temple, the priestly aristocracy and its role in Jewish life perished. The role of the Torah, the Jewish scriptures, became even more pronounced as the Torah was examined, debated, and commented upon with ever more vigor and zeal.

One final outbreak of violence against the Romans took place in 132 CE when Bar Kokhba, with the support of Rabbi Akiba, claimed that he was the long-awaited Messiah who would lead the people to throw off the yoke of their Roman oppressors and reestablish the independence of the Jewish nation. Bar Kokhba's efforts led to a second Jewish-Roman war that lasted three and a half years and produced the same results as did the first one. In 135 CE the Romans defeated the Jewish rebels, destroyed what remained of the city of Jerusalem, and sold countless Jews into slavery. Over the remains of the once-proud capital of Judaism, the Romans built a new city, naming it Aelia Capitolina. Any remaining Jews were driven out of the former city of Jerusalem and were not allowed to enter it again. The Jewish state came to a disastrous end, not to rise from the ashes again until the creation of the modern nation of Israel in 1948.

The Roman Empire

During the first century CE Rome witnessed the rise and fall of several emperors. At the turn of the century the emperor was Augustus (earlier called Octavian), who had become the sole ruler of the empire with his defeat of Mark Antony and Cleopatra at Actium in 31 BCE The reign of Augustus marked not only a new era in Roman politics, but also brought about a golden age of peace, prosperity, and stability to the Roman world. Philo of Alexandria, a Jewish philosopher of the time, described Augustus and his reign in glowing terms:

> This is he who exterminated wars both of the open kind and the covert which are brought about by the raids of brigands. This is he who cleared the sea of pirate ships and filled it with merchant vessels. This is he who reclaimed every state to liberty, who led disorder into order and brought gentle manners and harmony to all unsociable and brutish nations, who enlarged Hellas [Greece] by many a new Hellas and hellenized the outside world in its most important regions, the guardian of the peace, who dispensed their dues to

each and all, who did not hoard his favours but gave them to be common property, who kept nothing good and excellent hidden throughout his life. . . . The whole habitable world voted him no less than celestial honors.[3]

Other writers also leaped lavish praise on Augustus. The Priene inscription of 9 BCE, mentioned earlier in the discussion on the word *gospel*, states:

> . . . and since the Caesar through his appearance has exceeded the hopes of all former good messages, surpassing not only the benefactors who came before him, but also leaving no hope that anyone in the future would surpass him, and since for the world the birthday of the god was the beginning of his good messages, [may it therefore be decided that . . .].[4]

It was during the reign of Augustus that Jesus of Nazareth was born.

Following the death of Augustus in 14 CE, his son-in-law and adopted son Tiberius took over the reigns of Roman power. Although Tiberius attempted to continue the principles and practices of Augustus, he was not the popular and successful ruler that his predecessor had been. On one occasion, according to Josephus, Tiberius ordered the expulsion of all Jews from Rome due to the reported behavior of four con artists among them.[5] Tiberius was the emperor during the period of Jesus' adult life and at the time of his trial and crucifixion. He died in 37 CE.

Tiberius was succeeded in office by his twenty-five-year-old great-nephew Caligula (a nickname meaning "little boots," given to him by soldiers when he stayed in the army camp with his father). Soon after taking office, Caligula appointed his friend Agrippa I to the position of king over certain territories in Palestine. Caligula's reign was characterized by his bizarre behavior and pretentious claims to greatness. He claimed divine status and ordered that statues of himself be installed throughout the empire so that he might be worshiped. His order that such a statue be placed in the Jerusalem Temple was met by resolute but peaceful protest by the Jews. Fortunately for the Jews, the assassination of Caligula by his imperial guard in 41 CE prevented the order from being enforced.

Claudius, an uncle of Caligula, was chosen as the next emperor. He seems to have ruled well, effecting several changes in Roman administration and improvements in roads and aqueducts. He also invaded Britain and made it a Roman province. Unrest between Jews and Greeks in Alexandria, made worse by Caligula, Claudius dealt with sensibly and fairly. Several years later, according to the Roman historian Suetonius, he expelled the Jews from Rome, due to rioting "at the instigation of a certain Chrestus" (*Lives of the Caesars, Claudius* 25.4), possibly a reference to Christianity. Claudius died in 54 from eating poisoned mushrooms supplied by his wife Agrippina, whose son Nero he had earlier adopted.

Rome next saw one of its most infamous emperors with the accession of Nero to office. The early years of Nero's rule went well, primarily because of the assistance of people such as the philosopher and statesman Seneca. Soon, however, Nero's cruel and morally desolate nature became evident. Nero executed many people he viewed as threats, including his own mother. When a massive fire broke out in 64 CE that did major damage to Rome, Nero was rumored to have been responsible for it. In order to shift blame away from himself, Nero accused the Christians of setting the fire. As a consequence, Nero had many Christians arrested and punished. The Roman historian Tacitus describes Nero's cruelty toward the accused as follows: "They were covered with wild beasts' skins and torn to death by dogs; or they were fastened on crosses, and, when daylight failed were burned to serve as lamps by night. Nero had offered his Gardens for the spectacle, and gave an exhibition in his Circus, mixing with the crowd in the habit of a charioteer, or mounted on his car.".[6]

This act by Nero was apparently the first time the Roman government distinguished Christians from Jews. The persecution was of limited scope, affecting only Christians in Rome for a brief time. During the latter part of Nero's rule, the revolt of the Jews in Palestine broke out. When opposition to Nero continued to grow in Rome and a conspiracy against him developed, Nero committed suicide in 68 CE. For years afterward rumors persisted that Nero was not really dead or that he had come back to life and was plotting to gain control once more.

After a brief period of civil war during which time three different individuals were proclaimed emperor (Galba, Vitellius, and Otho), the general Vespasian, who was in Palestine in charge of suppressing the Jewish revolt, succeeded in claiming the office. Vespasian was an excellent emperor, rebuilding the portions of Rome destroyed in the civil war, implementing sound fiscal practices, and restoring order and confidence in the government. When he died in 79 CE, his son Titus, who had remained behind in Palestine and successfully brought to an end the Jewish-Roman war, became the emperor. He lasted only two years, however, before he died.

Titus was followed in 81 CE by Domitian, his brother. Well liked by the army (he had dramatically raised their pay), but despised by the senate (he exiled or executed several senators), Domitian governed with an autocratic hand. Roman writers portray him as demanding to be honored as a god, with punishments for those who failed to accord him the proper respect and dignity. Later Christian tradition remembered him as a persecutor of the church, although little evidence exists to support that claim. The book of Revelation, however, if written during his reign does reflect one writer's view that the emperor and the Roman Empire are the great beast that demands worship and that exterminates those who refuse. Domitian's reign ended in 96 CE when he fell victim to a conspiracy and was stabbed to death. Nerva, the next emperor, died two years after taking office.

The emperor who saw the end of the first century and beginning years of the second was Trajan, who ruled until 117 CE. Trajan was remembered by ancient writers as an excellent emperor who had a well-organized and efficiently run administration. At his death, Hadrian was named the new emperor, a position he held until his death in 138. During his reign the second Jewish-Roman war erupted, led by Bar Kokhba.

The Social World

Because the narrative setting of the Gospels is Palestinian Judaism of the first century CE, our study of the social world of the Gospels will focus on Palestinian Jewish society. Since the social world of some of the authors and original readers of the Gospels was the larger Roman society of the first century, however, we will occasionally broaden our perspective.

Family Life

The family was the basic unit of Palestinian society, often including father, mother, children, grandparents, and daughters-in-law. Within Judaism, marriage and procreation were understood as religious obligations, based on an understanding of Genesis 1:28 ("be fruitful and multiply") as a divine command. For this reason unmarried adults were the exception. Marriages were normally arranged by the parents, frequently when the children were rather young. Girls were often married between the ages of twelve and fourteen, and in some cases even earlier. Males were usually older when they married, around eighteen or twenty. Although polygyny (multiple wives) was acceptable under Jewish law, in reality it was rare due to practical and financial reasons. Betrothal was a formal arrangement and could be broken only by a divorce. From the standpoint of custom and law, betrothed couples had almost the status of a married couple. During the betrothal period, which could last for several years, the woman remained in her father's household and the relationship was not consummated sexually. The man presented the woman a marriage contract stating a specific sum of money that would be hers in the event of divorce or her husband's death. After the wedding, during which the bride was accompanied to the home of the groom's family and which included seven days of celebrations, the new couple lived with the groom's family, often in a side room or rooftop room that had been added for that purpose.

If a man died childless, his oldest brother was obligated to marry his widow and produce children in his name as a way of guaranteeing the continuance of the lineage of the deceased man. If a man refused to honor this obligation of levirate marriage (*levir* is a Latin word meaning "brother-in-law"), he must do so in a formal ceremony that released the widow. A widow could either remain with her deceased husband's family or return to her own father's household. A Jewish man could divorce his wife by giving her a bill of divorce, a written statement that he had divorced her and that she was free to remarry, although Jewish authorities disagreed over what were acceptable reasons for granting a divorce. Women could not divorce their husbands, although a provision was made whereby a woman could ask the court to intercede on her behalf and compel her husband to grant the divorce. (In Roman society, however, both men and women alike could initiate a divorce.)

When a person died, family members and close friends expressed their grief by rending or tearing their garments. Burials normally took place the same day as death. The corpse was prepared by being washed and wrapped in shrouds, and then buried in a wooden coffin. Tombs were often in caves, either natural ones that were adapted for a burial site, or ones excavated for that purpose. The funeral procession included paid mourners, usually women, who accompanied the coffin with loud wails and lamentations.

Education and Language

The extent of formal education and the establishment of schools in first-century Palestine is an issue that is strongly debated. S. Safrai, for example, claims, "As early as the first century CE and perhaps even earlier, the majority of the children received education at school."[7] As noted in the previous chapter, however, Shaye Cohen argues that for the most part elementary education was the responsibility of the family and likely consisted of little more than girls being trained in domestic duties and boys being given instruction in the father's trade. Why such a discrepancy in viewpoints? Part of the difference lies in Safrai's dependence on evidence from rabbinic literature dating from the second century CE and later. While Safrai correctly assumes that much of the rabbinic literature reflects oral traditions from the first century and earlier, one can never be sure what material comes from which time period. Thus conclusions about first-century practices drawn from statements in the rabbinic literature are methodologically suspect. Widespread education and schooling may have been the norm in first-century Palestine, but no compelling evidence to support that conclusion exists. Cohen's approach is more cautious and more in line with the evidence. He concludes that any teaching of children—whether it be reading and writing skills, the scriptures, or professional skills—was the task of the parents. Wealthy or extremely dedicated parents might be able to afford private tutoring for their children. Such privileged education would have been the exception rather than the norm, however.

The primary language of first-century Palestine was apparently Aramaic, one of the Semitic languages closely related to Hebrew. Aramaic had been the official language of the Persian Empire. During and after the exile, Aramaic began to replace Hebrew as the common language of the Jewish people, although Hebrew remained in some circles as the language of religious teaching and discourse and possibly as a spoken language among certain extremely pious or nationalistic Jews. By the first century many Jews of Palestine could no longer understand Hebrew. Thus the practice developed in the synagogues that after a text from the Hebrew scriptures was read, someone would stand and recite an Aramaic translation of the passage. These translations, which often included interpretive remarks as well, were later collected in written form and are known as Targums.

As a result of Hellenization following the time of Alexander the Great, Greek became the official language of the Mediterranean world. Those who operated in the circles of power in the Roman world would have been able to speak Greek, as would also the educated elite, and to varying degrees people involved in trade and commerce. In Palestine as well, Greek would not have been an uncommon sound. The uneducated, the poor, and the people who lived in the towns and villages, probably had little reason or desire to learn Greek and their use of that language would have been minimal. The educated, the priestly aristocracy, the wealthy, and the urban dwellers of cities such as Jerusalem and Caesarea likely knew and used a considerable amount of Greek.

Economic Life

The primary economic activity of Palestine was agriculture. Olives, wine, and grain (wheat and barley) were the chief products. Figs, dates, and various vegetables were also grown. Sheep, goats, and, to a much lesser extent, cattle were the major livestock that were raised, providing milk, meat, wool, and leather. Around the Sea of Galilee, fishing was an important livelihood.

The agricultural economy was sustained in various forms. Affluent landowners, including the Herodians and other wealthy proprietors, farmed their land using tenants, sharecroppers, day laborers, and slaves. On the other hand, poorer landowners in and around the towns and villages eked out a living, producing what crops and livestock their plots of land would support. If they were fortunate they might have surplus goods to sell in the marketplace. Unfortunately, however, their existence was a precarious one, "sometimes at subsistence level, subject as they were to the vagaries of weather, market prices, inflation, grasping rulers, wars, and heavy taxes (both civil and religious)."[8]

In addition to agricultural workers, the Palestinian economy was composed of merchants and craftspersons (carpenters, stonemasons, tanners, potters, butchers, weavers, bakers, metalworkers, cobblers, etc.), day laborers, and traveling craftsmen. Most of these individuals were likely in the same economic situation as the poorer landowning farmers, barely making enough to provide for their families from day to day, with little left over for any luxuries. In Jerusalem, the Temple contributed greatly to the economy, both directly and indirectly. Concerning the economic impact of the Temple, S. Applebaum writes,

> Besides purchasing considerable quantities of livestock for the public sacrifices, and supporting annually 7,000 priests and Levites, it kept busy a notable staff of physicians, scribes, maintenance workers, butchers, weavers, metalworkers, incense-makers and bakers of the shewbread. In the decades prior

to 66, the remodelling of the shrine employed, in addition to trained priests, 10,000 other labourers.[9]

In Jerusalem, as well as in other relatively large cities in Palestine (Tiberias, Caearea, Sepphoris) merchants, craftsmen, and skilled workers were numerous, particularly during boom building periods under the Herodians.

Most people of Palestine were not city dwellers, however. The majority of the population lived in towns and villages. Sean Freyne describes typical village life of Galilee during the first century when he writes:

Life within the village confines was far from idyllic. Dwellings were small and clustered together, and generally, living conditions must have been primitive, giving rise to frequent illness and a short life-expectation. Attacks from passing robbers or highwaymen were frequent, explaining the location of some of the more remote settlements—away from the road and high up on the slopes of the hills. Invading armies were also frequent sources of great harassment, as the villagers were compelled to make provisions available, irrespective of their own needs.

. . . In a word, life in a Galilean village was never easy and sometimes brutal, constantly under pressure from above, usually from the city or city-based people that threatened to deprive the less fortunate of the necessities of life, thus reducing them to penury. Enjoyment was confined to the odd visit of a wandering minstrel or the religious festival. Though fraught with danger, the pilgrimage to Jerusalem must have had a very definite social function for Galilean Jewish peasants, lifting them temporarily out of the narrow confines of village life and bestowing a sense of belonging to something greater. (Lk 2:41, 44)[10]

The transportation of goods and services, whether by merchants, traveling craftsmen, large landowners, or peasant farmers, was costly and labor-intensive. Over land, goods would be transported by donkey, mule, wagon, or camel. Transoceanic travel, obviously, was by ship, as were also journeys across the Sea of Galilee. The Dead Sea and the Jordan River were also used for transportation. By modern standards, travel in the ancient world was slow. Most people traveled by foot and could average 15 to 20 miles per day. The distance covered by persons riding on a donkey, a more common animal in ancient Palestine for human transport, would have been slightly higher. Individuals on horseback, not common transportation in Palestine, could perhaps travel 25 to 30 miles in a day.[11] Several highways and roads traversed Palestine, some of which were substantially improved by Roman road building techniques. Inns were available for travelers but were notoriously dirty and dangerous. If at all possible, a person usually stayed with friends or family members when overnight lodging was necessary.

The economic situation of the Palestinian people was worsened by the heavy religious obligations and civil taxes they had to bear. The variety of offerings of the Jewish sacrificial system (sin offerings, guilt offerings, grain offerings, thank offerings, burnt offerings) and the payment of tithes (a tenth of one's income and produce) were required of the religiously faithful. Furthermore, a Temple tax of a half-shekel was to be paid annually by every Jewish male twenty years old and above. In addition a "wood offering" was required annually to help supply the wood for the altar of burnt offering in the Temple.[12]

A variety of civil taxes was imposed on the people, either directly by the Roman governors or by the Herodian rulers. Among the taxes levied against the people were the *tributum soli* (a tax on crops), the *tributum capitis* (a tax on each person above a certain age), sales taxes, inheritance taxes, and tolls and duties on the transportation of goods (collected at border crossings, seaports, and at other locations). When all the civil and religious taxes and tithes are added up, the total burden on the average peasant farmer of Palestine was likely between 40 and 50 percent.[13] Such heavy taxation coupled with occasional droughts and poor crops would have driven many of the peasant farmers into debt as they borrowed heavily to meet their obligations. Mounting debts likely caused many to sell their meager plots of land and become landless tenants or day laborers.[14]

Tensions existed between the city dwellers and the rural people. The wealthy, who fed off the poor by means of loans, tenant-owner relationships, and taxes, were located in the cities. In general rural populations are more conservative, less likely to abandon traditional beliefs and practices. Cities, on the other hand, are more cosmopolitan, more accepting of change. In Palestine Hellenization was certainly more pronounced in the cities, although even the towns and villages did not go unaffected. Urban dwellers and rural inhabitants "were worlds apart, and everything, from accent, to gait, to dress, helped to accentuate those differences and underline the unequal relationships as far as the peasant was concerned. Consequently, the peasant viewed the city as dangerous and alien, and regarded its inhabitants with suspicion at best, and at worst with hostility."[15]

Social Status

Roman society was stratified by various social classes. At the top were the senatorial families, membership in which required possession of a certain amount of wealth. Next were the members of the equestrian order, from whose ranks the procurators or prefects of Roman provinces such as Judea were drawn. Below the equestrians were the members of the local senates. Plebians were the lower class of Rome, followed by the freedmen, that is, former slaves who had gained their freedom.

Palestinian society was not ordered according to the Roman social classes but had its own hierarchical social relationships. In Jewish Palestinian society the priesthood was the upper level of society. They offered sacrifices for the people, officiated and served in the Temple, bestowed blessings on the people, declared them ritually clean, and served as the link between the common people and God. Priesthood was based on heredity, thus entrance into this class was limited, although the number of individuals who were priests was so large that they were divided into twenty-four divisions and served in the Temple a week at a time on a rotating basis. The religious role of these priests bestowed on them a certain social status. They did not necessarily possess high economic status, however. A secondary level of Jewish "clergy" was the Levites, who were definitely lower in social status than the priests. These men served as singers, gatekeepers, watchmen, and custodians in the Temple. Like the priests, the Levites also were divided into twenty-four divisions, each division serving in the Temple one week at a time.

At the top of the priestly class was the high priest, who since postexilic times had exercised tremendous power in Palestinian society. The high priest was in charge of the Temple as well as of the Sanhedrin (see below). As the spiritual leader of Judaism, the high priest was the only person who could offer the sin offerings on behalf of the people on the Day of Atonement. He alone was allowed to enter the innermost part of the Jerusalem Temple, the Holy of Holies, and then only on the Day of Atonement. Former high priests (the office, which theoretically was a lifetime appointment, had become a political pawn in the hands of the Herodians and the Romans) and priests of the leading families of Jerusalem comprised an inner circle of "chief priests." This latter group of priests led by the high priest, together with the lay aristocracy of Jerusalem (wealthy, influential individuals who were not members of the priestly class), formed a socio-religious-political group in Palestine that exercised enormous control over the lives of the people. This upper strata of Jewish society had by necessity formed an uneasy alliance with the Roman authorities. The Roman procurator kept the high priest's sacred vestments locked away, allowing him to have them only on special festivals when they were needed. Furthermore, Rome had allowed the Jewish hierarchy to maintain a degree of autonomy over the religious and civil affairs of Palestine. Only if the Jewish power structure kept rebellious factions in check and supported the Roman authorities would such an arrangement be permitted to continue.

Because of the importance of the study of the scriptures within Judaism, special honor and status was enjoyed by those men who devoted their lives to the study and teaching of the Jewish scriptures. These individuals, the scribes, were the experts in Jewish law and Jewish religious practices. They functioned as guardians and conveyors of the religious traditions. They were also teachers, gathering around them a group of students who studied with the scribe for years in order that they too might become recognized masters of the tradition. These religious scholars rendered opinions on matters of religious regulation and ritual. Some were also priests, but most were lay scholars. Their power and influence derived not from their economic status but from their knowledge. Some of the scribes, in fact, were poor. Many seem to have supported themselves through some type of manual labor. (At least by the second century CE the title "rabbi" was applied to the experts in Jewish law. Originally the title simply meant something equivalent to "sir," but it later came to designate a teacher of the law. The evidence on its use and meaning in the first century CE is ambiguous.)

Below the priests, Levites, the lay aristocracy, and the scribes were the common people of society. These would have included the farmers, merchants, craftsmen, and others mentioned above. As in most societies, certain professions enjoyed more prestige or social status than others. Those who were day laborers, tenant farmers, and itinerant craftsmen would have held lower status than those who owned their plots of land and ran their own businesses.

Below the common people were the slaves. Slaves were abundant throughout the Roman Empire and were an important part of the ancient economy. Persons became slaves in a variety of ways: (1) One of the common means by which a person entered slavery was through conquest in time of war. Rome, like other nations, subjugated many of its conquered peoples and made them slaves. The Jewish population of Rome, in fact, likely arose in large part from the presence of Jewish slaves brought to Rome from Palestine. (2) Children born to women in slavery produced a large number of slaves. (3) Persons who could not pay their debts were sometimes sold into slavery. Children, especially daughters, were often sold into slavery to pay family debts. (4) An individual who was in serious financial difficulty could sell himself or herself into slavery, usually for a preset time period. (5) Unwanted infants who were left on their own to die were sometimes picked up and raised for sale as slaves. While common throughout the Roman world, such "exposure" of infants for death was abhorrent to the Jews. (6) Ancient sources indicate that kidnapping individuals for slavery was also practiced.

References in Jewish literature and the New Testament indicate that ownership of slaves was very common in Palestine, especially among the well-to-do, including the high priest. Most slaves of Jewish masters were gentile slaves, usually foreigners. These slaves were usually circumcised (male slaves) and treated as proselytes. Although the legal status of slaves was below that of people who were free, such may not have been the case in regard to social status. S. Scott Bartchy notes, "Despite the neat legal separation between owners and slaves, in none of the relevant cultures did persons in slavery constitute a social or economic class. . . . Slaves' individual honor, social status, and economic opportunities were entirely dependent on the status of their respective owners."[16] Slavery was normally not a lifelong condition. Individuals could be set free by their owner (and often were), they could buy their own freedom, or friends or relatives could purchase freedom for them.

Social/religious classifications divided Palestinian society on the basis of one's relationship to Judaism, as well. From a Jewish perspective humanity could be divided into several categories: full-blooded Jews, proselytes, "God-fearers," and gentiles. Full-blooded Jews would be those people who were born Jewish. Proselytes (a term that denotes someone who converts from one belief system or group to another) were non-Jews who became complete converts to Judaism. For men this would have included undergoing the ritual act of circumcision. The term "God-fearers" is sometimes used to describe non-Jews in the ancient world who were attracted to some of the elements of Judaism and adopted some Jewish beliefs and practices but stopped short of becoming full converts to Judaism. The last term, "gentiles," refers to anyone who is not Jewish. Strictly speaking, "God-fearers" are still gentiles, as well. Even within the borders of Palestine many gentiles could be found: Roman soldiers, inhabitants of the land whose ancestry was not Jewish, and people who migrated and settled in various areas of the land, particularly in the Hellenistic cities of Palestine. The region to the northeast of the Sea of Galilee, ruled over by the Herodian Philip from 4 BCE to 34 CE, was almost entirely a gentile population. From a strictly religious viewpoint, these categories represent a distinction in ritual purity, with gentiles at the impure end of the spectrum.

The Greco-Roman world was a patriarchal society in which the social status of women was inferior to that of men. Generally speaking, women in Roman society fared better than women in Palestine. In Roman society the education of young girls was permitted and even encouraged, especially among the upper class. Although the husband was definitely the head of the household, a woman had certain property rights, could divorce her husband, and enjoyed some freedoms and choices in lifestyle, including owning and operating businesses. Women, however, were not allowed to vote or to hold public office.

Within Jewish society the role of the woman was basically restricted to the home. Whereas women who fulfilled the roles of wife and mother well were highly praised and esteemed and women were given great responsibility within the home, women functioned in the larger society as second-class citizens. Rabbinic literature of the second century and later contains statements warning men about conversing with women, even their own wives, in public and exempting women from the obligation to fulfill the positive commandments of Jewish tradition. It also reflects the varying opinions of the rabbinic scholars over whether the testimony of women was acceptable in court or whether one should "waste" the teaching of the Jewish law on young women. Because these are later writings (even though some of the teachings are attributed to first-century and earlier scribes), one is not certain how accurately these reflect first-century beliefs or practices. Two aspects of religious life, however, give concrete evidence of the subordinate status of women in Jewish life. Circumcision, the physical sign of belonging to the covenant people of God, was a male only ritual. Obviously women could not share in this act. Temple life and leadership also excluded women. Women could not be priests or Levites. As is discussed below, the physical layout of the Temple excluded women from the inner parts of the Temple, restricting them to the Court of the Women.

The Religious World

Although other religious systems besides Judaism were widely known and practiced in the Roman world, and even within Palestine, Roman and Hellenistic temples and shrines could be found, Judaism was the major religious tradition of first-century Palestine. Obviously the complexities and varieties of Judaism cannot be adequately covered in the brief survey that follows. Our focus, then, will be on the major institutions, groups, and beliefs and practices within first-century Palestinian Judaism.

Institutions

The Temple. The most important religious institution for the Jewish people was the Jerusalem Temple. The Temple was the locus of the sacrificial system, the primary element of worship in ancient Judaism. The Jerusalem Temple was the only place where sacrifices could be offered. The Jewish people visited the Temple for a variety of reasons: to offer sacrifices, to present tithes and offerings, to fulfill religious vows, to pray and worship, for ritual cleansing and to be declared clean by the priests after certain forms of defilement (touching a corpse, unnatural bodily discharges, certain skin disorders), to observe the offering of sacrifices, to receive priestly blessings, and to hear or teach the Jewish scriptures. Teaching and discussions about the Jewish law often took place around the porticoes and in the porches of the Temple. In the outer court of the Temple one could buy animals that were acceptable for sacrifices (pigeons, doves, sheep), as well as oil and wine for offerings, and could exchange foreign currency for Jewish coins. (Foreign currency with human images stamped on it was unacceptable because this was seen as a violation of the commandment against "graven images" [Exod 20:4]. Jewish coins had no depictions of human figures or faces.)

In addition to its use for worship, the Temple was also a place for the study and teaching of the Jewish scriptures and a major financial center. The Temple treasuries contained huge sums of money, brought to the Temple as tithes and offerings by worshipers, contributed as gifts by foreign rulers and dignitaries, and sent as payment of the half-shekel tax on all Jewish males. The Temple also served as a depository of private funds, placed there for safekeeping because the people viewed it as a secure place because of its religious sanctity.

The Temple complex covered a large area, approximately 172,000 square yards.[17] The major portion of that area was open courtyards, surrounded by covered porticoes. The outermost court was called the Court of the Gentiles (see figure 2.1). Anyone could enter this part of the Temple. A stepped platform, surrounded by a low partition, separated this section of the Temple mount from the rest of the Temple. Placed along the partition were plaques in Greek and Latin that warned of the penalty of death for any gentile who crossed beyond that point. The next section of the Temple was the Court of the Women into which any Jewish person could enter. In this area most of the acts of community worship, with the exception of the sacrifices, took place. Beyond the Court of the Women, up a set of semicircular steps and through a great bronze gate was the Court of the Israelites, which was open only to Jewish men (women could apparently enter this area to observe the offering of sacrifices).[18] Further inside was the Court of the Priests, which contained the altar, where sacrifices were offered, the slaughter area, and a large basin that was use by the priests for ceremonial washings. The innermost part of the Temple, the Sanctuary, was the most sacred part of the Temple. Fronted by a porch, it contained two sections. The front section was known as the Holy Place. Only priests could enter this section, which contained an incense altar, a candelabrum, and a table for sacred bread, the "bread of the Presence." The back section was known as the Holy of Holies and was open only to the high priest, who entered this area only once a year, on the Day of Atonement.

The Sanhedrin. The Sanhedrin was another important institution in the life of Judaism. This Greek term refers to the ruling council within Judaism. Unfortunately our ancient sources (Josephus, the rabbinic writings, and the New Testament) do not agree on the function, membership, and even the name of this group. For this reason, some scholars posit that two or three governing councils operated in first-century Palestine, some with religious responsibilities, others with political responsibilities. It seems preferable, however, to explain the variations on the basis of confusion or errors on the part of the sources and to conclude that one governing body existed, realizing that this group may have changed somewhat over time and that the pre-70 CE Sanhedrin likely differed considerably from the post-70 institution.

The Sanhedrin was the chief judicial and legislative body within Judaism, interpreting the law, enacting laws, conducting trials, and imposing

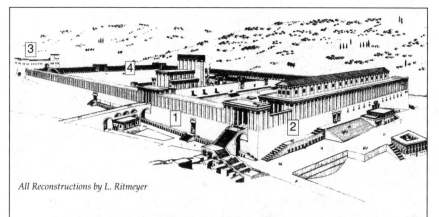

All Reconstructions by L. Ritmeyer

THE TEMPLE MOUNT AND TEMPLE OF HEROD THE GREAT

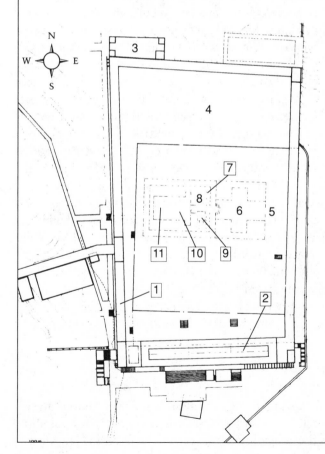

1. Western Wall
2. Royal Portico
3. Antonia Fortress
4. Court of the Gentiles
5. Beautiful Gate
6. Court of the Women
7. Court of Israel
8. Court of the Priests
9. Altar
10. Holy Place
11. Holy of Holies

punishment. It decided matters both religious and political. The Romans allowed conquered peoples a significant amount of self-rule. The Sanhedrin was the body that functioned in this way in Palestine. The Sanhedrin was composed of seventy members, primarily priests and scribes, plus the high priest who served as the leader of the Sanhedrin. Following the destruction of Jerusalem and the Temple in 70 CE, the Sanhedrin (or a somewhat similar group) was reorganized at Jamnia (or Yavneh), a city west of Jerusalem and close to the Mediterranean sea. At Jamnia over the next few decades Jewish scholars met to restructure Judaism following the debacle of the first Jewish-Roman war. With the demise of the Temple, leadership no longer was in the hands of the high priest and the priestly aristocracy. Instead, the major scribes or rabbis became the leading figures within Judaism.

Synagogues. Whereas the Temple was at least symbolically the most important institution within Judaism, for many Jews outside Jerusalem, and especially for Jews in the Diaspora (a Greek term meaning "dispersion" and used to refer to Jews outside Palestine), the synagogue exercised more influence over their lives. The origin of the synagogue is unclear. Some scholars have argued that the earliest synagogues arose during the exile or shortly thereafter as substitutes for the Temple, although the earliest inscriptions that refer to a synagogue come from the third century BCE. Egypt and the oldest archeological finds of a synagogue are from the first or second century BCE (from the Aegean island of Delos). By the first century CE, synagogues were widespread, both within Palestine and in the Diaspora. The remains of only three synagogues from as early as the first century CE have been found in Palestine. This suggests that during this period many private homes and perhaps some public buildings were used as meeting places for the Jews. The synagogues functioned as a place of prayer and study, a place for worship, a school, and a meeting house. In contrast to the Temple, which was led by priests, the synagogues were controlled by the congregation and the community who selected persons to serve in leadership roles. No sacrifices were offered in the synagogues. Scripture reading, sermons, and prayer were the main elements of synagogue worship.

Groups

As we have seen already, first-century Palestine exhibited a rich diversity—urban versus rural, the wealthy versus the poor, the powerful elite versus the powerless, the religiously clean versus the unclean, Jew versus gentile, Roman dominator versus the dominated Palestinian. Such variety was true within Palestinian Judaism as well. Judaism was not all of one stripe; various expressions of the Jewish faith coexisted and often competed.

Sadducees. The Sadducees (whose name was apparently derived from Zadok, one of the leading priests under David and Solomon) were for the most part the priestly, aristocratic party within Judaism. Josephus and the New Testament both report that the Sadducees rejected the belief in resurrection of the dead, and the New Testament adds that they also did not believe in angels or spirits.[19] Probably because the Sadducees were closely aligned with the Temple and seem to have been concentrated in and around Jerusalem, the fall of that city and the destruction of the Temple in 70 CE led to the demise of the Sadducees.

Pharisees. The Pharisees are presented often in Josephus and the New Testament as opponents of the Sadducees. In contrast to the Sadducees, the Pharisees accepted the idea of the resurrection of the dead. According to the ancient sources, the Pharisees had the support of the populace, whereas the Sadducees were the party of the wealthy. The two groups often disagreed over interpretations of the Jewish law. The Pharisees accepted the large body of oral interpretation of the Jewish scriptures (the "oral law") that had been handed down through various scribes. The Sadducees did not accept these interpretations as authoritative. The Pharisees and Sadducees vied for control over Judaism. Both groups were represented in the Sanhedrin. The form of Judaism that survived and became normative after 70 CE was Pharisaic Judaism.

The name "Pharisees" was derived from a Hebrew word meaning "separated one," indicating either their separation from everything ritually unclean or from other people. Unfortunately, because of the negative portrayal of the Pharisees in the New Testament, the word "Pharisee" has taken on a pejorative meaning today to indicate someone who is hypocritical or insincere. Such an understanding of the Pharisees, however, is inaccurate and prejudiced. The Pharisees should be viewed as a strict, pious group within Judaism who attempted to follow as closely as possible their understanding of the claims of God on their lives.

Essenes. Josephus and a few other ancient writers (Philo and Pliny the Elder) mention another group within Judaism, the Essenes, a group that is not mentioned in the New Testament nor in rabbinic sources. The Essenes, like the Pharisees, were strict followers of Judaism, although the two groups had major differences in beliefs and practices. The Essenes believed that Temple worship, and particularly the priesthood, had become corrupt. They therefore withdrew from mainstream Judaism. Some Essenes withdrew almost completely from mainstream society, forming their own closed communities in which individuals held property in common, followed rigid rules for behavior, worked at crafts and agriculture, shared communal meals, and emphasized the study of scripture. Other Essenes lived in towns and villages throughout Palestine and withdrew from society to a lesser extent. While some Essenes maintained celibate lifestyles, others did not.

According to most scholars, the community of Jews living at Qumran on the northwestern shore of the Dead Sea and who produced the Dead Sea Scrolls were Essenes. This community, probably originating in the last half of the second century BCE, was an apocalyptic group who saw themselves as the Children of Light preserving the pure form of Judaism. When the final, eschatological battle takes place, the Children of Light will be led by the archangel Michael to defeat the Children of Darkness, led by Belial. In 68 CE, during the first Jewish-Roman war, the Romans destroyed Qumran.

Sicarii and Zealots. Josephus mentions other groups that were operative in first-century Palestine, groups that could be labeled right-wing, nationalistic movements. The members of these groups were willing to use violence to help drive out the Romans. The Sicarii, whose name arose from the dagger or *sica* that they carried with them in order to kill Jewish sympathizers to the Romans, and the Zealots were both active in the first Jewish revolt against the Romans. The Sicarii were the ones who defended the fortress at Masada until it was overrun by the Romans in 74 CE.

Samaritans. Another group within Palestine was the Samaritans. The term Samaritan is used in two ways: to refer to the inhabitants of the region of Samaria, and to refer to members of a distinct religious community. The latter meaning is the one that concerns us here. The origin of the Samaritans is shrouded in uncertainty. The Hebrew Bible (2 Kings 17) claims that they were the descendants of foreigners who were settled in the land by the Assyrians subsequent to the Assyrian conquest of Israel and deportation of the Israelite people. The resultant religion of these transplants was syncretistic, mixing Israelite and foreign traditions. The Samaritans, however, dispute this, claiming that they are the true representatives of Israelite religion. Whatever their origins, by the first century CE the Samaritans were a separate, though closely related, religious group from the Judaism of Jerusalem. The Samaritans claimed that Mt. Gerizim (near the city of Shechem), not Jerusalem, was the correct place to worship God. They had even built a temple there but it was destroyed in 128 BCE by the Hasmonean ruler John Hyrcanus. In contrast to the Jews, the Samaritans accepted as authoritative scripture only the first five books, the Pentateuch or Torah. Animosity between the Jews and Samaritans ran high, with each group considering the other as heretical. (A small community of Samaritans still lives and worships near Mt. Gerizim today.)

Beliefs and Practices

Although Judaism of the first century was diverse in its beliefs and practices, in general several practices and attitudes were common among the Jewish people.

Monotheism. One of the characteristics that distinguished Jews from their neighbors in the ancient world was their monotheism, that is, the belief in only one god. The Hellenistic-Roman world was a polytheistic world. People believed in and worshiped many gods. Elaborate temples and sanctuaries to these gods and goddesses were built throughout the empire, including some areas of Palestine. The refusal of the Jews to acknowledge and honor other gods seemed very peculiar to most of the non-Jews. If worship of one god was commendable, worship of a multitude of gods would seem even more pious. Why risk the wrath of the gods by not recognizing and honoring them? Judaism, however, clung to its belief in the uniqueness and sovereignty of its god.

Scripture. A modern Jewish Bible contains three sections, the Torah (Law), the Nebiim (Prophets), and the Kethubim (Writings). Whereas the first two sections were probably universally accepted and recognized by the first century CE, the final section was still somewhat fluid. Some of the works in this section may not have been considered authoritative by all Jews. On the other hand, some works not in the present Hebrew Bible may have been considered authoritative by some Jewish groups. The most important part of the Jewish scriptures was the Torah, or the Pentateuch, the first five books. These comprised the heart of Judaism.

Eschatology. Eschatology refers to beliefs about the last days or the end times. Strictly speaking, the teachings in the Hebrew Bible deal more with the future than with end-time events. Although much variety can be found in the Hebrew Bible, in general the writers speak of a future time, often after God's punishment, when the land of Israel would be restored, peace and prosperity would reign, and the people would live in faithfulness to God. Some of these future scenarios contained an ideal king of the line of David who would rule over the land with justice and righteousness. This "prophetic eschatology" eventually gave way to apocalyptic eschatology, however. Following the return to Palestine after the exile, anticipated with such exalted expectations in Isaiah 40–55, the reality of the situation challenged the hopeful outlook that expected a renewed and glorious nation of Israel. Ultimately hope within history faded as people began to believe that this world was so evil and wicked that God would not salvage history. Hope was shifted from this world and this age to another world and another age. Hope lay beyond history. One day God would bring this world to a cataclysmic end, followed by the creation of a new world. Resurrection of the dead, a final judgment, rewards for the righteous, and punishments for the wicked were often components of apocalyptic eschatology.

A messiah figure may or may not be a part of Jewish eschatological expectations. The term *messiah* means "anointed," a person set apart for a special task (originally through the pouring or rubbing of oil on them). In the Hebrew Bible normally only kings are described as anointed, although on a few occasions priests and even a prophet are so described. The word *messiah* is never used in the Hebrew Bible for an ideal, future ruler, although the use of the term in the book of Psalms to describe the Davidic king likely contributed to the idea of a future, kingly Messiah. In later Jewish writings, the term *messiah* is only one of several terms that are used to describe God's eschatological agent or mediator. Further diversity is seen in the Dead Sea Scrolls from Qumran, which appear to speak of two expected Messiahs, a priestly and a kingly Messiah. In addition, the eschatological scenarios of many Jewish writings contain no messianic figure or other eschatological agent; God acts directly to accomplish God's purposes.

Worship. As discussed earlier, both the Temple and the synagogue were centers of worship for the Jewish people. The offering of sacrifices was the main element of Temple worship. Daily sacrifices as well as occasional sacrifices were offered in the Temple. The common people did not attend all these sacrificial offerings, rather the priests served as representatives of the people. In the synagogue they would gather for prayer, praise of God, scripture reading, and sermons.

Worship also occurred in the homes. The faithful Jew was expected to pray twice daily, in the morning and the afternoon at times corresponding to the *Tamid* offering, the daily burnt offering in the Jerusalem Temple. The Shema (a prayer drawn from Deut 6:4-9) was to be recited in the morning and at evening. Meals were prefaced and concluded with the pronouncement of blessings. Certain practices, while not explicitly worship, were intended to remind the people of their commitment to God. For example, the people were supposed to attach fringes or tassles (*tzitzit*) to the corners of their clothing, to place a *mezuzah* (a small box containing scripture verses) on their doorposts, and to wear *tefillin* or phylacteries (small capsules containing scripture verses that were bound to their arms and head).

Holy Days, Festivals, and Fasts. The most important day of the week within Judaism was the sabbath, the seventh day. On this day no work was permitted. The day was characterized by synagogue worship and family or group meals. Although the Jewish scriptures give little details about what one could or could not do on the sabbath, a large body of oral traditions arose to give guidance about the sabbath. Particularly for Jews in the Diaspora, observance of the sabbath was a distinctive practice that set them apart from other people.

The Jewish people celebrated several religious festivals each year. Passover, a spring festival, was a commemoration of the Israelite's exodus from Egypt. Passover itself lasted only one day. It was combined with the seven-day Feast of Unleavened Bread, and the term *Passover* came to be used for the entire period. Each family or group took a lamb to the Temple on the afternoon prior to the beginning of Passover. The lamb was ritually slaughtered by the priests and returned to the people to be roasted and eaten as a part of the Passover meal. The Feast of Pentecost (or Feast of Weeks) was a celebration of the spring grain harvest and occurred fifty days after Passover. The Feast of Tabernacles (or "Booths"), an autumn festival, was also originally an agricultural festival but was given a historical interpretation, commemorating the Israelite's wilderness wandering period when they lived in tents (booths). This seven-day festival was very popular and was celebrated by special ceremonies in the Temple and by the people living in special huts or booths erected for the occasion. These three festivals were known as pilgrim festivals because the people were expected to journey to Jerusalem to celebrate these festivals.

The Jewish New Year, or *Rosh ha-Shanah*, began in the fall on the first day of the Jewish month of Tishri. It stressed God's kingship over the earth and was heralded by the blowing of the *shofar*, or ram's horn. The Day of Atonement (*Yom Kippur*) occurred on the tenth day of Tishri. It was a day of fasting, prayers, and repentance. Only on this day did the high priest enter the most sacred part of the Jerusalem Temple, the Holy of Holies. Other festivals were the Feast of Dedication (*Hanukkah*), which commemorated the rededication of the Temple during the time of Judas Maccabaeus, the celebrations of the New Moon, and Purim, a carnival-like festival celebrating the story of Esther saving her people.

The people also demonstrated their religious commitment through fasting, both communal and individual. In addition to fasting on the Day of Atonement, the community would fast as a sign of national mourning or lamentation. Individuals would fast to express personal grief or sorrow or as expressions of religious devotion.

Ritual Purity. Judaism possessed a variety of rules and regulations intended to separate that which was sacred ("set apart") from that which was profane, or common. Purity laws served this purpose. They delineated what was "clean" and what was "unclean." Purity laws were a way of drawing boundaries, of segregating people, places, animals, food, and objects. The categorization of people into Jews, proselytes, "God-fearers," and gentiles is an example of drawing boundaries around people. The divisions in the Temple—Court of the Gentiles, Court of the Women, Court of the Israelites, etc.—defined varying degrees of sacred space. Jewish customs declared certain foods acceptable or not, based upon whether they were considered ritually clean or unclean. Regulations specified when and under what circumstances certain foods, utensils, and clothing could be used. Procedures were spelled out for how an item or person that had been defiled, that is rendered unclean, could be declared clean once more. These procedures might involve washing, waiting a specified period of time, or offering a sacrifice. All these regulations about clean and unclean were attempts to provide an order to life and to be reminders that there is a sacred dimension to life that should not be forgotten.

Chapter 3

❖

The Gospel of Mark

Since Mark was the earliest Gospel written and in the opinion of most scholars was a source used by the authors of Matthew and Luke, we will begin our examination of the Gospels with Mark. For many years Mark was the neglected Gospel. In the early church Mark was understood primarily as a condensed version of Matthew that added little to what could be found in Matthew. Mark was seen, therefore, to be of less importance than the other Gospels. The early church leaders seldom quoted from the Gospel of Mark in any of their writings and no known commentary was written on the Gospel of Mark until the fifth century CE. This attitude toward Mark began to change in the nineteenth century when scholars decided that Mark was the first Gospel written. It thus was given priority in attempts to reconstruct the life of the historical Jesus. Furthermore, the belief that Matthew and Luke were dependent on Mark propelled Mark's Gospel to prominence. Today, the Gospel of Mark is highly regarded, not because it is thought to be more accurate historically than the others, but because most scholars accept the theory that Matthew and Luke used Mark as a source and because scholars have come to appreciate the literary and narrative skills of the author of Mark.

Social Setting

Date of Writing

In the previous chapter we attempted to describe in broad terms the historical, social, and religious world of the first century, particularly first-century Palestine. Can we locate the writing of Mark's Gospel more specifically in that first-century world? When and where was it written? What was the community to which it was addressed? External evidence for dating the Gospel of Mark is scant. The earliest copy we possess is a manuscript dating from the early to middle part of the third century. Several leaders of the church in the late-second century refer to the Gospel of Mark in their writings, including Papias, whose writing from the middle of the second century is quoted by Eusebius. Papias, as we have seen, associates the writing of the Gospel with Mark's recollection of the teaching and preaching of Peter. Assuming that Peter died during the Neronian persecution of 64 CE and that Mark would have been written shortly thereafter, some interpreters have argued for a date of the Gospel around 64 CE. As we have noted, however, the Papias tradition is very suspect and should not be used as a basis for dating the Gospel.

Lacking sufficient evidence to date Mark, we must turn to clues within the Gospel itself. Here we do not fare much better. Chapter 13, with its references to persecution, suffering, war, and the destruction of the Jerusalem Temple, perhaps contains some hints about when the work was written. Many scholars have argued that the references to persecution and suffering would fit well the period of persecution when Christians in Rome suffered at the hands of Nero. They argue that Mark saw a parallel between the sufferings of contemporary followers of Jesus and the sufferings and death of Jesus himself. According to this view, one of the purposes of his work was to offer hope and encouragement to beleaguered believers by correlating their sufferings with those of Jesus. The references to suffering and war might also relate to the situation in Palestine during the first Jewish-Roman war. The predictions of the destruction of the Temple are usually viewed as indications that the work was written shortly before or immediately after the Romans destroyed the Temple in 70 CE. Since Mark's reference to the fall of Jerusalem is rather general, compared to the description in Luke 21:20-24 (and perhaps also Matt 22:7 and Luke 19:43), he must have written his Gospel prior to the fall of Jerusalem in 70 CE. Other scholars interpret the statement in 13:14 about "the desolating sacrilege set up [or "standing"] where it [or "he"] ought not to be," which is borrowed from the book of Daniel (9:27; 11:31; 12:11), as referring to the entrance of Titus into the sacred precinct of the Temple, the Holy of Holies. On that basis they argue for a date shortly after 70 CE. Thus even though scholars disagree, most would opt for a date somewhere between 65 and 72 CE. Sometime around 70 CE is likely the nearest we can come to ascertaining the date for the writing of Mark.

Place of Writing

The place of writing of this Gospel is also uncertain. The Gospels give no indication that they were written in one location but addressed to people in another location (as was the case with the letters of Paul). For this reason, we can reasonably assume that the community for which a Gospel was written was also the community in which the Gospel writer lived. Tradition, based on the comments of Papias, Irenaeus, and others, claims Rome as the location for the writing of Mark. Modern scholars have sought support for this claim within the Gospel itself. Some readers have pointed to the presence in Mark of several Latinisms or Latin loan-words as an indication that the Gospel originated in Rome. Such Latinisms were found throughout the Roman Empire, however, even occurring in the Hebrew Talmud. The presence of these terms in Mark provides no clue to location. Reference to one particular Roman custom, however, may point to a Roman origin. In the Markan version of Jesus' teaching on divorce, the presumption is that women, as well as men, may initiate divorce (10:12; cf. Matt 19:9; Luke 16:18). Wives could divorce their husbands according to Roman law, but not according to Jewish law.

The Gospel's special interest in persecution and suffering also has been used as support for a Roman provenance. The predictions of Jesus' suffering and death (8:31; 9:31; 10:33-34), the statements about the necessity of suffering for the disciples of Jesus (8:34-38; 10:38-45), and the predictions of their impending persecution (13:9-13) are evidence of this emphasis. Perhaps Mark's emphasis on suffering and persecution reflects the situation of his readers; that is, they too were experiencing persecution. The condition of the Christians in Rome during the Neronian persecution of 64 would certainly fit this situation. (This persecution setting would also apply, however, to Palestine and possibly Syria during the Roman-Jewish war of 66–74 CE.)

More recently, scholars have proposed other locations for the composition of the Gospel. The two most popular suggestions are Galilee (primarily because of the prominence and significance of Galilee in the Gospel) and Syria. The latter suggestion explains the Semitic flavor of the Gospel and its interest in rural Galilee (just south of Syria), yet it avoids the problem of the author's inaccurate information about Galilean geography.[1] Although both proposals have strong proponents, neither has yet convinced most scholars.

Although no specific location for the writing of Mark can be ascertained, the evidence of the Gospel itself points to a non-Palestinian location for the writing of the Gospel. Such evidence would include the author's erroneous statements about Palestinian geography, the translation of Aramaic words (3:17; 7:11; 14:36; 15:34) and the composition of the work in Greek.

Intended Readers

The explanation of Jewish customs in the Gospel (7:3-4; 14:12; 15:42) leads to the conclusion that the original readers were mainly gentiles. Furthermore, Mark's readers were concerned about persecution and suffering, which apparently contributed to heightened apocalyptic concerns about the end times.

Taken together, these clues, along with the evidence for the location of writing, suggest that the community out of which the Gospel of Mark arose was a Christian community, primarily gentile, located outside Palestine, and one which was experiencing or expecting persecution.

Telling the Story

The way a story is told is often as important as its contents. A good storyteller gives the readers or hearers clues to important ideas and motifs, provides helps for interpreting the story, and arranges the story in ways that facilitate understanding and memory. In the past, Mark's skill as a story-teller has often been disparaged. He has been portrayed more as a compiler of traditional materials than as a skilled author. Some scholars have claimed that Mark's major accomplishment was to string together the material he found in his sources, exercising little creative control over the material. This approach focuses on trying to determine the sources Mark used (source criticism) and examining the changes Mark may have made in those sources (redaction criticism).

More recently, scholars have begun to appreciate Mark's literary skill. Leaving aside the question of sources, these scholars examine how Mark tells his story of Jesus, how he arranges his material, and how he presents the major and minor characters. These scholars (literary critics and narra-tive critics) are convinced that Mark has intentionally crafted a narrative about Jesus, rather than simply collected, rearranged, and edited source materials. They look for clues to the plot or story line of Mark's Gospel; they isolate stylistic characteristics and structuring devices in the work; and they examine the narrative settings of the story. Rather than explaining the events in the Gospel simply as historical occurrences, or the arrangement of the Gospel on the basis of chronology or sources, these scholars attempt to enter the story world of the Gospel and listen to the story Mark tells. In the opinion of these scholars, the author was a skillful literary artist, a masterful storyteller, full of creativity and insight. Such an approach—a literary study—is basically the one followed in this work also.

How does Mark tell his story of Jesus? What elements of Markan style or ways of structuring the story aid in interpreting the text? The following paragraphs will highlight a few of the major elements of Mark's narrative.

Urgency

Readers of Mark's Gospel have often commented on the sense of urgency in this Gospel. Events move at a rapid pace, the chronological setting is compressed, and the characters hurry from one scene to the next, leaving the readers little time to catch their breath. Several stylistic factors contribute to this feeling of urgency, which is particularly strong in the first half of the book. Mark has a fondness for the word *immediately* (often obscured in English translations). In the opening chapter of Mark we are told that after his baptism, Jesus "immediately" saw the heavens opened; the Spirit "immediately" drove him into the wilderness; Simon and Andrew "immediately" left their fishing nets and followed Jesus; when Jesus saw James and John, he "immediately" called them; "immediately" on the sabbath Jesus entered the synagogue; in the synagogue there was "immediately" a man with an unclean spirit; "immediately" Jesus' fame spread throughout the region; "immediately" Jesus left the synagogue; the disciples told Jesus "immediately" about Peter's mother-in-law's fever; Jesus healed a leper and "immediately" the leprosy left him; Jesus sent the healed man away "immediately." The Greek word *euthys* ("immediately") occurs forty-two times in the Gospel of Mark, with all but seven of those occurrences found in the first nine chapters of the Gospel. Mark's predilection for this word is even more obvious when one compares Mark with Matthew and Luke, both of which are considerably longer than Mark. Matthew uses *euthys* only seven times, whereas Luke uses the word only once in his entire

Gospel. Obviously the use of "immediately" is a part of Mark's writing style, rather than a historical description.

Another aspect of Markan style that adds to the sense of urgency is Mark's sentence structure. Mark frequently connects sentences and clauses with the word *and* (*kai* in Greek). This creates a run-on effect so that the action seldom completely stops. Translators of the Greek text often ignore the presence of *kai* because its overuse makes the writing appear clumsy and awkward. Although Mark's fondness for using *kai* as a connective contributes to an inelegant writing style, it functions to draw the reader into the story and helps the reader sense the urgency of the Gospel message: "The time is fulfilled, and the kingdom of God has come near" (Mark 1:15).

Likewise, Mark chose to concentrate on the activities of Jesus. Jesus is constantly on the move in the Gospel of Mark. He is busy teaching, preaching, and healing. Although Mark emphasizes the role of teacher for Jesus, he seldom gives any extensive teaching of Jesus. This busy pace of the Gospel adds to the urgency felt by the reader.

Mark also varies the story time or chronological setting of his narrative. The first part of the Gospel rushes through several months of Jesus' activities in Galilee as he moves around the Sea of Galilee and beyond, proclaiming the news about the kingdom of God, calling disciples, and healing the sick. In the latter half of the Gospel, the pace slows as Mark describes the events leading up to Jesus' trial and crucifixion. Whereas the events of the first ten chapters occur over a period of months, the activities of the last six chapters, including the passion narrative, occupy only a few days. By slowing the pace, Mark calls the reader to pay attention to these events. As Elizabeth Struthers Malbon explains,

> A modern-day analogy would be a filmmaker's skillful use of slow motion photography to suggest the profound significance of a climaxing series of scenes. The more detailed setting of scenes in time and space of the Markan passion narrative is the implied author's plea to the implied reader: slow down; take this in; to understand anything of the story, you must understand this. It is another form of urgency.[2]

Series of Three

Commentators have often noted Mark's fondness for a threefold presentation of sayings and events. Examples include Jesus predicting his death three times (8:31; 9:31; 10:33-34); Peter denying Jesus three times (14:68,

70, 71); three opinions about Jesus (8:28); three times in Gethsemane Jesus goes off alone to pray and returns three times to find Peter, James, and John asleep (14:32-42); at Jesus' trial Pilate asks the crowd three questions (15:9, 12, 14); Mark mentions three, three-hour intervals during Jesus' crucifixion (15:25, 33, 34). By means of this threefold pattern Mark calls attention to particular ideas or themes. The reader cannot fail to take note of these repeated sayings or events.

Intercalation

Mark employs the literary technique of intercalation, the bracketing of one narrative by the beginning and ending of a second narrative. For example, in chapter 5 Mark begins to narrate the story of the healing of Jairus' daughter. In the middle of the story, another healing episode is told. The end of the chapter then returns to the initial story, giving its conclusion. These "Markan sandwiches" serve not only to create suspense for the reader, but also are interpretive devices. The two episodes are held in tension and provide commentary on each other by means of contrast or similarity.

One of the best examples of this framing technique is the cursing of the fig tree and the cleansing of the Temple, described in 11:12-25. As Jesus and his disciples are going into Jerusalem from Bethany, Jesus curses a fig tree because it is barren. Proceeding into Jerusalem, Jesus goes to the Temple, becomes angry at the abuses he sees, and drives out the money changers and merchants. After this so-called "cleansing of the Temple," Jesus retires to Bethany for the evening. The next morning as he and his disciples are returning to Jerusalem, the disciples notice the fig tree has completely withered and died. Taken as a historical occurrence, this cursing of the fig tree raises problems for the interpreter. Why would Jesus have expected to find figs on the tree when the text clearly states that it was not the season for figs? Furthermore, this use of miraculous power is out of character with the Jesus presented in the Gospels. The cursing of the fig tree appears to be the impetuous act of an impatient person disappointed at not finding figs to eat when he wants them. If, however, the cursing of the fig tree is understood primarily as a literary device that Mark uses to interpret the Temple episode, then the purpose of the story becomes clearer. By surrounding the Temple episode with the story of the cursing of the fig tree, Mark is indicating to his readers that Jesus' activity in the

Temple was not merely a cleansing of a system with minor problems. Rather, Jesus' activities and prophetic announcements in the Temple were a sign of the demise of the entire religious system, including the Temple. As the fig tree had been cursed because of its failure to bear fruit, likewise the Temple system was now "cursed" and would "wither" because it had failed to produce the fruits of righteousness. The two stories interpret each other.

Notice that in the cursing of the fig tree episode, as well as in the other instances of intercalation, the relationship between the inner and outer stories is not specified. Rather, the reader is left to ponder, and sometimes to puzzle, over the connections between the intercalated stories. Additional examples of Mark's use of intercalation are found in 3:20-35; 6:7-31; 14:1-11; and 14:53-72.

Irony

Irony occurs when a speaker makes a statement that has an unintended, and often opposite, meaning to the literal or surface meaning, or when an incongruity exists between what the characters in a story know or understand, and what the readers of the story know or understand. Mark makes extensive use of irony. In 15:18 the soldiers mockingly hail Jesus as the "King of the Jews." What the soldiers say as a taunt, the reader understands to be the true identity of Jesus. A similar use of irony occurs when the bystanders at the cross of Jesus mock him by saying, "He saved others; he cannot save himself. Let the Messiah, the King of Israel, come down from the cross now, so that we may see and believe" (15:31-32). The actions of the disciples throughout the Gospel also are filled with irony. They are the ones who are the closest to Jesus, the ones who should understand his task and his mission. Yet they are often the very ones who misunderstand and who fail in their commitment to Jesus.

The Narrator

Readers of the Gospels who are accustomed to thinking of these writings as accurate historical documents have perhaps never noticed the role of the narrator in the Gospels. The narrator is not the actual writer or storyteller, but is a literary device of the author. A narrator performs an important task, telling the story from a certain point of view and providing clues for the reader on the meaning of the text. In some works, the narrator is a limited narrator, that is one who views the story from the same perspective as the characters in the story. A limited narrator has no inside knowledge that is not available to the characters of the story. In some cases, the narrator is actually one of the characters in the story. In other works, the narrator is "invisible" to the characters in the story, one who stands outside the story and narrates the events. Such outside narrators are often omniscient storytellers. They know more than the characters in the story know and share their special knowledge with the readers.

In Mark, as in the other Gospels as well, the narrator is of the latter type. His narrator is omniscient, giving the reader insights that are not available to the characters of the story. For example, the narrator informs the readers not only about the public speeches and activities of the various characters, but even shares the private thoughts and actions of many of the characters. The narrator in Mark also guides the reader in interpreting the story, providing clues and explanations. Sometimes these interpretive helps are obvious, as when the narrator pauses in his story to offer a parenthetical aside to the reader. The best example of this technique is in 13:14 where the narrator directly addresses the reader with the remark, "Let the reader understand." By this remark the narrator calls the reader's attention to the passage and encourages the reader to look closely for the meaning of the text. In other places in the Gospel, Mark's narrator pauses to interpret Aramaic words or to explain Jewish customs. He also interprets the significance of events or sayings. For example in 7:19, the narrator comments on Jesus' teaching on clean and unclean with the words, "Thus he declared all foods clean." As readers we see the story through the eyes of the narrator, adopting the narrator's point of view as our own. Jesus is the "good guy" and Jesus' opponents are the "bad guys"; that is the way the narrator wants us to perceive them.

Characters

The plot of a story unfolds through the activities and words of its main characters. In the Gospel of Mark the major characters are Jesus, his disciples, and the religious and political authorities. In addition, a diverse group of minor characters (such as the crowds, a Roman centurion, a Syrophoenician woman, and a synagogue leader named Jairus) populate the story. The central character is Jesus, whom the narrator identifies in the opening verse as "Jesus Christ [or, Messiah], the Son of God." One of the major issues in Mark's Gospel is the identity of Jesus. Although we, the readers, are told at the outset who Jesus is, the characters in the story are not privy to that information. They struggle to make sense of this man who teaches with such authority, who heals the sick, who casts out demons, who forgives sins, who commands the forces of nature, and who finally suffers and dies.

The disciples play an ambiguous role in Mark. On the one hand, they are positive characters. They respond affirmatively to Jesus' invitation to follow him, they stay with him throughout his ministry, they are sent out on a preaching and teaching mission by Jesus, and they are privy to special teachings and instructions by Jesus. On the other hand, the disciples are often slow to understand Jesus and his ministry, they have to ask for explanations of his teachings, they continually disappoint and fail Jesus, and eventually one of them even betrays Jesus to his enemies. We will pay particular attention to the disciples as we read and comment on Mark's Gospel.

The religious and political leaders in Mark are negative characters. Jesus is a threat to their power and authority. The conflict between Jesus and the religious authorities is a major part of the plot of the Gospel. This conflict begins as early as chapter 2 in the Gospel, intensifies throughout Jesus' ministry, and culminates in his trial and execution. The conflict between Jesus and the authorities is part of a larger conflict in the Gospel, a conflict between those who "set their minds on divine things" and those who "set their minds on human things" (cf. Mark 8:33). The religious and political authorities are representatives of the latter group. Their opposition to Jesus is evidence of their opposition to God. Mark's Gospel participates in an apocalyptic worldview that perceives that a cosmic struggle is taking place between God and Satan. Those who recognize the true significance of Jesus and follow him are on the side of God, whereas those who are opponents of Jesus are allies of Satan. Note that even Peter, when he opposes Jesus, is identified with Satan (Mark 8:33).

Whereas the authorities in Mark represent those who "set their minds on human things," the minor characters as a whole are portrayed as those who "set their minds on divine things." The men who bring a paralytic for healing are noticed for their faith (2:5); a demoniac named Legion goes about proclaiming the power of Jesus in healing him (5:20); a woman is praised for her faith that allows her to be healed (5:34); a synagogue leader's faith results in the healing of his daughter (5:35-42); a Syrophoenician woman persists and is successful in her efforts to get Jesus to heal her daughter (7:24-30); and the centurion at Jesus' crucifixion proclaims, "Truly this man was God's Son!" (15:39).

The portrayal of the minor figures in Mark is different from the portrayal of the anonymous "crowds" who follow Jesus. Whereas the minor characters are generally characterized in a positive way, the crowds are more ambiguous. Their response to Jesus is one of amazement, surprise, and wonder. They are at best tentative, fickle followers, ones whose commitment is shallow. They are interested in Jesus' ability to provide food and healing for them. Eventually they turn away from Jesus, even joining in the demand for his execution (15:13). In the imagery of one of Jesus' parables from chapter 4, the seed never takes root in these persons.

Structure

Students of Mark's Gospel have struggled to determine the underlying arrangement of the material in the Gospel. A careful reading of the text reveals that the Gospel is obviously not arranged in a strict historical, chronological, or geographical order. (Note the problems, for instance, in trying to follow the geographical references in 6:45 and 6:53, in which the disciples are supposedly headed across the sea to Bethsaida but end up at Gennesaret; or the chronological problems inherent in trying to reconstruct the events of 4:35–6:6, in which, according to the most natural reading of the text, all the events described in that section of the text occur in the course of a single evening.) Although scholars agree that the arrangement of Mark's Gospel is due to his own literary or theological purposes, attempts to reach a consensus on the Markan structure have not been successful. The outline of Mark followed in this study conforms to some of the obvious shifts or breaks in the narrative.

Major Themes in the Gospel of Mark

By his selection, arrangement, and alteration of traditions about Jesus, the author of the Gospel of Mark emphasized several key ideas about Jesus and his ministry.

Identity of Jesus

Throughout the Gospel of Mark the question of Jesus' identity is continually raised. From the amazed reaction following Jesus' first miracle in Capernaum to the centurion's declaration at the foot of the cross, the characters in the Gospel struggle to understand who Jesus is. As readers of the Gospel, we are told at the outset who he is: he is Jesus Christ, the Son of God. In addition to "Christ" and "Son of God," Mark uses other titles to identify Jesus without ever explaining what those titles mean, titles such as "Son of Man" and "Son of David." How would a first-century reader have understood those terms? Even more important, what seems to be their meaning as they are used in the Gospel of Mark?

Messiah. The Hebrew word for "messiah," which in Greek is *christos*, means "anointed one." In ancient times individuals were set apart for special service by anointing their heads with oil. Kings, priests, and others were often anointed as they assumed their roles. In the Hebrew Bible the Davidic king is often referred to as Yahweh's anointed, indicating his role as God's special representative. Within Judaism the idea developed that in the future a special anointed one, or Messiah, from God would appear who would usher in God's final kingdom. Jewish literature from the Hellenistic and Roman eras indicate that a diversity of views about the Messiah was prevalent. The Messiah may be of supernatural or of human origin. He may function as a king, an eschatological judge, or as a conquering, military figure—sometimes as a combination of these three. He may even be a priestly figure.

In the Gospel of Mark the title "Messiah" is applied to Jesus only four times—in the titular verse of chapter 1, by Peter at Caesarea Philippi (8:29), in a question from the high priest directed to Jesus at his trial (14:61), and in a sarcastic taunt at his crucifixion (15:32). Even so, the title is important for Mark, otherwise why would Mark begin his Gospel with that declaration of Jesus' identity? Furthermore in Mark, Jesus unequivocally accepts that identification when asked by the high priest. That Mark understands Messiah as a royal designation for Jesus can be seen in its combination with "the King of Israel" in 15:32. Jesus is the kingly Messiah, anointed at his baptism. For Mark, Jesus is indeed the Messiah, but a different kind of Messiah. He is not primarily a messiah of conquering and glory, but a messiah of suffering and sacrifice, as Jesus' response to Peter's use of the term at Caesarea Philippi makes clear.

Son of God. The phrase "Son of God" is much more frequent in Mark than is the title "Messiah." When Jesus is recognized by the demons whom he casts out, they identify him as "the Son of God" (3:11; 5:7; cf. 1:24). Like the term "Messiah," "Son of God" also appears in 1:1 (although some ancient copies of Mark lack the words "Son of God") and in the high priest's question to Jesus at his trial (14:61). Even more significant, at both Jesus' baptism and his transfiguration, a heavenly voice, the voice of God, identifies him as "my Son, the beloved" (1:11; 9:7). Finally, the centurion at the cross proclaims, "Truly this man was God's Son!" (15:39).

In the Hebrew Bible the phrase "Son of God" is applied to Davidic kings, who were seen as adopted sons of God. Although the term can be used in a more generalized way to refer to the faithful of Israel as "sons of God," royal connotations are the most characteristic aspect of the designation "son of God." In Mark the author draws a parallel between "Son of God" and "Messiah," as evidenced by 1:1 and 14:61. As with the term "Messiah," however, the identification of Jesus as Son of God needs to be further defined. Jesus' sonship is most clearly evident in his suffering and crucifixion, a point made clear by the centurion's recognition at the cross that Jesus is God's Son.

Son of David. In 2 Samuel 7, God speaking through the prophet Nathan promises to David that God would establish a Davidic dynasty whereby a Davidic king would rule forever. This promise became the basis for the Davidic messianic hopes, that is, the belief that God would one day raise up a new "Son of David" who would rule as a victorious king and would restore Israel to international prominence. In the story in Mark's Gospel of the healing of blind Bartimaeus (10:46-52), Bartimaeus cries out to Jesus, calling him Son of David. Mark gives no reaction to this designation. Two chapters later, however, Mark presents Jesus questioning how the Messiah could be David's son (12:35-37). Since for Mark, Jesus is indeed the Messiah, this is tantamount to declaring that Jesus is not the Son of David, or at least greatly modifying the idea. Why? Because for Mark, Jesus is not the earthly, conquering king of Davidic expectations. His kingship is of a different nature, one characterized by suffering and death.

Son of Man. The most frequently found title in the Gospel of Mark is "Son of Man." It is Jesus' favorite self-designation in the Gospel. This title is also one of the most disputed aspects of New Testament scholarship.

Critical scholars have raised many questions, both about the authenticity of the Son of Man sayings in the Gospels and about their meaning. The phrase "son of man" could be used in Hebrew or Aramaic to mean simply "mortal" or "human being." Some scholars have argued that Jesus applies this phrase to himself because it is does not carry any specific connotation, thus allowing him to define the title in his own terms. Other scholars have found the clue for its meaning in Daniel 7, where "one like a son of man" (NRSV: "one like a human being") comes on the clouds as an eschatological figure to whom God's final kingdom is given. According to these scholars, Jesus interpreted his ministry in terms of this eschatological Son of Man figure.

Although we cannot ascertain whether Jesus viewed himself in terms of this apocalyptic figure from Daniel, Mark apparently saw in this Danielic figure an appropriate designation for Jesus. Like the Danielic "son of man," Jesus ushers in God's final kingdom. Mark is careful, however, to qualify this picture of a glorious "Son of Man." In Mark the Son of Man is not only the one who "comes in the glory of his Father with the holy angels" (8:38) but also the one who "must undergo great suffering, and be rejected by the elders, the chief priests, and the scribes, and be killed, and after three days rise again" (8:31).

Messianic Secret

The phrase "messianic secret" was coined by Wilhelm Wrede in his 1901 study of the Gospel of Mark to describe the frequent commands to silence in the Gospel concerning the identity of Jesus.[3] Demons who confess the identity of Jesus are ordered to keep silent (1:25, 34; 3:12); persons who are healed are commanded to keep quiet (1:44; 5:43; 7:36); and the disciples are told not to disclose his identity (8:30; 9:9). Modern scholars studying the Gospel of Mark are usually convinced that these commands to secrecy owe more to Mark's literary and theological concerns than they do to any actual attempt on Jesus' part to command secrecy.

In Mark's view, Jesus cannot be adequately understood apart from his suffering and death. Any identity of Jesus that does not include the cross is inadequate. He was not just another miracle worker, or teacher, or prophet. Even the titles "Messiah," "Son of God," or "Son of Man" can be misleading, for they too must be interpreted in the light of Jesus' death and resurrection. Thus the commands to silence are Mark's way of reminding the readers that premature evaluations of Jesus are faulty. A true under-standing of Jesus can be obtained only when one has reached the end of the story. That is why the only time that a human character in the Gospel identifies Jesus as the Son of God occurs at the foot of the cross, for only then is his "sonship" accurately understood.

Suffering

Suffering is a dominant motif throughout the Gospel of Mark. John the Baptist, the forerunner of Jesus, is imprisoned and beheaded. On three different occasions, Jesus predicts his own rejection, suffering, and death (8:31; 9:31; 10:33-34). The impending death of Jesus looms so large over the Gospel of Mark, particularly in the latter half, that earlier scholars sometimes referred to the Gospel as a passion narrative with an extended introduction. While such a description fails to do justice to the literary and theological complexities of the Gospel, it does highlight the Gospel's emphasis on the death of Jesus. Furthermore, not only are the disciples of Jesus warned to expect suffering and persecution (10:39; 13:9-23), but all who would be followers of Jesus must be willing to suffer and even die for his cause (8:34-38).

This emphasis on suffering in the Gospel of Mark is certainly consistent with Mark's overall understanding of Jesus—he was the suffering Son of Man who "came not to be served but to serve, and to give his life a ransom for many" (10:45). Some scholars have suggested a historical reason for Mark's emphasis on suffering, seeing in this a reflection of the situation in Mark's community where the believers were themselves experiencing suffering and persecution. In the midst of this situation those early Chris-tians were likely tempted to compromise their faith, or at least were questioning why they were suffering. Mark points them to Jesus, who himself suffered and died a martyr's death and who called them to follow in his footsteps.

Discipleship

One of the first activities of Jesus in the Gospel of Mark is to call others to follow him, to become disciples. As noted at the beginning of our study of this Gospel, the presentation of the disciples in Mark is rather ambiguous. On the one hand the disciples are presented positively in that they accept Jesus' invitation to follow him and stay with him to learn from him and even minister with him. This positive portrayal is overshadowed, however, by the repeated failures and misunderstandings of the disciples. They are continually having to ask Jesus to explain his teachings to them. They are astonished by his actions. They fail to comprehend or even accept his predictions of his impending suffering. During his last days with them, they repeatedly fail and even betray him—Peter, James, and John fall asleep during his time of agony in the Garden of Gethsemane; Peter denies him three times; Judas betrays him to his enemies; they all run away and desert him when he is arrested; and at the cross, no disciple is present.

Why such a negative portrayal of the disciples? The answer likely lies in the centrality of the cross for Mark. The failure of the disciples to adequately understand Jesus was inevitable apart from Jesus' death and resurrection. The cross was the interpretive key not only to an understanding of Jesus, but also to an understanding of true discipleship. Prior to Jesus' death, all evaluations of him are, at best, only partial and thus inadequate. Furthermore, the failure of the disciples is perhaps a part of Mark's pastoral word to his community, as well as to modern readers. The path of discipleship is not an easy path. Failures and misunderstandings occur "on the way." This unflattering portrait of the disciples perhaps served (and continues to serve) as a word of encouragement to Mark's readers when they, like the first disciples, wavered in their commitment to Jesus. Mark's Gospel reminded them that the way of discipleship was filled with difficulties, disappointment, and failures.

Outline of the Gospel of Mark

The following outline will serve as the basis for our closer examination of the Gospel of Mark. Readers are encouraged to read the text of the Gospel in conjunction with the Reading Guide that follows the outline.

    I.   Prologue (1:1-13)
    II.   Jesus Begins His Ministry (1:14–3:6)
    III. Jesus Continues His Ministry in Galilee (3:7–6:6)
    IV.   Jesus Expands His Ministry Beyond Galilee (6:7–8:21)
    V.   Jesus Turns Toward Jerusalem (8:22–10:52)
    VI.   Jesus Teaches in Jerusalem (11:1–13:37)
    VII. Jesus Faces Death (14:1–15:47)
    VIII. Jesus Is Resurrected (16:1-8)

Reading Guide to the Gospel of Mark

Prologue (1:1-13)

Mark begins his Gospel in a clear, straightforward manner, leaving the reader with little doubt about the purpose of his work. The focus of Mark's story is "the good news [or "gospel"] of Jesus Christ, the Son of God" (1:1). The central character of the story (Jesus) is not only introduced, but also identified (Christ, or Messiah, and Son of God). Exactly what these titles mean, we are not told. That will have to be determined later, after we have heard Mark's story. But by declaring at the outset that Jesus is Messiah and Son of God, the narrator lets us know that Jesus is a person of importance and authority. Furthermore, the narrator's point of view concerning Jesus and his message is readily apparent. The narrator is no disinterested observer. Rather, he informs the reader that the story of Jesus is "good news." Three episodes make up this first section of the Gospel: the work of John the Baptist (1:4-8), the baptism of Jesus (1:9-11), and the temptation of Jesus (1:12-13).

The significance of John the Baptist is indicated by the quotation from the Hebrew scriptures that connects v. 1 to John.[4] He is God's messenger who was sent to prepare the way of the Lord (the latter title understood by Mark as a reference to Jesus). In biblical tradition the wilderness is both a place of divine salvation (the place of the exodus from Egypt, when the redemptive power of God was dramatically evidenced) and a place of divine testing, even danger.[5] The former connotation of the wilderness is present in this scene. The appearance of John and Jesus in the wilderness are signals that a new redemptive activity of God is about to begin. This, indeed, is the "beginning of the good news." John fulfills his role of forerunner by calling the people to repent (turn away) from their sins and be baptized and by pointing beyond himself to a greater one who is still to come.

As we will see later, the baptism of Jesus by John created theological problems for the other evangelists, but apparently not for Mark. Mark states without comment that Jesus came to John and was baptized by him. After his baptism two important events occur: the Spirit of God descends upon him and a heavenly voice proclaims him to be God's beloved Son. In the story world apparently only Jesus is aware of these occurrences, because no mention is made of any reaction by John or the onlookers. We the readers, however, are privy to this information, information that confirms what we were told in v. 1 about the significance of Jesus.

The last scene of the prologue is the briefest of the three. In a graphic description, the narrator says that "the Spirit immediately drove him out into the wilderness" (1:12). The second association of wilderness mentioned above is operative here. The wilderness is a place of testing, as Jesus is tested for forty days by Satan. Mark hints here at what will become clear in the remainder of the Gospel: Jesus is involved in a cosmic struggle with evil, a battle with Satan, the outcome of which has already been decided. Here at the outset Jesus has defeated Satan. He has entered Satan's house, plundered his property and tied him up (3:27). Because in Israel's past the wilderness had been the place of God's deliverance of the people (i.e, after the exodus from Egypt), the author of Isaiah 40 spoke of God's future deliverance as also occurring in the wilderness. For Mark, then, Jesus' encounter with Satan in the wilderness is a sign that the anticipated end time has begun.

Jesus Begins His Ministry (1:14–3:6)

After preparing the way for Jesus, John fades away in the story. The departure of John from the narrative is rather abrupt—"after John was arrested"—leaving the reader with many unanswered questions: Why was John arrested? Who arrested him? What happens to him? These questions are not answered until later in the Gospel (6:14-29). Whereas the starkness of Mark's treatment of John here is perhaps puzzling to the reader, it points to what we already know: the major focus of the story is on Jesus, who now arrives on center stage proclaiming "the good news of God." What was hinted at in the encounter between Jesus and Satan in the wilderness is now announced plainly by Jesus, "The time is fulfilled, and the kingdom of God has come near" (1:15). The phrase "kingdom of God" refers not to a location or an area, but to a realm of authority. It denotes the rule of God in the lives of people. For Mark, the rule of God is already at hand in the acts and teachings of Jesus. One's response to Jesus ("repent and believe in the good news") determines whether one participates in this kingdom.

The first act of Jesus' ministry according to Mark is to call others to follow him, to join him in the work of God. As readers, we also hear the invitation and are drawn into the story to follow along and see where the way of Jesus leads. In 1:16-20 Simon, Andrew, James, and John respond positively to Jesus' invitation. Later in this same section, Levi the tax collector also heeds the call to become a follower of Jesus (2:13-17).

In addition to the calling of disciples, two major themes are evident in 1:14–3:6. The first is the positive, even incredulous, response of the people to Jesus' teachings, healings, and exorcisms. The crowds "were astounded at his teaching" (1:22); they "were all amazed, and they kept on asking one another, 'What is this? A new teaching—with authority! He commands even the unclean spirits, and they obey him' " (1:27). Jesus becomes so popular with the masses that his fame spreads throughout Galilee. He achieves celebrity status and cannot go out freely in public because the people are thronging after him. At first glance this popular response to Jesus seems good; it means that Jesus is a "success." We learn, however, that such is not the case. Jesus does not want to remain with the adoring crowds who want his healing touch. Rather he must go on to other towns to preach his message there. As will become obvious in the course of Mark's story, the clamoring crowd is a fickle crowd.

The second major theme in this section is the conflict that Jesus encounters. Conflict in these stories is of two types. The exorcisms that Jesus performs are a part of the conflict that was introduced in Jesus' temptation in the wilderness. The demons, or unclean spirits, are in league with Satan, their ruler. People in the ancient world believed in the existence of these supernatural forces. Demons were thought to be responsible for certain illnesses and diseases that afflicted people. For this reason healings and exorcisms are closely related in the Gospels. Modern readers often find these stories of demon possession strange or even ludicrous because such beliefs are not a part of the modern worldview. If we are going to appreciate Mark's story, however, we must be willing to suspend our disbelief and enter imaginatively into Mark's story world, a world in which the cosmic struggle between the forces of Satan and the forces of God is very real. Jesus is able to cast out demons because he has already defeated Satan. He operates with the power and authority of God, which the people do not fully understand. They are simply amazed. The unclean spirits, on the other hand, recognize Jesus for who he is—"the Holy One of God" (1:24).

The other conflict that occurs in this section is the controversy between Jesus and the religious authorities. Jesus, who speaks with such authority, is a threat to the established authority and power base of the religious leadership. The controversies involve Jesus' claim to forgive sins, his association with the religious outcasts, the failure of his disciples to observe the religious practice of fasting, and Jesus' violation of strict rules regarding the sabbath. The opposition of the religious leaders, which begins with their disgruntled "questioning in their hearts" (2:6), escalates rapidly in their ensuing encounters with Jesus. By the time we reach the last episode in this section, the leaders have decided that Jesus is too great a danger. He must be eliminated, so they plot how they can destroy him.

These two groups in the Gospel of Mark who are in opposition to Jesus—the demons and the religious leaders—are simply two aspects of the same conflict. Those who are not on the side of God are on the side of Satan; by opposing Jesus, they are opposing God.

Finally, we should note a premonition that is given of something that will become increasingly prominent in the Gospel. In a controversy with the religious leaders, Jesus defends his disciples' lack of fasting by explaining that fasting is inappropriate when the bridegroom is present. He notes, however, "The days will come when the bridegroom is taken away from them" (2:20), a hint not only to the characters in the story, but to the readers of the Gospel as well, of the approaching death of Jesus. Even in this early section, the cross is already casting its long shadow across the pages of Mark's Gospel.

Jesus Continues His Ministry in Galilee (3:7–6:6)

Many of the themes and activities from the previous section are present in this section of the Gospel as well—healings and exorcisms, popularity with the crowds, choosing disciples, and opposition and rejection. Much of the activity in this section is located around the Sea of Galilee. Jesus' fame has spread so widely that "great numbers from Judea, Jerusalem, Idumea, beyond the Jordan, and the region around Tyre and Sidon" (3:8) come seeking him. While the crowds continue to be enamored with Jesus, the opposite reaction to him is voiced by the religious authorities and even by his own family. In 3:21 we are told that Jesus' family comes to take him because they think he has "gone out of his mind" (3:21). (The NRSV translation shifts the negative evaluation about Jesus from his family to the anonymous "people." The Greek phrase almost certainly refers to Jesus' family.) Scribes from Jerusalem also respond negatively to Jesus, accusing him of being under the power of Beelzebul (used here as another name for Satan).

Mark has structured these two episodes using the technique of intercalation. Verses 20 and 21 introduce Jesus' family who, after hearing about

Jesus, leave to bring him home. The scene then shifts to the scribes from Jerusalem and Jesus' response to them. Jesus' family then arrives, leading Jesus to declare that his real family is composed of "whoever does the will of God" (3:35). The effect of the sandwiching of these two stories is to highlight the rejection of Jesus. Both the failure of his family to recognize the importance of his work and the refusal of the religious leaders to accept his authority and teaching are two sides of the same coin—resistance to the will of God. Those who refuse to accept the will of God—embodied in the preaching and teaching of Jesus—are "outsiders," beyond the bounds of the kingdom of God. On the other hand, those who respond affirmatively to Jesus and his teaching are the "insiders."

Chapter 4 contains the largest collection of parables and the longest teaching section in the Gospel of Mark. The most prominent parable is the parable of the sower, which along with its interpretation comprises almost half the chapter. Following as it does immediately after the saying about who is Jesus' "brother and sister and mother" (3:35), this parable functions as further elaboration on "insiders" and "outsiders." Insiders are those who hear the word of Jesus and respond faithfully, allowing the teaching of Jesus to bear fruit in their lives. The outsiders are those who, for a variety of reasons, fail to bear fruit. The twelve disciples along with "those who were around" Jesus (v. 10) are part of the insiders to whom has been given the "secret of the kingdom of God" (v. 11), which has been hidden from those who are outside.

What is this "secret" or "mystery" (Greek: *mystērion*) that is given to the insiders? We, as readers, are not explicitly told. Furthermore, as the remainder of the Gospel demonstrates, the response of the disciples indicates that they do not have a clear grasp of the "secret" either. Mark perhaps gives us a clue, however, by his arrangement of the material in his Gospel. Following the interpretation of the parable of the sower, Jesus is presented as saying, "Is a lamp brought in to be put under the bushel basket, or under the bed, and not on the lampstand? For there is nothing hidden, except to be disclosed; nor is anything secret, except to come to light" (4:21-22). The Greek text actually reads, "Does a lamp come . . . ?" which is a strange choice of verbs. A lamp may be brought, but it does not come in on its own! In the Gospel, Jesus is the one who comes and thus the one who is to be disclosed. He himself is the secret that is given to the disciples and those with them. One's response to this "secret" indicates one's response to the kingdom of God. The other parables in the chapter are parables about the certainty of the kingdom of God, offering reassurance that the work of God in and through Jesus might seem small and insignificant, but eventually its success is certain.

Immediately after these parables Mark includes a story that demonstrates how inadequately the disciples have grasped the "secret" of Jesus. Caught in a fierce storm while at sea, they are frightened and reprimand Jesus for his seeming unconcern. After calming the storm, Jesus says, "Why are you afraid? Have you still no faith?" (4:40). Puzzled, the disciples ask one another, "Who then is this, that even the wind and the sea obey him?" (4:41). Supposedly being "insiders," the disciples ask the same question that others in the Gospel have been asking.

Jesus' power and the necessity of a faith response to Jesus are emphasized in the other stories of this section. Chapter 5 contains the most dramatic exorcism in the Gospel, the story of Jesus casting out the legion of demons from the man living among the tombs in "the country of the Gerasenes" (5:1)[6]. Once again the demons recognize Jesus, identifying him as "Jesus, Son of the Most High God" (5:7). Even though they are many, they are no match for Jesus, who sends them out of the man and into a herd of pigs. Like the earlier exorcism (1:21-28), this episode reveals Jesus' triumph over the forces of Satan.

After crossing back over to the other side of the Sea of Galilee, Jesus performs two healings, both of which emphasize faith. These two stories are another example of Mark's use of intercalation. Jesus is confronted by Jairus, a synagogue leader, who begs him to come and heal his dying daughter. Jesus' journey to the man's house is interrupted, however, by a sick woman who reaches out in faith to touch Jesus' cloak in order to be healed. Jesus responds to her with the words, "Your faith has made you well" (5:34). At that point, someone comes to inform Jairus that his daughter has already died. Jesus speaks up and instructs Jairus, "Do not fear, only believe." The story concludes with Jesus bringing the dead girl back to life. Some readers have suggested that the intermingling of these two stories is historical: Jesus was actually interrupted on his way to the home of Jairus. Because of Mark's disregard of actual historical or chronological connections elsewhere in the Gospel, coupled with his affinity for intercalation, the more likely understanding of these two events is that the placement of the stories is the work of Mark, who sandwiched them together as a way of reinforcing the teaching on faith.

The faith of Jairus and the woman throw into even sharper relief the earlier lack of faith of the disciples when Jesus stilled the storm. Furthermore, the lack of faith of the disciples coupled with the absence of faith of the people in Jesus' hometown (6:1-6) form an *inclusio* in which these two stories of unbelief bracket the two episodes of faith. Those who are the most likely candidates to believe in Jesus—his disciples and the people of his hometown—are failures, whereas those who have no connection to him demonstrate true faith.

Jesus Expands His Ministry Beyond Galilee (6:7–8:21)

Jesus sends the twelve disciples, who are named in 3:16-19, on a special mission of preaching, healing, and casting out demons. Again Mark interrupts one story by inserting another in the middle. This time the account of the disciples on mission is interrupted by a narration of the arrest and death of John the Baptist. After describing John's fate, Mark then returns to the disciples, telling us that they reported back to Jesus after their missionary journey. What purpose does this intercalation serve? Perhaps it is a way of foreshadowing the death of Jesus. As Mark showed at the beginning of the Gospel, the lives and ministries of John the Baptist and Jesus are connected. As John's ministry led to his death, so the ministry of Jesus, here expanded by his disciples, will ultimately end in death.

The story of the feeding of the five thousand (6:30-44) is the only miracle story that is repeated in all four Gospels. The story is rich in reminders of the exodus of the Hebrew people from Egypt, the central event in the salvation history of Israel, when God provided manna for them in the wilderness. Here Jesus provides bread (and fish) for the crowds. In the evening, while Jesus is on land the disciples are in a boat crossing to the other side of the sea. When they encounter difficulty due to a strong wind, they see Jesus walking on the water, but they fail to recognize him. They think he is a ghost. He speaks to them, gets into their boat, and the wind subsides. Mark says of them, "They were utterly astounded, for they did not understand about the loaves, but their hearts were hardened" (6:51-52). As in the earlier episode when Jesus calmed the sea, once more the disciples fail to understand Jesus adequately and to trust him. They have failed to understand the power and authority of Jesus manifested in his feeding of the five thousand.

The episode in chapter 7 about what is ritually clean or unclean might seem disconnected to the surrounding episodes. It serves, however, as preparation for Jesus' movement into specifically gentile territory. The declaration by Jesus in 7:1-23 that all foods are clean is expanded in his response to the Syrophoenician woman to demonstrate that all persons are clean. This woman who comes to Jesus asking that he cast a demon out of her daughter is non-Jewish. She is a "Gentile, of Syrophoenician origin" (7:26). Jesus initially refuses to grant her request, claiming that it would not be fair to spend his energies on gentiles ("the dogs") while Jews ("the children") were still in need. After the woman's witty repartee—"Sir, even the dogs under the table eat the children's crumbs" (7:28)—Jesus concedes and heals her daughter. (This woman is the only person in the Gospel to get the best of Jesus in an argument.)

Although Mark's geographical references are confused (Jesus travels north to get south, going from Tyre to the Sea of Galilee by way of Sidon), the next episode clearly places Jesus still in a gentile area. Encountering a man who is deaf and who has speech difficulties, Jesus heals him. The response of the people—astonishment—parallels the reaction of the people of Galilee to Jesus' teaching and healing.

Chapter 8 contains another feeding miracle. This time Jesus is said to feed four thousand people instead of five thousand. Most scholars understand these two stories to be variants of the same tradition. Rather than treat them as one incident, Mark presents them as two separate miraculous events. In Mark's telling of the stories, the first feeding occurred in Jewish territory (note the significance in that story of the twelve baskets of leftovers, reminiscent of the twelve tribes of Israel). The feeding of the four thousand, however, occurs in gentile territory, reinforcing the declaration that not only are all foods clean, but all persons are clean and acceptable to God as well. On the purely historical level, the acceptance of these two incidents raises major problems (aside from the issue of miracles in general). If the disciples had already seen Jesus feed the five thousand, why do they again see no solution when four thousand need to be fed? How can the disciples be so dense? The duplication of the feeding, however, is a part of Mark's story world, not the historical world. By placing both stories in his Gospel, Mark leads us to ask those very questions about the disciples. "How can they be so unperceptive?" Like Jesus in the story, we want to ask, "Do you still not perceive or understand? Are your hearts hardened? Do you have eyes, and fail to see? Do you have ears, and fail to hear?" (8:17-18).

Sadly, the answer is yes. The disciples seem to have moved from being "insiders" to being "outsiders."

Jesus Turns Toward Jerusalem (8:22–10:52)

In this central section of the Gospel, Jesus turns toward Jerusalem both literally and figuratively. In 10:1 Jesus leaves Galilee and heads south, going "to the region of Judea and beyond the Jordan." In 10:32 we are specifically told that he is on the way to Jerusalem. A definite geographical shift is taking place then in this section. A different kind of shift takes place as well. Jerusalem is the place of Jesus' death. Three times in this section Jesus will tell his disciples about his impending death. The tragic events in Jerusalem begin to overshadow the Gospel more and more.

A Markan *inclusio* defines the boundaries of this section. Stories of Jesus healing a blind man both open (8:22-26) and close (10:46-52) this portion of the Gospel (the only two instances of Jesus healing a blind person in Mark). The first of these two stories appears rather odd. After reading several accounts of the power of Jesus to heal various diseases, cast out demons, raise the dead, and calm the storms, we encounter here an instance in which Jesus' healing is initially only partially effective. Jesus must lay his hands on the man's eyes a second time before the man's vision is completely restored. Throughout this section the disciples are presented as failing to understand Jesus. This comes as no surprise to the reader. Already we have seen the bewilderment, lack of understanding, and unbelief of the disciples. Immediately prior to this section, Jesus has even accused them of being blind ("Do you have eyes, and fail to see?" 8:18). Perhaps that is a clue to the meaning of this section. Jesus is trying to open the blind eyes of his disciples. As Jesus brings physical sight to the two men at the beginning and end of this section, so he likewise is trying to bring spiritual sight to his disciples. Like the man in the first episode, the blindness of the disciples is a tough case! They too will need a "second touch" before they accurately understand Jesus.

Likewise, for us as readers a two-stage insight into Jesus is offered in the Gospel. The image of Jesus we obtain from the first half of the Gospel is one of his power—he heals, he commands the forces of nature, he forgives sins, he raises the dead, he overcomes demons. This image is not sufficient, however. We need a "second touch" from the latter half of the Gospel to show us that Jesus is accurately understood only in the context of suffering and self-sacrifice. Lack of awareness of Jesus' suffering and self-sacrifice is also the reason for the blurred spiritual vision of the disciples.

From 8:27 to 10:45 Mark structures his material into a threefold pattern: (1) Jesus predicts his suffering, death, and resurrection, (2) the disciples fail to understand Jesus and his teachings, and (3) Jesus teaches about discipleship. This threefold pattern is itself repeated three times in this section: 8:27-38; 9:30-37; 10:32-45. The first example of this threefold pattern, Peter's so-called "confession" of Jesus at Caesarea Philippi, has often been seen as the central focus of the Gospel, both because of its location (it occurs approximately in the middle of the Gospel) and because of its content (Peter's confession of Jesus as the Messiah). Whereas it is true that the scene at Caesarea is a dramatic and important moment in the Gospel, it is not, however, the theological focus of the Gospel. For one thing, as noted above, this scene is only one of three episodes in this section with similar emphases. For another, the confession that Peter makes is, in the overall presentation of the Gospel, an inadequate confession. Peter's sight is still blurry. His vision needs a "second touch." Immediately following Peter's claim that Jesus is the Messiah, Jesus gives his first passion prediction, teaching the disciples that suffering, rejection, and death lie ahead for him. Coming as it does immediately after Peter's confession, the statement on suffering serves as a corrective to Peter's understanding of Jesus. Jesus' "messiahship" involves suffering and even death, an idea that Peter cannot accept. Peter's rebuke of Jesus in response to the statements of suffering indicate that Peter has still not grasped the true identity and mission of Jesus. In fact, Peter speaks more with the voice of Satan than with the voice of God (8:33). Peter is representative of all the disciples here. His failure is their failure as well.

The second passion prediction of Jesus also highlights the failure of the disciples. Mark has placed it next to a report of an argument the disciples had among themselves about who among them was the greatest. The contrast between Jesus' suffering and rejection and the disciples' failure could hardly be greater. A similar contrast occurs with the third passion prediction. After we read about Jesus telling the disciples about what is to happen to him, the very next scene shows James and John asking Jesus for privileged status: "Grant us to sit, one at your right hand and one at your left, in your glory" (10:37). When the other disciples hear about this, they become angry with James and John. Our impression is not that they are angry because they sense the inappropriateness of the request of James and

John, but because they do not want James and John to have an unfair advantage! This episode becomes the occasion for Jesus to teach the disciples about the meaning of true discipleship. He tells them, "Whoever wishes to become great among you must be your servant, and whoever wishes to be first among you must be slave of all. For the Son of Man came not to be served but to serve, and to give his life a ransom for many" (10:43-45).

By the time we get to the end of chapter 10 with the story of the healing of blind Bartimaeus, we recognize clearly that Bartimaeus is not the only person in the story who is blind and needs to gain sight. The disciples have repeatedly shown their lack of insight, both by their actions and by their words. As readers, we are left wondering, "Will the disciples ever see or will they forever remain blind?" The healing of Bartimaeus offers hope that the disciples as well might finally have their eyes opened. Bartimaeus becomes a paradigm for discipleship. Because of his faith, he is able to see and follows Jesus "on the way" (10:52).

One other scene in this section of the Gospel deserves our attention. The transfiguration of Jesus is described in 9:2-8. Jesus takes three disciples, Peter, James, and John, with him up a high mountain where he suddenly appears transfigured, or changed, before them. Along with him appear Elijah and Moses. Overwhelmed by this scene of Jesus' exaltation, Peter says to Jesus, "Let us make three dwellings, one for you, one for Moses, and one for Elijah" (9:5). In the context of the Gospel, Peter's remark is unacceptable for it represents once more his failure to grasp the way of Jesus. Peter wants to hang on to this moment of glory, to preserve it. A glorified Jesus is what Peter seeks. But as we have seen throughout this section, the way of Jesus is the way of the cross. Jesus, and those who would be his disciples, must come down from the mountain and follow the path of suffering. This scene also serves to legitimate the identity of Jesus. As at the baptism of Jesus, so here a voice speaks from above declaring, "This is my Son, the Beloved."

Jesus Teaches in Jerusalem (11:1–13:37)

This section of the Gospel opens with what has traditionally been called Jesus' triumphal entry into Jerusalem. Riding toward Jerusalem on a donkey, Jesus is hailed by the crowd (apparently including his followers) in messianic terms: "Blessed is the one who comes in the name of the Lord!

Blessed is the coming kingdom of our ancestor David!" (11:9-10). Is this a correct interpretation of Jesus, or has the crowd misunderstood? In light of what we have seen in the rest of the Gospel, we should be suspicious of their accolades. Werner Kelber is likely correct in his assessment of this scene when he writes:

> In the context of Mark's story the acclamation scene is one of supreme irony. It is Jesus' followers who continuing to mistake his identity turn his journey to Jerusalem into a triumphal celebration. Those who acclaim Jesus' Davidic messiahship perpetuate an attitude shown earlier by the refusal to listen to the passion-resurrection predictions. As far as the followers are concerned, Jesus enters Jerusalem in order to establish the Kingdom in power. That is cause for celebration. As far as Jesus is concerned, he enters into suffering and death. He will not be King until he is nailed to the cross.[7]

If the crowd hails Jesus in messianic terms while he is on his way into Jerusalem, the opposite reaction is true of the religious leaders once Jesus actually arrives in the city. The opposition and conflict between Jesus and the authorities that has been building throughout the Gospel now increases dramatically. The contrast between the reaction of the crowds and the reaction of the religious leaders is stark. The first time we read about the leaders in this section we are told that the chief priests and the scribes "kept looking for a way to kill him; for they were afraid of him, because the whole crowd was spellbound by his teaching" (11:18).

Jesus' opposition to the religious status quo is demonstrated in a dramatic way in an episode often called "the cleansing of the Temple." This episode is "sandwiched" between the two parts of another story, Jesus' cursing of the fig tree, and together they form one of the best-known examples of Markan intercalation. We have already discussed these episodes and their meaning (see pp. 79-80). These stories indicate that the Temple and the religious authorities have failed. The Temple elite have utilized the Temple for their own purposes. They have seen it as a place of security, giving them divine protection in spite of their unrighteousness and abuses. Furthermore, the Temple has failed because it is not "a house of prayer for all the nations," for gentiles are excluded from all but its outer courts. Jesus' actions are not simply a cleansing or reform of the Temple system. Jesus shuts down Temple worship and declares it invalid.

Whether the disciples understand the significance of this prophetic act of Jesus is not stated. The religious authorities certainly do, for it is at this point in the narrative that Mark tells us that the chief priests and the scribes look for a way to kill Jesus. They recognize the grave threat to their system that he poses. Jesus is not just a misguided simpleton; he is a dangerous zealot and he must be stopped. At the end of chapter 11 and throughout chapter 12 Mark presents story after story in which the religious authorities argue with Jesus and try to entrap him in his teachings. Jesus always outmaneuvers them. He tells a parable depicting their rejection of God's messengers, points out their hypocrisy, and warns the people to beware of them. The reader now has no question about the standpoint of the religious authorities. In their opposition to Jesus they align themselves with those who set their minds "not on divine things but on human things" (8:33). As such, they are in league with Satan and not with God.

The Gospel of Mark demands a choice on the part of the reader, as well. The Gospel urges the reader to follow the path of the scribe described in 12:28-34 and the poor widow in 12:41-44. The scribe is declared to be "not far from the kingdom of God" (12:34) because he recognizes that what is necessary is not "burnt offerings and sacrifices" but loving God and neighbor. The poor widow exemplifies true discipleship in her willingness to give all that she possesses to God.

One of the most difficult chapters in the Gospel of Mark is chapter 13, sometimes called the "Little Apocalypse" due to the apocalyptic nature of its contents. After coming out of the Temple, one of Jesus' disciples exclaims, "Look, Teacher, what large stones and what large buildings!" (13:1). The reaction of the disciple is understandable for the Temple complex built by Herod was certainly an impressive sight. The limestone blocks of which the Temple wall was constructed were large, approximately fifteen feet long and three to four feet high, although one block in the remaining portion of the western wall is forty feet long. A saying recorded in later rabbinic writings states, "No one has seen a truly beautiful building unless he has seen the Temple."[8] In the context of Mark's Gospel, however, the remark of the disciple is painfully ironic. Jesus' words and actions in chapters 11 and 12 have demonstrated the failure of the Temple and predicted its demise. The way of Jesus and the way of the Temple are at odds with each other. Yet what is the response of the disciple? He is enamored with the Temple. The disciple's lack of understanding is reinforced by Jesus' response: "Not one stone will be left here upon another; all will be thrown down" (13:2).

After they have crossed over to the Mount of Olives, Jesus' disciples ask him about his prediction of the Temple's destruction ("when will this be") and the events of the end time ("all these things"). As was apparently true of some Jewish people of the time, the disciples connected the demise of the Temple with the coming of God's final kingdom. The problems facing the reader in trying to understand the remainder of this chapter are numerous, certainly beyond the scope of what we can adequately discuss here. Several key ideas can be highlighted, however. First, two different scenarios are discussed in this chapter—the events preliminary to the end and the end of the age itself. Interpreters of Mark do not agree on which verses relate to which scenario. Second, references to events contemporaneous with the time of the writing of the Gospel of Mark appear to have been woven into the chapter (persecution, arrest, false messiahs). Some scholars interpret the warning in v. 14 about "the desolating sacrilege set up where it ought not to be" to be a reference to the conquest of the Temple by the Roman general Titus in 70 CE. Such a reference is possible, but not certain.

Third, Mark seems to be interested in defusing intense apocalyptic expectation. In Mark's community were likely persons who were interpreting the troubles they were facing as signs that the end of the age was upon them and that the return of Christ had already happened. Mark quotes Jesus as saying, "This must take place, but the end is still to come" (v. 7); and "This is but the beginning of the birth pangs" (v. 8). Furthermore only God knows when the end will actually occur (v. 32). Apocalyptic fervor that claimed that the end was already at hand was mistaken. The events Mark's community was experiencing were only preliminary events. Fourth, Mark does not deny the return of Christ. On the contrary, he says that the proper attitude of followers of Jesus is one of watchful anticipation. They are to "keep awake" and be ready because no one knows when the Son of Man will come.

Jesus Faces Death (14:1–15:47)

This section of the Gospel begins on a somber note, informing us in 14:1 that "the chief priests and the scribes were looking for a way to arrest Jesus by stealth and kill him." The next scene continues this foreboding feeling. Jesus is at Bethany, visiting in the home of Simon the leper, when a woman comes to Jesus with a bottle of expensive ointment, which she pours over

Jesus' head. When she is scolded by the bystanders for wasting such expensive ointment instead of selling it to benefit the poor, Jesus defends her action, seeing in her act an anticipatory gesture. Jesus states, "She has done what she could; she has anointed my body beforehand for its burial" (14:8).

This act of unselfish homage is in contrast to the activity of Judas Iscariot, one of the twelve, described in the following verses. Whereas the woman was unconcerned about money in her effort to honor Jesus, Judas plots to betray Jesus to his enemies and is promised a reward of money (14:10-11).

Jesus' last meal with his disciples, which in Mark is a Passover meal, becomes the occasion for Jesus' prediction that one of the twelve will betray him (14:17-25). The bread and wine that are served at the meal are interpreted by Jesus as symbols of his sacrificial death. After the meal, they leave the upper room and go to the Mount of Olives where the failure of the disciples is emphasized again (14:26-31). This time Jesus foretells that all of them will desert him. When Peter challenges Jesus, Jesus responds with an additional prediction: not once but three times Peter will deny Jesus. In light of the past performance of the disciples, the reader expects Jesus' prediction to be fulfilled.

The next two scenes in the Gospel paint some of the harshest portraits of the disciples. In Gethsemane, Jesus goes off to pray, agonizing over his impending fate (14:32-42). Leaving behind the other disciples, he takes with him the inner circle of Peter, James, and John. After describing for them the gravity of the situation, Jesus asks them to remain awake while he goes aside to pray. Three times he returns to them, only to find them asleep. In the moment of Jesus' deepest struggle and agony, the disciples fail him. The following scene (14:43-50) describes the arrest of Jesus by the religious authorities, who arrive with Judas, who points Jesus out with a kiss. As if this betrayal by one of the twelve were not enough, Mark tells us, "All of them deserted him and fled" (14:50). The declaration by Peter and echoed by the rest, "Even though I must die with you, I will not deny you" (14:31), rings hollow.

Jesus is taken that evening to be interrogated by the high priest and other members of the religious establishment who eventually "condemned him as deserving death" (14:64). Mark has juxtaposed Jesus' appearance before the religious authorities and Peter's denial of Jesus in the courtyard below. At the same time that Jesus is willing to confess his identity ("the Messiah, the Son of the Blessed One" and "the Son of Man" 14:61-62) even when it means death, Peter denies his own identity and his identification with Jesus in order to save his own life.

The next morning Jesus is taken before Pilate, the Roman governor (15:1-20). Throughout the trial Pilate and his soldiers mock Jesus by calling him "the King of the Jews." The irony of this statement is obvious to the readers, who by now have come to realize that for Mark that is indeed who Jesus is. The crowd, which throughout the Gospel has been enamored with Jesus, now demonstrates its fickleness. They, too, join in the demands for Jesus' crucifixion. Yielding to their cries, Pilate hands Jesus over to his soldiers to be crucified, who, along with the crowd, continue to taunt Jesus even after he is nailed to the cross.

Darkness descends upon the Gospel, in the same way that Mark says that "darkness came over the whole land" unnaturally (15:33). Jesus, deserted by friends, family, and disciples and seemingly abandoned even by God, cries out in agony, "My God, my God, why have you forsaken me?" (15:34). When Jesus dies, Mark states that "the curtain of the temple was torn in two, from top to bottom" (15:38). As the heavens were ripped apart at Jesus' baptism and the Spirit descended upon Jesus, so now at his death his spirit or breath leaves and the tapestry separating the Holy of Holies from the Holy Place in the Temple is ripped apart. The destruction of the Temple predicted by Jesus in his attack upon the animal sellers and money changers is here connected with the death of Jesus. His death on the cross signals the end of the Temple. Seeing Jesus die, a Roman centurion makes the statement, "Truly this man was God's Son!" (15:39). Is this another case of verbal irony, a situation where the character in the story makes a sarcastic statement that is in reality a true statement? Or are we to understand that the centurion realizes the truth of what he says? Mark leaves the answer in ambiguity. Whether the statement is ironic or not, for Mark it is an accurate assessment of Jesus. In his death, he has indeed become the Son of God. The moment of his humiliation has become the moment of his enthronement and exaltation.

The only supporters of Jesus whom Mark mentions who were present at the crucifixion were several women, including those who "used to follow him and provided for him when he was in Galilee" (15:41). Joseph of Arimathea, described as "a respected member of the council, who was also himself waiting expectantly for the kingdom of God" (15:43), takes the dead body of Jesus and, after wrapping it in linen, buries it in a rock tomb.

Jesus Is Resurrected (16:1-8)

According to the Markan time frame, Jesus is crucified Friday morning and buried late that afternoon before the Jewish sabbath began at sundown. Early on Sunday morning (the sabbath ended at sunset on Saturday), three of the women who had been present at the crucifixion hasten to the tomb to anoint the body with the proper spices, which due to the shortness of time had not been done before the sabbath began. When they arrive at the tomb they are surprised to find the large stone, used to seal the tomb, has been rolled back. Inside the tomb they are greeted by a young man dressed in a white robe who tells them that Jesus is no longer there, but has been raised. He instructs them to go tell the disciples "that he is going ahead of you to Galilee; there you will see him, just as he told you" (16:7). Frightened and amazed the women run out of the tomb. Verse 8 ends with the words, "And they said nothing to anyone, for they were afraid."

The earliest and best extant ancient manuscripts of the Gospel of Mark end at verse 8. Other ancient manuscripts continue with verses 9-20, known by scholars as the "longer ending" of Mark. Another ending, consisting of two sentences and called the "shorter ending" of Mark, is found in a small number of manuscripts. Most New Testament critics are convinced that neither the "longer ending" nor the "shorter ending" of Mark is original to the Gospel. Both were composed later by individuals who felt a need to complete what seemed lacking in Mark. Did Mark originally end with verse 8, or was the remainder of Mark's Gospel lost? Most scholars opt for the former view.[9]

How do we understand this strange ending of the Gospel of Mark? Mark ends with an affirmation of the resurrection of Jesus but with no resurrection appearance stories as are found in the other canonical Gospels. Instead, the Gospel ends on a note of fear and silence. Yet there is "gospel" or "good news" here as well. The words of the young man at the tomb to the women are surprising words in the context of the actions of the disciples. The disciples, who misunderstood and failed Jesus and finally deserted him, certainly do not deserve a second chance. But that is what they receive in the promise of Jesus (given earlier in 14:28). Even for disciples who fail, even those who fail as badly as Peter, there is good news!

But perhaps such an interpretation places an unwarranted happy ending on the Gospel of Mark. The Gospel ends with verse 8, not with verse 7. Do the women ever tell what they know? Do they remain in terror and fear? Do the disciples ever go to Galilee, or do they remain failures? The fulfillment of Jesus' promise is not described in Mark. Mark's ending is an ambiguous ending, one that continues to challenge readers of the Gospel. The open-ended nature of the Gospel of Mark is perhaps the author's way of drawing the readers into the story, forcing them to complete the story in their own lives. Will they become faithful disciples who follow Jesus and proclaim what they have seen and heard, or will they flee in fear and silence? The ending of the Gospel is continually being written.

Chapter 4

❖

The Gospel of Matthew

The Gospel of Matthew quickly became the favorite Gospel in the early church. Writers from the early centuries of the church quoted extensively from Matthew. In lists and collections of the Gospels, the Gospel of Matthew was regularly placed prominently as the first Gospel. An examination of the contents of this Gospel reveals why the church favored and relied on this Gospel so heavily: (1) The organization of the Gospel lends itself to the teaching and preaching needs of the church—five major blocks of teaching material, including the well-known Sermon on the Mount. (2) This Gospel (unlike the other three) specifically addresses issues of church authority and discipline (16:13-20; 18:15-35). (3) Material in Matthew (the Lord's Prayer, the Beatitudes) served the worship needs of the church. (4) In comparison to Mark especially, the Gospel of Matthew was seen as a more complete presentation of the life and teachings of Jesus.

This Gospel, the second longest of the four canonical Gospels, continues to exert a strong influence. For example, most people familiar with the Lord's Prayer and the Beatitudes usually identify with the Matthean version rather than the Lukan version of these sayings. In addition, stories unique to Matthew—such as the visit of the wise men to the infant Jesus and Peter's attempt to walk on water—are widely known and alluded to, even by people who do not know their origin in the Gospel of Matthew.

Social Setting

Date of Writing

Attempts to date the composition of the Gospel of Matthew usually begin with the assumption that Matthew was dependent on the Gospel of Mark, written around 70 CE. A few years after that event would be the earliest date that could be assigned to Matthew. Since not all scholars accept the theory of Markan priority, however, other evidence for dating needs to be examined. The latest date possible for the writing of Matthew is fixed by the apparent use of the Gospel of Matthew by Ignatius, bishop of Antioch, in his letters written around 107 CE; so the Gospel of Matthew was likely written no later than the end of the first century. Further evidence is found in the Gospel itself. The author of Matthew seems to have inserted into the parable of the marriage feast (22:1-14) the statement that the king "burned their city" (v. 7), likely indicating an awareness of the destruction of Jerusalem by the Romans in 70 CE. A similar historical allusion is possibly present in the reference to the desolating sacrilege "standing in the holy place" (24:15), a more specific reference to the destruction of the Temple than that found in the parallel passage in Mark 13:14.

The tension between Judaism and Christianity reflected in the Gospel of Matthew is consistent with the last quarter of the first century. For example, in Matthew on several occasions the narrator or Jesus refers to the Jewish synagogues as "their" synagogue or "your" synagogue (4:23; 9:35; 10:17; 12:9; 13:54; 23:34), thus indicating a distinction between the Jewish community and the implied readers of Matthew's Gospel. This antipathy toward Judaism is noticeable also in the story of the scribe or lawyer who comes to Jesus and asks about the greatest commandment. The Markan Jesus praises the man, saying, "You are not far from the kingdom of God" (12:34). In Matthew, however, Jesus gives no word of praise to the man (22:34-40; in Luke 10:28, Jesus compliments the man for giving the correct answer).

Some interpreters of Matthew have also pointed to aspects of this Gospel that seem to indicate later theological development within the church, such as the Gospel's advanced ecclesiology (teachings about the church) and the trinitarian baptismal formula in 28:19. Because of these internal and external clues, many scholars opt for a date around 85–90 CE for the writing of Matthew's Gospel. That appears to be a reasonable conclusion.

Intended Readers

What was the nature of the community to which this Gospel was addressed? A fair inference to be drawn from the use of Greek as the language of the Gospel is that the community itself was predominantly Greek-speaking. Jack Dean Kingsbury, by studying clues in the Gospel and comparing Matthew to Mark and Luke, has drawn the following picture of the Matthean community.[1]

First, the community was composed of individuals from both Jewish and gentile backgrounds. Evidence indicating Jewish concerns includes the respectful substitute of "kingdom of Heaven" for "kingdom of God," and following the Jewish custom of not saying the divine name. Also, Jesus is presented as one who upholds the Jewish law and the traditions of the elders, except in cases where he considers it contrary to the will of God. Furthermore, Matthew leaves unexplained certain Jewish customs and phrases (cf. 5:22; 15:2; 23:5; 27:6). On the other hand, that Matthew's community also contained gentile members is suggested by the attention paid to gentiles. In the genealogy of Jesus in chapter 1, Matthew includes four non-Israelite women. Also prominent in the birth narrative is the presence of the wise men "from the East," likely meaning Persia, but obviously of non-Jewish origin. When Jesus is entreated by a Roman centurion to heal his servant, Jesus says approvingly, "In no one in Israel have I found such faith" (8:10). On several occasions in the Gospel, Jesus indicates that the good news is to be proclaimed to all the world (24:14; 26:13; 28:19-20).

Second, the Matthean community was likely a materially prosperous group. In the Sermon on the Mount, the Lukan Jesus pronounces a blessing on the poor (6:20); in Matthew Jesus blesses "the poor in spirit" (5:3). When Matthew mentions various types of money, his amounts are vastly more than the amounts in the parallel passages in Mark and Luke (cf. Mark 6:8 with Matt 10:9; Luke 19:11-27 with Matt 25:14-30). In the parable of the great dinner in Luke (14:16-24), the king sends his slave to bring in the "poor, the crippled, the blind, and the lame." In Matthew's parable of the wedding feast (22:1-14), likely a variant of the parable in Luke, the king sends the slaves to "invite everyone you find to the wedding banquet," with no specific mention made of the poor. Finally, in distinction from Mark and Luke, when Matthew identifies Joseph of Arimathea he calls him a rich man (27:57). These instances are not significant individually, but taken together they imply a community that was comfortable with wealth.

Third, Matthew's community was urban instead of rural. Kingsbury points out that Mark uses the Greek word *polis* ("city") eight times and the word *kome* ("village") seven times. In comparison Matthew uses the word for "village" only four times but the word for "city" twenty-six times. Kingsbury surmises, then, that the community of Matthew was a prosperous, urban, Greek-speaking community composed of persons of Jewish and gentile backgrounds.

Concerns about the Jewish Torah, the relationship between Judaism and Christianity, and issues of religious authority and leadership that are found in Matthew have caused some scholars to see the restructuring and reinterpretation of Judaism following the first Jewish-Roman war as the possible background for Matthew's Gospel.[2] Jewish leaders met at Jamnia (or Yavneh) in 90 CE to preserve and restructure Judaism in the wake of the destruction of the Temple and the end of the sacrificial system. As the leaders at Jamnia wrestled with the question of what it meant to be the people of God, heirs of the Torah tradition, Matthew and his community were also grappling with similar questions. They, too, saw themselves as the people of God, as ones committed to the Torah and the will of God. Yet their answers to the question of what defined the people of God was different from the answers that became associated with normative Judaism. The centrality of Jesus and the inclusion of gentiles in the Christian community were elements of the church's beliefs that differentiated Christianity from Judaism. What we find in the Gospel of Matthew, then, is perhaps evidence of a community deeply rooted in Judaism, engaged in the struggle to define itself over against its sibling religious faith that became rabbinic Judaism.

Place of Writing

Where might such a community have been located? Over the years scholars have suggested various locales: Palestine, or more specifically Jerusalem or Caesarea Maritima; Phoenicia; Alexandria; Edessa; Pella; or Syria. The last suggestion has been most widely followed by modern scholars, most of whom narrow the location to the Syrian capital of Antioch. This location has been attractive because it was a large urban area that was primarily Greek-speaking and contained a sizable Jewish population. Furthermore the city was the center of one of the earliest Christian mission efforts to gentiles. The mixed Jewish-gentile community that seems to be the audience of the Gospel would be consistent with a city like Antioch. As strong a candidate as Antioch seems to be, however, even proponents of this view admit that the identification of Antioch or any other locale for the writing of the Gospel is little more than an educated guess.

Features of Matthew's Gospel

The reader of Matthew who is familiar with the Gospel of Mark will find many similarities between the two works. The central character in each is Jesus. They both follow the same basic chronological outline of his life and ministry. Many of the same incidents and sayings appear in these two Gospels. In fact, more than 90 percent of the contents of Mark appears in Matthew. As we discussed earlier, this is one of the reasons most New Testament scholars are convinced that the author of Matthew used a copy of Mark when writing his Gospel.

On the other hand, the reader of Matthew will also notice several major differences between Mark and Matthew. Obviously Matthew is much longer than Mark. This additional material in Matthew was likely derived from Q, the source the author of Matthew had in common with the author of Luke, and from special sources or information available to the author of Matthew. Two of the most obvious additions to Matthew are the birth narrative and the resurrection appearance stories.

Even when Matthew includes the same sayings or incidents that are found in Mark, Matthew often changes them. For instance, the miracle stories in Matthew are more abbreviated than they are in Mark. In addition, the sense of urgency and action contained in Mark is not so prominent in Matthew. Furthermore, Matthew stresses the teachings of Jesus instead of the activity of Jesus. This emphasis on Jesus' teachings is seen both in the larger amount of teachings in Matthew and in the way in which Matthew has arranged this material. The following sections will highlight some additional special features of the Gospel of Matthew.

Use of Scripture

More than any other Gospel writer, Matthew likes to quote from the Hebrew Bible. A stereotyped formula, with variations, often introduces these quotations: "This was to fulfill what had been spoken by the Lord through the prophet." Jesus is seen as the fulfillment of these biblical texts. The reader who is familiar with these texts that are cited will likely be puzzled by the way in which Matthew uses them. In many cases the historical and literary contexts of the passages are ignored in Matthew's reuse of the texts. Matthew takes a passage referring to an earlier historical situation and reinterprets it as a reference to Jesus. For example, in telling the story of the journey of Mary, Joseph, and Jesus to Egypt (2:13-15), Matthew views this as a fulfillment of the words in Hosea 11:1, "Out of Egypt I have called my son." In the context of the book of Hosea, these words have nothing to do with a messianic prophecy. Rather they are a reference to God's bringing the Hebrew people out of bondage in Egypt and leading them into the land of Canaan. Matthew ignores the original meaning in order to make the text applicable to Jesus.

Matthew's interpretation of the Hebrew Bible, in which he views ancient texts as having contemporary referents, is similar to the approach followed by the members of the Qumran community who produced the Dead Sea Scrolls. In the *peshers*, or commentaries, on biblical texts produced by this community they frequently interpreted historical statements in biblical passages as references to present or future events. Specifically they interpreted the texts as describing events of the latter days of history, the time in which they viewed themselves as living. Although Matthew's interpretive methods are likely to be unconvincing to the modern reader, we must realize that Matthew's intended readers probably would have found his approach persuasive.

More important than their credibility to modern readers is the function of these scriptural texts in the Gospel of Matthew. Like others in the early church, Matthew turned to the Hebrew Bible to understand the identity and significance of Jesus. Matthew understood God's saving activity in the world to be divided into two broad periods, the period of prophecy and the period of fulfillment. In this understanding of salvation history, the Hebrew Bible contains prophecies about the activities of God in the future, specifically in the "last days," the eschatological period. Because he saw Jesus as the bearer of God's salvation, that is, as the long-awaited fulfillment of prophetic hopes, Matthew was able to interpret Jesus as the literal fulfillment of statements in the Hebrew Bible. As Matthew makes clear, he sees Jesus as "Emmanuel"—"God is with us" (1:23).

Characters

Many of the same characters that populate the Gospel of Mark are present in Matthew as well. In both works the central character is Jesus. Although both Gospels apply the titles Son of God, Messiah, Son of David, and Son of Man to Jesus, the presentations of Jesus differ in the two works. As we shall see as we survey Matthew's writing, the Jesus of Matthew does more teaching than he does in Mark. Also the Matthean Jesus is more concerned with the theme of righteousness and fulfilling the law than is the Markan Jesus.

The disciples are certainly portrayed differently in Matthew than they are in Mark. The negative image of the disciples shown by Mark is frequently softened. For example, in Mark's Gospel, James and John go to Jesus and ask to sit at Jesus' right and his left when he comes in glory (10:35-40). In Matthew, however, this selfish act by the disciples is missing. Instead, their *mother* asks for this special privilege for them (20:20-23). Both Mark and Matthew contain the story of Jesus calming the storm at sea (Mark 4:35-41; Matt 8:23-27). In Mark, Jesus criticizes the disciples as people who have "no faith." In Matthew, they are simply those who have "little faith." Throughout the Gospel of Matthew the disciples may disappoint Jesus, may desert him, and may fail to understand him fully, but they always remain as ones who at least have a "little faith" (cf. 6:30; 8:26; 14:31; 16:8). The final portrayal of them at the end of the Gospel is a positive one. They are sent out to continue the work of Jesus.

The religious authorities are negative characters in Matthew, as they are in Mark. The polemic against the religious leaders is sharper in Matthew, however, than it is in Mark. Particularly harsh are the denunciations of the scribes and Pharisees in chapter 23, where they are called "hypocrites," "blind guides," "snakes," and a "brood of vipers." The animosity and opposition to Jesus exhibited by the religious authorities is the major conflict that drives the plot of Matthew's Gospel. Jesus condemns the leaders both for their false understanding of the Jewish law and for their failure to follow their own teachings. Whereas in the Gospel of Matthew Jesus is presented as being righteous in both word and deed, the opposite is true of the religious leaders who oppose him. They are failures in both their teachings and their actions.

Many scholars understand the harsh rhetoric in Matthew against the religious leaders as a reflection of the actual situation of the original readers of Matthew's Gospel. Matthew's community was at odds with the Jewish community under the leadership of the Pharisees. Both groups saw themselves as faithful followers of the way of God, rival claimants to being the true Israel of God. Both groups were involved in defining who they were over against the other. And both groups saw the other as false or erroneous. The tension and rivalry between Matthew's community and the synagogue leadership is evident in the strong criticisms and denunciations of the religious leaders in the Gospel.

Structure

Although the Gospel of Matthew is similar in form and contents to the Gospel of Mark, Matthew is not simply a copy of Mark with slight variations. Rather, the arrangement and composition of Matthew's Gospel display the creativity and literary skills of its author. The author of this Gospel had a real penchant for organization, grouping together material that was similar in form (the Beatitudes in 5:3-12; contrasting sayings in 5:21-48; parables in 13:1-52; woes in 23:1-36) and in content (discipleship in 10:1-42; teachings about the church in 18:1-35; denunciations of the religious leaders in 23:1-39; and eschatological instruction in chapters 24 and 25). Some of these groupings Matthew may have found in his sources. Due to the prevalence of these collections and a different arrangement of the materials at times in Mark and Luke, however, one is led to conclude that Matthew is largely responsible for the skillful organization of the Gospel of Matthew.

In regard to the larger structure of the Gospel of Matthew, two widely followed proposals have been suggested. The first proposal is based on the repeated occurrence in Matthew of the statement, "Now when Jesus had finished saying these things. . . ." This statement (with slight variations) appears five times in the Gospel (7:28; 11:1; 13:53; 19:1; 26:1). These sayings divide the Gospel of Matthew into five major sections (3:1–7:29; 8:1–11:1; 11:2–13:53; 13:54–19:2; and 19:3–26:2), each containing narrative material and teaching (or discourse) material. These five sections are preceded by stories of the birth of Jesus (chaps. 1–2) and followed by the account of Jesus' death and resurrection (26:3–28:20).

The second proposed structure for the Gospel notes the appearance in 4:17 and in 16:21 of the statement, "From that time on Jesus began. . . ." One of the major proponents of the latter proposal argues that both occurrences of this set phrase or formula signal to the reader transitions in Matthew's Gospel that divide the work into three sections. Each section describes a different phase of the ministry of Jesus. The beginning phase (1:1–4:16) deals with events prior to the ministry of Jesus; the middle phase (4:17–16:20) presents Jesus' ministry in Galilee and his rejection by the religious leaders; the final phase (16:21–28:20) is concerned with Jesus' journey to Jerusalem and his death and resurrection.[3]

Neither of these two proposals is totally satisfactory. The first proposal has been criticized for relegating the accounts of Jesus' birth and his death to the minor roles of prologue and epilogue. Furthermore, chapter 23 does not fit neatly into this pattern of alternating narrative with discourse. Some scholars group this chapter with the narrative section, others with discourse material. The tripartite division, on the other hand, while it is attractive because of its simplicity and its attention to the narrative flow of the text, is ultimately unconvincing. The phrases at 4:17 and 16:21 that supposedly demarcate the phases of Jesus' ministry do not seem to bear that much weight in Matthew's Gospel. These phrases ("from that time on Jesus began") indicate shifts in the story time of the Gospel, that is, in Matthew's telling of the events of Jesus. The two occurrences of the phrase, however, do not seem to be major structuring devices for Matthew.

Dissatisfaction with both of these proposals has led other scholars to argue that the key to Matthew's structure is found in symmetrical or triadic arrangements of the material. Unconvinced by any of these proposals, Robert Gundry has even suggested that the author of this Gospel had no explicit structure in mind and that we would be better off not trying to impose a structure where one does not exist.[4]

Even though the author's structural plan of the Gospel is somewhat unclear, the fivefold repetition of the stereotyped expression, "Now when Jesus had finished saying these things," strongly suggests that Matthew grouped his material into sections demarcated by these sayings. The outline proposed in this study follows that pattern. Although this suggested outline is not without difficulties, it does recognize the importance of the stereo-typed expression mentioned above and highlights the combination of narrative and teaching material in the Gospel. Furthermore, this arrangement brings into focus the emphasis that Matthew places on the teachings of Jesus.

Major Themes in the Gospel of Matthew

Although Matthew tells many of the same stories as Mark and includes many of the same sayings of Jesus, the Gospel of Matthew is clearly different from the Gospel of Mark. Some of these differences can be attributed to different social and historical settings, but much of the originality of this work is due to Matthew's creative arrangement of his material and his emphasis of key ideas and themes.

Identity of Jesus

Messiah. From the opening verse of this Gospel, the narrator clearly states his evaluation of Jesus. He is "the Messiah, the son of David, the son of Abraham." As Messiah and Son of David, Jesus is the long-awaited agent of God who brings salvation to God's people. He is the royal Messiah who enters Jerusalem, not as a military conqueror, but as the humble prince of peace foretold by the prophet Zechariah. Because he is the Davidic Messiah, he is then the "king of the Jews," an identification that is made at his birth (2:2) and again at his death (27:11, 29, 37, 42). In him are fulfilled all the promises made to Israel, not only the messianic hopes and the promises to Israel, but also the promise of a blessing to all peoples. As son of Abraham, he is the one through whom God's promise of a blessing for all the nations (Gen 22:18) is realized.

Son of God. Also important to Matthew is the title "Son of God." (Notice that Matthew adds the title in several places where it is not found in Mark: 14:33; 16:16; 27:40, 43.) The story of Jesus' miraculous conception indicates that Jesus was God's Son from birth. Later at his baptism, his transfiguration, his trial, and his crucifixion, Jesus is also identified as God's Son. After Jesus walks on the water, the disciples confess he is the Son of God (14:33). At Caesarea Philippi, Peter confesses that Jesus is not only the Messiah, but also "the Son of the living God" (16:16).

What does "Son of God" mean for Matthew? The title likely carried, in part, kingly, messianic overtones. The royal connotations of this title can be seen in the announcement made at Jesus' baptism and transfiguration, "This is my Son." This pronouncement is an adaptation of Psalm 2:7, a royal psalm used at the coronation of a king of Israel, celebrating his status as God's newly adopted son. For Matthew the title also signifies Jesus' status as the obedient one. Because he is the supremely obedient Son of God, Jesus possesses a unique relationship to God, whom he addresses as Father. This uniqueness is most clearly expressed in 11:27, "All things have been handed over to me by my Father; and no one knows the Son except the

Father, and no one knows the Father except the Son and anyone to whom the Son chooses to reveal him."

Does "Son of God" carry divine status in Matthew? The evidence is not clear. For Matthew, Jesus' sonship may be functional (he is God's Son because he is obedient to God) rather than ontological (Jesus' very nature is divine). The former view seems present in the Gospel of Mark. The Gospel of Matthew, however, while still holding a functional view, seems to be moving in the direction of an ontological understanding of Jesus as the Son of God. The Matthean story of the virginal conception of Jesus could be seen as suggesting that Jesus is by nature divine. Also, Matthew's version of the story of the rich young man who comes to Jesus (19:16-22) points in the same direction. In Mark's account (10:17-22), in response to being addressed as "Good Teacher," Jesus says, "Why do you call me good? No one is good but God alone," thus apparently denying divine status to himself. In Matthew the young man does not call Jesus good and Jesus' question is "Why do you ask me about what is good?" Matthew perhaps changed the Markan text because he was uncomfortable with the implication that Jesus did not accept divine status.

Son of David. The title "Son of David" is important for Matthew: he applies this title to Jesus in the opening verse of his Gospel, and seven more times throughout the work Jesus is called "Son of David." This title emphasizes that Jesus is the fulfillment of the hopes of a royal Messiah of the line of David. This title by itself, however, is an insufficient identification of Jesus. It can be used by some who continue to have an inadequate understanding of Jesus. In the story of Jesus' entry into Jerusalem, the crowds hail Jesus as the "Son of David" (21:1-11). Their lack of true understanding, however, is seen by their further identification of him as only "the prophet Jesus from Nazareth in Galilee" (21:11). Their complicity in his trial and condemnation demonstrate further that they have no real understanding of who Jesus is. On the other hand, other characters in the Gospel use the title in a way that indicates they are more perceptive in their understanding of Jesus. The Canaanite woman (15:21-28) and the two blind men of Jericho (20:29-34) who also address Jesus as "Son of David" exhibit true faith. Not only do they call Jesus "Son of David" but also "Lord." The title "Son of David," then, needs to be joined with other titles of Jesus for an accurate understanding of Jesus. Jesus is indeed the

"Son of David," but in a way that alters and surpasses the expectations of the people.

Son of Man. The phrase "Son of Man" also is applied to Jesus in Matthew, quite often by Jesus himself. Although the title is used to describe Jesus during his earthly ministry and in reference to his suffering, death, and resurrection, for Matthew the title especially refers to Jesus as the apocalyptic Son of Man figure (cf. Dan 7:13-14) who will come at the end of the age "with power and great glory" on the clouds from heaven (24:30). He will then serve as eschatological judge of the world (Matt 25:31-46).

Higher Righteousness

Matthew describes Joseph as "a righteous man" (1:19) and explains Jesus' baptism as necessary "to fulfill all righteousness" (3:15). In the Sermon on the Mount Jesus mentions righteousness several times, specifically telling his disciples that their righteousness must surpass that of the scribes and Pharisees (5:20). This righteousness that Jesus expects to be evident in both one's words and deeds must be authentic righteousness, not simply religious acts done for the sake of public show. To be righteous is to do the will of God, and in Matthew the supreme example of one who does the will of God is Jesus.

Discipleship

Matthew portrays the disciples more positively than does Mark. The disciples in Matthew may fail and may be slow to understand, but they are still ones who have "little faith." They are not complete failures. They are "disciples-in-training" who are continuing to grow in their understanding and their faithfulness. In contrast to the Gospel of Mark where the last act of the disciples is their desertion and denial of Jesus, in Matthew the last scene is the commissioning of the disciples to go out to make more disciples. Early in the Gospel when the disciples are sent out on mission they are authorized to preach and heal, but teaching is not mentioned. Now at the end, after the disciples have been taught by Jesus, they are specifically commissioned to teach new followers "to obey everything that I have commanded you" (28:20). Thus in Matthew there is both a call to be a disciple—which means hearing the teaching of Jesus and following it—and a call to make new disciples.

Church and Synagogue

The Gospel of Matthew is the only Gospel to use the word "church" (16:18; 18:17). These passages give special prominence to Peter and provide guidance in matters of church discipline. Even though the word "church" (*ekklēsia*) only occurs in these two verses, the entire Gospel is a church document, dealing with concerns of Matthew's community and providing guidance and instructions for this Christian community.

One of the problematic issues in reading the Gospel of Matthew is the harsh polemic directed against the synagogue and the Jewish leadership. As mentioned above, Matthew often emotionally distances Jesus (and the reader) from the synagogues by referring to "their" synagogues or "your" synagogues (4:23; 9:35; 10:17; 12:9; 13:54; 23:34) as if Jesus himself were not Jewish. Throughout the Gospel the religious leaders are described in extremely harsh and negative terms, culminating in the woes and denunciations in chapter 23. In the passion narrative Matthew goes to great lengths to portray the guilt of the Jewish people for the death of Jesus.

Unfortunately, this harsh rhetoric of Matthew's Gospel has been responsible for much anti-Semitism throughout history, as Christians have used these passages (particularly 27:25) as rationale to heap verbal or physical abuse upon Jews and Judaism. Certainly such a response to the Gospel of Matthew is deplorable. Recently, scholars have paid special attention to this aspect of the Gospel of Matthew (as well as other New Testament texts), not in order to excuse the hostility, but in an attempt to understand its origin and function in the Gospel. This language likely reflects more the situation of Matthew's community than the situation of Jesus. Almost all Matthean scholars agree that the Gospel of Matthew gives evidence of a tension between post-70 CE Judaism and Matthew's Christian community. Opinions are divided over whether a definitive split had already occurred between the two groups. Regardless of whether the split is final or not, the rhetoric of Matthew's Gospel is that of a minority group (the Christian community) that is alienated from the dominant group (mainstream Judaism) and is trying to establish its own worldview as the correct one. Both groups claim to be the true heirs of Judaism. The church's claim that Jesus was the Messiah and the authoritative teacher of the law was a major point of contention between the two groups. Matthew's church was trying to understand the rejection of Jesus by the rest of Judaism. The church was moving beyond its Jewish roots and embracing a gentile mission. This, too, added to the tension.

In trying to understand Matthew's attack on the Jewish leaders, readers must remember that early Christianity was a Jewish sect, born and nurtured within Judaism. The Jewish group at Qumran that produced the Dead Sea Scrolls (likely the Essenes) used vitriolic language to describe the rest of Judaism whom they saw as "children of darkness" and their leaders as the "Wicked Priest" and "the Liar." These opponents they described as "lying interpreters," "seekers of falsehood," and "teachers of lies."[5] In the same vein, Matthew also used harsh language to propagandize against the current Jewish leadership. Since Matthew's community was strongly Jewish in origin if not in current composition, the struggle between the synagogue and the church was more like a struggle between two rival Jewish groups than a struggle between two different religions. Thus when we read the Gospel of Matthew, we should understand the polemics against the Jewish leaders not as attacks on the Jewish people as a whole, but as attempts by Matthew to "demonize" the Jewish leaders in order to "win points" in his argument that the Christian community is the true community of God.

Outline of the Gospel of Matthew

The following outline will serve as the basis for our closer examination of the Gospel of Matthew. Readers are encouraged to read the text of the Gospel in conjunction with the Reading Guide that follows the outline.

   I.   The Birth and Infancy of Jesus (1:1–2:23)
   II. A Higher Righteousness (3:1–7:29)
        A. Narrative (3:1–4:25)
        B. Teaching (5:1–7:29)
   III. Discipleship (8:1–11:1)
        A. Narrative (8:1–9:35)
        B. Teaching (9:36–11:1)
   IV. The Kingdom of Heaven (11:2–13:53)
        A. Narrative (11:2–12:50)
        B. Teaching (13:1-53)
   V.   Instructions for the Christian Community (13:54–19:2)
        A. Narrative (13:54–17:27)
        B. Teaching (18:1–19:2)
   VI. The End of the Age (19:3–26:2)
        A. Narrative (19:3–23:39)
        B. Teaching (24:1–26:2)
   VII. The Death and Resurrection of Jesus (26:3–28:20)

Reading Guide to the Gospel of Matthew

The Birth and Infancy of Jesus (1:1–2:23)

The first sentence of Matthew's Gospel introduces the readers to the main character of the story. Matthew's Gospel is a story about "Jesus the Messiah, the son of David, the son of Abraham." All three of these titles are important in this Gospel, which presents Jesus as the royal Messiah of the line of David, the fulfillment of God's promises from the time of Abraham. The genealogy of Jesus that appears in chapter 1 is often skipped over or read hurriedly by readers who see it as nothing more than a list of boring "begats" (according to the KJV translation). This genealogy, however, reflects the editorial hand of Matthew, who through his arrangement and selection of the names has crafted a theological statement about Jesus. Verse 17 calls the reader's attention to the groupings of the names in the genealogy. They are arranged in three groups of fourteen generations each. The significance of this arrangement probably lies in the ancient practice of *gematria* in which letters could have numerical values. By counting the numerical value of the individual letters in a person's name one could arrive at a numerical value for the name. In Hebrew, the numerical value of the name of David is fourteen. By his artificial arrangement of the names in the genealogy (some generations were omitted in order to construct this pattern of fourteen), Matthew is claiming that in Jesus the Davidic Messiah has come.[6]

One other aspect of the Matthean genealogy is of interest. In addition to Mary, the mother of Jesus, Matthew lists four women in Jesus' family tree—Tamar, Rahab, Ruth, and the wife of Uriah (i.e., Bathsheba). Matthew's list is unusual in that biblical genealogies do not normally include women. Why has Matthew included these women? Two features stand out about the women Matthew has chosen to include. First, all of these women are described in the Bible as being non-Israelites, or they were remembered that way in later Jewish tradition. The inclusion of these non-Israelite women hints at the universality of the message of Jesus, a subordinate motif in the Gospel of Matthew. Second, there is something questionable or even scandalous about the sexual history of each of these women. By mentioning these particular women, Matthew was perhaps preparing for the questionable circumstances of the pregnancy of Mary. Furthermore, by including these women Matthew might have been pointing out that God can use unusual means and imperfect persons to accomplish God's plans.

The events leading up to the birth of Jesus focus on Joseph, Jesus' father, who is described as "a righteous man" (1:19). An angel appears to him in a dream announcing the pregnancy of Mary and declaring that the child is to be named Jesus, "for he will save his people from their sins" (1:21). By explaining the name to the readers, Matthew lets them know the significance of this child that is to be born. Through him, who is also identified as Emmanuel ("God is with us"), God will bring salvation to the world. Whereas in the Gospel of Mark, Jesus' divine sonship is manifested at his baptism when the heavenly voice proclaims him to be God's Son, in Matthew the status of Jesus as God's Son is moved back to his conception.

The appearance of the Magi, or wise men, in Bethlehem following the birth of Jesus highlights the various responses to Jesus. The wise men, symbolic of those who faithfully follow Jesus, come to worship this "king of the Jews" (2:2); Herod, the king of Judea, on the other hand, seeks to kill him. His actions prepare us for the rejection and eventual death of Jesus. Throughout this section, Matthew is intent on showing that events in the early life of Jesus are fulfillments of the Hebrew Bible. The exodus motif is strong in this chapter. Like the ancient Hebrews, Jesus and his family travel to Egypt and then return to the land of Palestine. Matthew even applies to Jesus the words which the prophet Hosea applied to the Hebrews in Egypt, "Out of Egypt I have called my son."

A Higher Righteousness (3:1–7:29)

Narrative (3:1–4:25). Matthew's story moves swiftly from the birth of Jesus to his baptism by John the Baptist. Matthew's account of John is fuller than Mark's version. The Pharisees and Sadducees who come to John the Baptist, lumped together almost as one group, are harshly condemned by John. His criticism of them prefigures Jesus' criticism of and conflict with the religious authorities. In presenting the story of Jesus' baptism, Matthew answers a question that might have troubled his readers: Why should Jesus, John the Baptist's superior, be baptized by John, especially since this was a baptism signifying repentance for sins? To deal with this issue Matthew has John express reservations about baptizing Jesus. The answer that the Matthean Jesus gives highlights a theme we have already encountered, but which becomes even more important in this section of the Gospel. Jesus is to be baptized in order "to fulfill all righteousness" (3:15). Like Joseph before him (1:19), Jesus is presented as one who is righteous and obedient to God. At his baptism, the heavenly voice speaks not to Jesus only (cf. Mark 1:11, "You are my Son, the Beloved") but apparently to others as well ("This is my Son, the Beloved"). What is surprising, though, is that in the remainder of the Gospel, no one, including John the Baptist (cf. Matt 11:2-6), seems to have been informed by this pronouncement. Only Satan appears to know the identity of Jesus (4:3, 6).

Again, Matthew (as well as Luke) gives a fuller narrative than Mark of Jesus' testing in the wilderness (4:1-11). In Matthew the story of Jesus' temptation serves to reinforce for the reader the image of Jesus as the one who "fulfills all righteousness." Regardless of what temptations Satan lays before him, Jesus remains the supremely obedient Son of God, answering each of Satan's temptings with a quotation from scripture. "If you are the Son of God," Satan says as he tempts Jesus the first two times. Because we the readers have already heard the divine voice at Jesus' baptism identify Jesus as God's Son, we recognize the irony in these words of Satan: they are a true identification of Jesus. His faithfulness during the time of testing validates this identification. Jesus' forty days and forty nights in the wilderness is reminiscent of the Hebrew's forty years of wandering in the wilderness after the exodus from Egypt. Whereas the Israelites were often unfaithful and rebelled against God, Jesus exemplifies the obedient Son.

Throughout the opening sections of the Gospel, the narrator is intent on presenting the life of Jesus as a fulfillment of the Hebrew scriptures. In accordance with this plan, the narrator interprets Jesus' move from Nazareth to Capernaum (4:13) as a fulfillment of a passage from Isaiah 9. The text in Isaiah celebrates the coming of God's salvation to Zebulun and Naphtali, old tribal lands in the territory of Galilee. Matthew sees Jesus, the bearer of God's salvation, fulfilling these words of hope by his move to Capernaum, a city in Galilee. The use of the Isaiah quotation is perhaps intended also to explain why the Messiah would be active in Galilee, known more for its rebelliousness and religious laxity than for its spirituality, rather than in Jerusalem or Judea. The narrator sees Jesus' activity in Galilee as divinely ordained. In Galilee Jesus continues the work of John the Baptist, proclaiming the same message, "Repent, for the kingdom of heaven has come near" (4:17; cf. 3:2). Verses 18-24 provide a summary of the activities of Jesus in Galilee. He calls disciples, teaches, proclaims the good news of the kingdom, and performs healings. Consequently, his fame spreads from Galilee into Syria and beyond, with the result that "great crowds followed him from Galilee, the Decapolis, Jerusalem, Judea, and from beyond the Jordan" (4:25).

Teaching (5:1–7:29). Chapters 5–7 comprise the first major teaching section in Matthew's Gospel. Whereas the narrative section of 3:1–4:25 has demonstrated the righteousness of Jesus in his actions, the thrust of chapters 5–7 is to make clear the demand for righteousness in Jesus' teachings. This section of the Gospel is normally called the Sermon on the Mount. Because many of the sayings contained in Matthew's Sermon can be found in the Gospel of Luke, most scholars assume that Matthew and Luke are dependent on the source Q for the form and contents of these sayings. In Luke the sayings are not grouped together as they are in Matthew, but are scattered throughout his Gospel. Most scholars believe that the "Sermon on the Mount" was never delivered orally as one sermon or teaching, but represents a collection of sayings from throughout Jesus' ministry, supplemented with additional material from the early Christian communities and from the Gospel writers themselves. How much of Matthew's Sermon on the Mount actually derives from the historical Jesus is a debated question. As Matthew presents the material, however, these sayings highlight the ethical demands of those who are followers of Jesus. The righteousness expected of Jesus' followers is a higher righteousness, one that "exceeds that of the scribes and Pharisees" (5:20).

The first part of Matthew's Sermon on the Mount consists of a collection of nine sayings known as the Beatitudes (named after the opening word in Latin translations, meaning "blessed"). These sayings announce God's favor or grace upon those who pursue the way of Jesus, the way of righteousness. A comparison of the Beatitudes in Matthew with the parallel passages in Luke has led most scholars to conclude that the Lukan versions are closer to the original Q form of the sayings. Matthew has often generalized and spiritualized these blessings. Compare for example Luke's concrete "Blessed are you who are poor" (6:20) with Matthew's "Blessed are the poor in spirit" (5:3); or Luke's "Blessed are you who are hungry now" (6:21) with Matthew's "Blessed are those who hunger and thirst for righteousness" (5:6). Matthew makes clear that these blessings are promised for those who are earnest and sincere in their desire to be a part of God's community, who desire it so badly they can taste it! The reader quickly realizes, however, that to be a part of God's kingdom is not always easy, for the last two beatitudes caution that to be obedient followers of God sometimes includes persecution and suffering.

The next part of the Sermon on the Mount (5:21-48) contains a series of antitheses, pitting traditional religious views against Jesus' interpretation of God's requirements. Cast in the form, "You have heard that it was said. . . . But I say to you," these sayings underscore the radical nature of Jesus' demands on his disciples. Jesus holds his disciples to a higher standard than that of the religious leaders of his day. For example, the Jewish law prohibited adultery. Jesus goes beyond this standard, demanding that his followers not even look at another person with lustful thoughts. Matthew is careful to show that even though Jesus is at odds with the religious interpreters of his day, he does not cast the Jewish law aside (cf. 5:17-20). He intensifies, rather than abrogates the demands of the law. For Jesus, the problem is not with the law but with its interpretation.

The remainder of the Sermon on the Mount likewise portrays Jesus' intense demands and calls to obedience for his disciples. Their piety is to be deep and genuine, not casuistic or only for show as is the case with those Jesus denounces as "hypocrites." Who are these hypocrites? Because in 5:20 Jesus has already warned that his disciples' righteousness must exceed "that of the scribes and Pharisees," the reader assumes that they are the same ones being labeled here as hypocrites. As we will see later in the Gospel, these two groups are stereotyped in Matthew's Gospel as the enemies of Jesus.

Doing the will of God is summarized in the saying usually referred to as the "Golden Rule": "In everything do to others as you would have them do to you; for this is the law and the prophets" (7:12). Once again Matthew presents a Jesus who does not abolish the "law and the prophets" but rather fulfills them and expects the same from his followers. Jesus calls for radical obedience from his followers, an obedience that is demonstrated not just by words but, most important, by actions. Jesus declares, "Not everyone who says to me, 'Lord, Lord,' will enter the kingdom of heaven, but only the one who does the will of my Father in heaven" (7:21).

The Sermon on the Mount in Matthew has made clear to the reader not only Jesus' demands for righteousness, but also the authority with which he speaks. Jesus speaks with a commanding voice, setting aside former interpretations in order to elucidate plainly the will of God. The reader can understand the reaction of the crowds—they "were astounded at his teaching, for he taught them as one having authority, and not as their scribes" (7:28-29)—for Matthew has clearly portrayed a Jesus who speaks with authority.

Discipleship (8:1–11:1)

Narrative (8:1–9:35). Following the first teaching section, Matthew picks up again the narrative of Jesus' activity. The authority of Jesus that was evidenced in his teaching in the Sermon on the Mount is likewise evident in his activity, which Matthew presents in nine miracle stories in this section.[7] Matthew has arranged these stories into three groups, each group containing three stories. The first group (8:1-17) contains stories of Jesus healing a leper, the paralyzed servant of a Roman centurion, and Peter's mother-in-law who is sick with a fever. The emphasis on Jesus' authority is particularly clear in the second healing as the centurion identifies with Jesus as one who is also a person of authority, who can utter commands and people obey. This healing episode also points to a theme that will become more important later in Matthew's Gospel, the mission of the church to the gentiles, for Jesus says about the Roman centurion, "Truly I tell you, in no one in Israel have I found such faith. I tell you, many will come from east and west and will eat with Abraham and Isaac and Jacob in the kingdom of heaven" (8:10-11). Matthew sees Jesus' healings as a fulfillment of the scriptures; specifically he interprets Jesus in terms of the suffering servant figure in Isaiah 53 (8:17; cf. 12:18-21).

The second group of miracle stories (8:23–9:8) depicts not only Jesus' power over illness and disease, but also his power over nature and his authority to forgive sins. The first act of power in this second trilogy is Jesus calming the storm at sea (8:23-27). The disciples ask in amazement, "What sort of man is this, that even the winds and the sea obey him?" (8:27). The reader shares perhaps some of the amazement of the disciples, yet the reader knows "what sort of man is this," because the narrator has made it clear already: this man is God's Son, the Messiah. His power is demonstrated further as he heals two demoniacs (8:28-34) and cures a paralyzed man (9:1-8). After the latter event, the crowds "were filled with awe, and they glorified God, who had given such authority to human beings" (9:8). The reader is likely surprised to find such a saying, that God had given the authority to forgive sin to human beings. Why do the crowds extend this to "human beings" and not just to Jesus? Likely, this is a reflection of

Matthew's situation, in which now the authority to forgive sins belonged also to the followers of Jesus, that is, the church.

In the final triplet of miracle stories (9:18-34), Jesus raises a girl from the dead and heals a woman with chronic hemorrhages (9:18-26), gives sight to the blind (9:27-31), and speech to one who was mute (9:32-34). Once again Jesus' power causes the people to respond in amazement. The opposite reaction arises from the Pharisees, however, who attribute Jesus' power not to God but to Satan, "the ruler of the demons" (9:34).

Between each of the three groups of miracle stories a section on discipleship is inserted. The brief episode following the first group of miracle stories (8:18-22) underscores the radical demands of following Jesus. To be a disciple of Jesus requires that one be willing to give up home, security, and even family obligations. Nothing is to take precedence over the kingdom of God. After the second collection of stories, the Gospel gives a brief description of Matthew's call to be a disciple (9:9). Matthew's response exemplifies that of the faithful disciple—he leaves behind the old way of life to become a follower of Jesus. His response is in contrast to that of the Pharisees who, as Jesus eats in what is presumably Matthew's house (9:10-13), criticize him for eating with social and religious outcasts ("tax collectors and sinners").

As was the case with the first narrative section, this narrative section ends with a summary statement about the work of Jesus, "Then Jesus went about all the cities and villages, teaching in their synagogues, and proclaiming the good news of the kingdom, and curing every disease and every sickness" (9:35; cf. 4:23).

Teaching (9:36–11:1). Once again the sight of the crowds leads to a major discourse. On this occasion, Jesus calls together his disciples and sends them out on a mission to preach and to heal. Prior to their departure, he instructs them as to their mission. This section of Matthew has sometimes been called the "missionary discourse" because it contains specific instructions for the disciples as they are sent out. Like John the Baptist (3:2) and Jesus (4:17), the disciples proclaim, "The kingdom of heaven has come near" (10:7). As their message is the same, so will be their reception: persecution and rejection will befall them. This type of treatment they are to expect, for "a disciple is not above the teacher, nor a slave above the master. . . . If they have called the master of the house Beelzebul, how much more will they malign those of his household" (10:24-25). True discipleship may well be costly discipleship, requiring a complete restructuring of commitments and priorities (10:34-39).

The reader of Matthew may be puzzled by one aspect of Jesus' instructions to his disciples, his command that they "go nowhere among the Gentiles, and enter no town of the Samaritans, but go rather to the lost sheep of the house of Israel" (10:5-6). We have already seen hints in Matthew's Gospel of a more inclusive spirit, "good news" that applies to Jew and gentile alike. What are we to make of this command to exclusiveness? As we shall see at the end of Matthew (28:19), after Jesus' resurrection the disciples are sent out to "make disciples of all nations." Their field of activity is to extend beyond the Jewish people. The restriction of the mission to the Jewish people may have been a part of the historical Jesus' own understanding. Matthew, however, sees that as a temporary restriction. The post-resurrection task of the disciples includes proclamation to all people.

Interestingly, even though Jesus gives the disciples lengthy instructions about the work they are being sent out to do, the actual mission is never described. We are told at the beginning of the discourse (v. 5) that Jesus sends them out, but after he finishes giving instructions, the mission seems to be forgotten. Neither their departure nor their return is mentioned. Perhaps, as some commentators have proposed, by not describing the mission or its completion Matthew suggests that the missionary task is open-ended. The charge to Jesus' followers continues to the time of the readers and even beyond. Matthew signals the end of this discourse with the formula, "Now when Jesus had finished . . ." (11:1).

The Kingdom of Heaven (11:2–13:53)

In the discourse material of this third section, Matthew has collected several parables of Jesus. The theme of the parables is the kingdom of heaven. The "kingdom of heaven" is Matthew's preferred term for what elsewhere is called the "kingdom of God." Matthew's preference for "kingdom of heaven" is likely due to his Jewish concerns. Pious Jews normally avoided saying the name of God. Instead, some circumlocution was used—the Name, the Holy One, or Heaven. Thus kingdom of heaven is synonymous with kingdom of God.

Narrative (11:2–12:50). The narrative material preceding the parables focuses on those who reject Jesus and his teachings, thereby rejecting the kingdom of God. The reader has been prepared for this theme of rejection and conflict by the earlier negative response to Jesus on the part of the scribes, Pharisees, and Sadducees. John the Baptist, whom we have not heard from since the baptism of Jesus, now reappears. Without any explanation, the narrator states that John is now in prison (11:2). From there, he sends his disciples to Jesus (explicitly identified by the narrator as "the Messiah") to ask if Jesus is indeed "the one who is to come," that is, the anticipated Messiah. Jesus answers by pointing to what he has done, inviting comparison with expectations found in the book of Isaiah (Isa 29:18-19; 35:5-6; 61:1-2) of events that would take place when God appeared to God's people. Jesus' statement, "And blessed is anyone who takes no offense at me" (11:6), hints of what is to come in the remainder of this chapter and in chapter 12. Over and over again, we meet people who do take offense at Jesus. These stories illustrate the negative response of many of the people to Jesus.

Some of the people ("this generation") are like children who are never satisfied, complaining about John the Baptist for his strictness in food and drink, while at the same time condemning Jesus because he is not strict enough (11:16-19). The inhabitants of Chorazin, Bethsaida, and Capernaum likewise reject Jesus. They refuse to accept his message and believe, even after they have seen the mighty works he has done (11:20-24). Even though Jesus pronounces judgment upon these who reject him, he offers rest and relief to any who would come to him, for his "yoke is easy" and his "burden is light" (11:30). The term "yoke" was sometimes used in reference to the Jewish law, a yoke that may have seemed too heavy to bear, particularly as the law was interpreted and applied by the religious leaders. In contrast, Jesus offers his followers an easy yoke. They are to learn from him what the demands of God truly are.

Examples of how the law was made into a heavy yoke are given in the controversy stories in chapter 12. In two stories (12:1-8, 9-14), Jesus is attacked by the Pharisees because of his failure to adhere to their regulations concerning the keeping of the sabbath. In both cases, Jesus is more interested in meeting the needs of people than in rigidly adhering to rules. As in 9:13, Jesus accuses the religious leaders of not understanding the true desires of God contained in the scriptures, for their actions demonstrate they have failed to comprehend the words of the prophet Hosea, "I desire mercy and not sacrifice" (12:7; Hos 6:6). The opposition to Jesus by the Pharisees is now unmistakable to the readers. The narrator informs us that after their encounters with Jesus, "the Pharisees went out and conspired against him, how to destroy him" (12:14).

Later in the chapter the Pharisees reappear, again criticizing Jesus, this time accusing him of being in league with "Beelzebul, the ruler of the demons" (12:24). Jesus denounces them as a "brood of vipers," whose evil deeds and words are evidence that they are not a part of the kingdom of God. The reader should note the contrast here: the righteousness of Jesus is demonstrated in words and deeds, whereas the evil of the religious leaders is evidenced in their words and deeds. In both cases, the saying of Jesus is fulfilled: "The tree is known by its fruit" (12:33). When the scribes and Pharisees demand a sign from Jesus to authenticate his authority and identity (12:38), the irony is obvious to the reader. Matthew has already given us many "signs" to show that Jesus is indeed the "one who is to come." The truth that the scribes and Pharisees refuse to see and accept Matthew has made abundantly clear to the readers. We are not surprised then when Jesus refuses to produce further evidence for this "evil and adulterous generation" (12:39). These religious leaders are in contrast to Jesus' disciples, whom he describes as his true family for they are the ones who do the will of God (12:49-50).

Teaching (13:1-53). Chapter 13 contains Matthew's third major teaching block, in which he has gathered several parables of Jesus, all of which attempt to elucidate the kingdom of heaven. These seven parables portray the various responses to the kingdom, describe the certainty of the coming of the kingdom, or point to the extreme value of the kingdom. The parable of the sower is interpreted by Jesus as an allegory in which the different types of soil represent the different responses of people to the message of the kingdom of God. A widely held view is that this allegorical interpretation, as well as the one attached to the parable of the net (vv. 49-50), belongs not to the historical Jesus but to later church tradition. Although this explanation for the origin of the interpretation may be true, Matthew sees the appropriateness of this allegorical interpretation for the purpose of his narrative. It serves as encouragement and warning to the readers of the Gospel who are themselves encountering difficulties in being faithful hearers of the word.

Although parables appear elsewhere in Matthew as well, they are given more prominence in chapter 13 than anywhere else. Not only do more parables appear here, but the reason for Jesus' use of parables is explained.

Whereas in Mark 4:11-12 and Luke 8:10 Jesus says that he speaks in parables in order that the people will not understand, in Matthew Jesus explains that he speaks in parables *because* the people have failed to understand his message (13:10-15). As a result of the people's failure to respond positively to Jesus, he gives his teachings specifically to those who do understand, the disciples (and to us, the readers).

Asked by Jesus whether they have understood all that he has been teaching them, the disciples reply, "Yes" (13:51). Their response is in sharp contrast to the response both of the religious leaders who have been antagonistic to Jesus and of the larger audience (the people of Israel) who are accused of not perceiving, listening, nor understanding the message of Jesus (13:13). The disciples are presented in a very positive light in this chapter. Jesus says to them, "Blessed are your eyes, for they see, and your ears, for they hear" (13:16). The reader will understand that the disciples are examples of one who "brings out of his treasure what is new and what is old" (13:52), for they have heard and accepted the new teachings of Jesus, while at the same time have not forsaken the instructions of God revealed in the Torah.

Instructions for the Christian Community (13:54–19:2)

Narrative (13:54–17:27). The narrative material in this section continues the theme of the responses to Jesus featured in the preceding material. In the first pericope Jesus goes to his hometown, where his teaching in the synagogue results in disbelief and rejection. "Where did this man get this wisdom and these deeds of power?" they ask (13:54). These characters in the story may not know the answer, but Matthew has made it plain to his readers. Jesus' teaching and mighty deeds are evidence of the power of God at work in him. The second pericope shows that Herod Antipas, the ruler of Galilee, is also puzzled by Jesus, thinking he must be John the Baptist, raised from the dead (14:1-2). We are told that Herod had been responsible for the death of John the Baptist (14:3-12). The reader, remembering the close connections between John and Jesus, and remembering that the religious leaders have already plotted the death of Jesus, should sense an ominous mood in the narrative.

The third pericope in this section (14:13-21), the feeding of the five thousand, demonstrates another response to Jesus. (Actually the text says that five thousand men were present, plus the women and children.)

Because of his ability to heal the sick, Jesus is popular with the crowds who follow after him and give him little rest. In Matthew the nameless "crowds" play an ambiguous role. They seem to follow Jesus for the wrong reasons, seeking only to be healed or fed. They are among the ones described as deaf, blind, and imperceptive to the teachings of Jesus (chap. 13). Yet these crowds are also potential followers of Jesus. They are astounded at his teaching, recognizing that he speaks with fresh authority (7:28-29). They praise "the God of Israel" on account of his healings (15:31). Furthermore, in contrast to the religious leaders, they are usually not antagonistic to Jesus.

A positive response to Jesus is seen in the next episode, the story of Jesus walking on the water (14:22-33). Unique to Matthew's version of this story is the attempt of Peter to walk on water. Initially successful, he fails when he breaks his concentration on Jesus. Peter, described here as having "little faith," is symbolic of all the disciples. They too were characterized earlier as having "little faith" (14:31; cf. 8:26). Furthermore, for Matthew this story likely reflects the experience of all followers of Jesus (the post-Easter church) who, beset by troubles and "storms," must put their faith in Jesus. This episode ends with the disciples worshiping Jesus and saying, "Truly you are the Son of God." Even though they are of "little faith" they make the correct confession of the identity of Jesus. (Contrast this response by the disciples with their response in a similar scene earlier in the Gospel at 8:23-27. In that scene after Jesus has calmed the storm at sea, the disciples do not worship, but only wonder in amazement, asking who this man could be.)

The positive response to Jesus by the disciples and the crowds throws into even sharper relief the reaction of the Pharisees and scribes described in the next scene (15:1-20). These religious leaders come to Jesus and question him about his disciples violating the traditions of the elders. In reply Jesus accuses the leaders of being hypocrites, guilty of honoring God with their words but not their actions (15:8-9). They have failed to comprehend the true demands of God. What is worse, they lead others as well to disobey God. Jesus denounces them as "blind guides of the blind" (15:14). The request by Peter for an explanation causes Jesus to ask, "Are you also still without understanding? Do you not see . . . ?" (15:16-17). The reader is reminded that the disciples are not perfect examples of faithfulness. They are still ones of "little faith" who need further guidance and teaching.

When Jesus leaves and goes to Tyre and Sidon (gentile territory), he encounters the unexpected—a woman who has great faith (15:21-28). (Notice how she addresses Jesus: "Lord, Son of David.") What is even more surprising is that she is non-Jewish. At first Jesus refuses to respond to her request to heal her daughter, saying, "I was sent only to the lost sheep of the house of Israel" (15:24). The woman is persistent, and after a brief verbal exchange, Jesus grants her request. While the religious leaders continue in their refusal to understand and believe, here Matthew provides an example of even a gentile who responds correctly to Jesus.

The reader may be puzzled why Jesus, who had earlier allowed his disciples to minister only to the house of Israel, would now concede to the woman's request. Two points should be noted. First, Jesus does not seek the woman out; she comes to him. Second, in the context of Matthew's Gospel, this action on the part of Jesus perhaps prepares for the missionary charge given to the disciples at the end of the Gospel. After his resurrection, Jesus commands them to go to all nations with their message. They are to follow in the steps of Jesus, who has already begun an outreach beyond the confines of Israel to all people.

After another feeding of the crowds by Jesus, numbering four thousand men plus the women and children (15:32-39), the Pharisees and Sadducees come to Jesus to put him to a test (16:1-4). They ask again for a sign. As before, Jesus refuses their request and warns his disciples to "beware of the yeast of the Pharisees and Sadducees" (16:6). Their failure to understand this statement results in Jesus again characterizing them as people of little faith (16:8).

This struggling faith of the disciples reaches a high point in the following scene where in response to Jesus' question, Peter identifies Jesus as "the Messiah, the Son of the living God" (16:16). The difference in the Matthean and Markan accounts of this episode underscores the difference in the portrayal of the disciples in these two Gospels. Whereas both Gospels contain Peter's rebuke of Jesus and Jesus' criticism in return of Peter, Mark makes this episode an integral part of the confession scene. In Matthew the correction of Peter appears to be unconnected chronologically with the confession. "From that time on" in Matthew 16:21 separates the two scenes. Even more importantly, in Matthew's account immediately after Peter's confession (which is itself a fuller confession than in Mark), Jesus heaps high praise on Peter saying, "Blessed are you, Simon son of Jonah! For flesh and blood has not revealed this to you, but my Father in heaven" (16:17).

In Mark the confession of Peter is inadequate; in Matthew the confession is presented as evidence of Peter's faith.

In a play on words, Jesus says, "You are Peter [Greek, *Petros*], and on this rock [Greek, *petra*] I will build my church" (16:18). Peter is an example of the type of faith that is necessary for the followers of Jesus. Jesus confers on him the power to "bind" and "loose," technical rabbinical terms meaning the authority to declare what things are permitted and what things are forbidden. This overwhelmingly positive portrayal of Peter is tempered, however, by the subsequent rebuke scene (16:21-23) in which Peter is not able to accept Jesus' prediction of his own suffering and death. Once more, the faith of Peter is faith "in process," still in need of growth and correction. Peter must learn that the way of discipleship is the way of self-sacrifice that ultimately may lead to a cross.

The fragility of the disciple's faith is evident in the next two stories that Matthew narrates. In the first story, the scene of the transfiguration of Jesus (17:1-8), Peter's offer to build three dwellings (one each for Jesus, Moses, and Elijah) is an inappropriate response. While he is still speaking, a heavenly voice interrupts, instructing the disciples, "This is my Son, the Beloved; with him I am well pleased; listen to him!" (17:5). As Jack Dean Kingsbury notes:

> Within the context of Matthew's story, the purpose of the announcement is to confirm to the three the truth of the confession Peter made on behalf of all the disciples near Caesarea Philippi that Jesus is God's Son. The purpose of the injunction ["listen to him!"] is to exhort the three to receive and not to reject, as Peter did, the new word Jesus delivered to the disciples; that he, whom they rightly perceive to be the Messiah Son of God, has been ordained by God to submit to suffering and death in Jerusalem.[8]

The second story that highlights the limited faith of the disciples concerns their inability to perform a healing (17:14-21). After Jesus descends from the mountain with Peter, James, and John, he heals an epileptic child whom his disciples had been unable to cure because they had "little faith" (17:20). In Matthew this incident is another opportunity to show that the disciples still have much to learn about being followers of Jesus.

The final pericope in chapter 17 is a strange story (17:24-27). After a discussion about whether Jesus is obliged to pay the annual half-shekel Temple tax required of all Jewish males, twenty years old and older, Jesus directs Peter to cast a net into the sea. He is told he will find in the mouth of the first fish he catches the exact amount of money needed to pay the tax for both Jesus and Peter! Scholars have suggested several reasons for this story. Some claim it was recounted by Matthew because it features Peter and highlights his prominence, while others argue that the theme of avoiding scandal or offense explains its presence here. Perhaps Matthew used it as a way to tell Jewish Christians in his community "not to offend Jews by refusing to participate in the collection of contributions throughout Jewry in support of the Patriarchy at Jamnia."[9] Or Matthew may have retained the story simply to remind the readers generally of "the obligation of disciples to avoid giving scandal."[10] Avoiding offense is one of the themes of the following chapter; thus this incident may prepare for Jesus' teaching in chapter 18.

Teaching (18:1–19:2). The large teaching section in chapter 18, the fourth in Matthew's Gospel, provides guidelines for how the followers of Jesus are to relate to each other. Its major themes are humility and forgiveness. The disciples come to Jesus wanting to know who is the greatest in the kingdom of heaven (18:1). Jesus says that even to enter God's kingdom one must become like a child, that is, one who trusts completely in someone else—in this case, in God. One who can become humble like a child becomes great in the eyes of God. In verses 6-14 the term "child" seems to be used metaphorically to refer to vulnerable, weak, neglected and even insignificant followers of Jesus. These persons are not to be ignored or despised in the Christian community. Those who would cause them to stumble (literally, "scandalize" or offend them) are in danger of eternal punishment. The community of faith is to look after these weaker members and not let them go astray.

What is the community, the church, to do when one of their members sins against someone in the church? A threefold procedure is outlined whereby the community is to try to regain the errant member (18:15-20). If all else fails, the community is to exclude the recalcitrant individual. The major concern of the community, however, should be reconciliation and forgiveness. That is made even clearer by the following teaching of Jesus (18:21-35). In response to a question from Peter about the number of times one must forgive another member of the church, Jesus tells a parable about a man who refuses to forgive a small debt owed him, even after he has a tremendous debt that he owes forgiven. The point of the story is that the munificence of God's forgiveness of humanity's sinfulness should lead one always to be willing to forgive. This is the higher righteousness that is expected of the followers of Jesus.

The End of the Age (19:3–26:2)

Narrative (19:1–26:2). The previous section ended by significantly noting that Jesus leaves Galilee and heads toward Judea. The Galilean ministry is finished; Jerusalem lies ahead. Matthew now describes several incidents that occur on the way to Jerusalem. The Pharisees once more put Jesus to the test, this time over the question of divorce. Jesus demonstrates again the freshness of his teaching, claiming that divorce should be avoided because it is contrary to God's intention (19:3-12). In another scene, the disciples speak harshly to those who try to bring children to him (19:13-15). The reader is perhaps surprised by this action, since in the previous chapter Jesus had said, "Whoever welcomes one such child in my name welcomes me" (18:5). This attitude is further evidence of the immature faith of the disciples. The coming to Jesus of a rich young man (19:16-22) becomes another teaching moment for the disciples, as Jesus warns them of the dangers of possessions and the need for total commitment to the kingdom of God (19:23-30).

The journey to Jerusalem serves as the setting for Jesus' third prediction of his impending suffering and death (20:17-19). Although the reader is not told explicitly of the disciples' response to this announcement, the juxtaposition of the following incident describing the desire for special privilege and position (20:20-28) gives the impression once more that the faith of the disciples is still incomplete. Notice that in Matthew this pericope is not as negative toward the disciples as is the parallel passage in Mark (10:35-45). In Mark, James and John approach Jesus asking for privileged positions. Matthew, on the other hand, reports that their mother was the one seeking special status for them. The disciples' jockeying for the best seats in the coming kingdom reflects the opposite attitude from that which should characterize the followers of Jesus. In God's kingdom, humility and service, not positions of power and prestige, indicate greatness. Jesus, himself, is the model, for he "came not to be served but to serve, and to give his life a ransom for many" (20:28). Matthew presents, parallel to the two brothers who seek greatness, two blind men who seek healing (20:29-34). (In Mark's version of the story there is only one blind man.)

Both the disciples and the blind men "need Jesus' healing touch that they may see the truth."[11]

When Jesus finally arrives at Jerusalem, he rides into the city in fulfill-ment of a statement from the prophet Zechariah (21:1-9; Zech 9:9). (Oddly, Matthew misinterprets the synonymous parallelism of the Hebrew text and pictures Jesus riding in on two animals at the same time!) The crowds welcome Jesus as "the Son of David" and "the one who comes in the name of the Lord!" (21:9). The reader recognizes the truth in these claims more than the crowds do, for when asked who Jesus is, the crowds reply that he is a prophet from Nazareth (21:11). In the next scene (21:12-17) the religious leaders refuse to see what even the children confess, that Jesus is indeed the "Son of David."

The episode of the cursing of the fig tree (21:18-22), found also in Mark, becomes in Matthew an opportunity to teach the disciples about the need for a stronger faith, a faith that is not weakened by doubt. Upon entering the Temple, Jesus confronts the religious leaders, who are variously iden-tified as "the chief priests and the elders of the people" (21:23), "the chief priests and the Pharisees" (21:45), and "the Sadducees" (22:23). Jesus tells three parables directed against these religious leaders (21:28-32, 33-44; 22:1-14). These parables condemn the leaders for their failure to do the will of God and for their rejection of God's true messengers (including Jesus himself). Recognizing that the parables are aimed at them, the leaders become even more antagonistic, wanting to arrest Jesus but hesitating to do so because of his popularity with the crowds. Biding their time, they try to entrap him with questions about paying taxes, life after resurrection, and the identity of the greatest commandment. Jesus deftly avoids their traps, amazing the crowds and sometimes even the leaders with his answers. He accuses the religious leaders of knowing "neither the scriptures nor the power of God" (22:29). Jesus so successfully answers their challenges that from then on they do not dare ask him anything else (22:46). This negative portrait of the religious leaders comes as no surprise to the reader. Matthew has revealed this developing conflict throughout his story. The concentra-tion of these negative portrayals in this section prepares the way for the denunciations of these leaders by Jesus in chapter 23.

Some scholars group chapter 23 with the two following chapters to form the fifth and final discourse section in Matthew. Others see the discourse beginning in chapter 24. Although the choice is not clear, we have opted not to place chapter 23 as a part of the final discourse because a new physical setting is described at the beginning of chapter 24. The "woes" that are directed at the scribes and Pharisees in chapter 23 are some of the harshest denunciations in the Gospel. As earlier in the Gospel, the scribes and Pharisees are accused of being blind guides and hypocrites, not only guilty of shallowness and insincerity but also responsible for keeping others out of the kingdom of God. The supposed righteousness of the scribes and Pharisees is exposed as only a facade. Jesus tells them, "So you also on the outside look righteous to others, but inside you are full of hypocrisy and lawlessness" (23:28). Jesus accuses these leaders of being just like their ancestors who persecuted and killed God's prophets. They, like their ancestors, are guilty of rejecting God. For that reason they are denounced as being a "brood of vipers" (23:33).

The reader will remember similar warnings about these religious leaders in the Sermon on the Mount where Jesus warned that anyone who wanted to be a part of the kingdom of God must exhibit a righteousness that exceeds that of the scribes and Pharisees (5:20). The reader will also hear in these denunciations some instructions on how life in the new community of God is to be lived, much of which has already been delivered earlier in the Gospel. Disciples of Jesus are to avoid ostentatious displays of piety and honorific titles and customs that elevate certain individuals over others. They are to be self-sacrificing and humble. Their commitment to God must be evident in their deeds and not just in their words. They are to pay careful attention to "the weightier matters of the law: justice and mercy and faith" (23:23).

Teaching (24:1–26:2). The subject of the final teaching block in Matthew is end-time events. The material in 24:4-28 is a listing of events that are to happen before the end comes. These signs, typical in apocalyptic writings, are not indications that the end has arrived, but are only preliminary events, "the beginning of the birth pangs" (24:8). Jesus warns his disciples not to be misled by the claims of false prophets or false messiahs. Likewise, they should not be misled into thinking that the calamities that he describes mean that the end is at hand. The coming of the Son of Man in the end time will be a public, cosmic event that will be unmistakable. Since no one, not even the Son, knows when that day will come, the task of the follower of Jesus is to be ready.

The material in 24:45–25:30 emphasizes the theme of the delay of the coming of the Son of Man, and thus tempers somewhat the urgency of the preceding section of this eschatological discourse. No one knows when the end will be and thus one must always be ready, even if the coming of the Son of Man is delayed. One does not want to be caught unprepared like the foolish bridesmaids who missed the wedding because they slept when the groom was delayed (25:1-13). Nor does one want to be like the slave who during the interim his master was absent made unwise use of those things entrusted to him (25:14-30). This emphasis in this section on the delay of the return of the Son of Man has often been interpreted as Matthew's challenge to his readers whose commitment and zeal had begun to wane because the expected imminent return of Christ had not yet occurred.

The last section of this teaching episode is the parable of the last judgment (25:31-46), in which Jesus warns that in the final judgment the criterion by which people will be judged will be the extent of their caring response to people in need—the hungry, the thirsty, the strangers, the naked, the sick, and the imprisoned. Showing love to people in need, Jesus says, is the way his followers show love for him. True righteousness, as we have been told before (22:39), consists in loving one's neighbor. This final section of Matthew's Gospel ends on an ominous note: "You know that after two days the Passover is coming, and the Son of Man will be handed over to be crucified" (26:2). The reader anticipates that the plot is moving toward its climax.

The Death and Resurrection of Jesus (26:3–28:20)

Immediately after Jesus' statement about his crucifixion (26:2), the narrator informs us that indeed the chief priests and the elders were plotting how they might arrest Jesus and kill him. The following two incidents add to the tension. An unnamed woman at Bethany anoints the head of Jesus with costly perfume. True to form, the disciples misunderstand the significance of this act and complain about the waste. Jesus, on the other hand, interprets this act of devotion as a preparation for his burial (26:6-13). Judas Iscariot then goes to the chief priests and offers to betray Jesus to them (26:14-16).

Jesus' impending death hangs heavy over the last supper that Jesus eats with his disciples, presented in Matthew as a Passover meal. Jesus warns his disciples that one of them will deny him, a statement that catches them by surprise and leads each to ask, "Surely not I, Lord?" (26:22). Matthew reports that when Judas asks the question, he addresses Jesus not as Lord as the other disciples do, but as rabbi. Throughout Matthew's Gospel, the title "Lord" has been reserved for use by those who recognize the authority of Jesus. "Rabbi" on the other hand, appears elsewhere in Matthew only in a negative context (23:7, 8). By this subtle shift, the narrator indicates his evaluation of Judas. Whereas the other disciples may have faith that is incomplete and sometimes prone to doubt, they are still disciples who can call Jesus "Lord." Judas, however, has now moved from the group who responds positively to Jesus to the group who opposes him. Jesus interprets the bread and wine at their meal in symbolic terms: the bread represents his body; the wine represents his blood, which atones for the sins of humanity.

Leaving the upper room where they shared the Passover meal, Jesus and the disciples go to the Mount of Olives, where Jesus predicts that all the disciples will desert him that very night (26:31). Because we the readers have come to trust the statements of Jesus, the protests of the disciples that they will remain faithful to Jesus even to the death ring hollow. We are not surprised, then, when these predictions of Jesus later prove accurate. In the very next scene (26:36-46), in fact, the inner group of Jesus' disciples cannot even stay awake in support of Jesus while he is agonizing in prayer in Gethsemane (an area on the Mount of Olives). Jesus' prayer in Gethsemane reinforces the image of Jesus as the obedient and righteous Son as three times in prayer he submits to the will of God.

Judas arrives, again calling Jesus "rabbi," and in an ironic gesture identifies Jesus with a kiss. Returning the irony, Jesus addresses Judas as "friend." Jesus does not resist arrest nor does he allow his disciples to resist. Even at his arrest, Jesus is in charge, for if he so chose, he could call on God who would "send me more than twelve legions of angels" (26:53). Jesus, however, goes without resistance in order that "the scriptures of the prophets may be fulfilled" (26:56).

Taken to the house of the high priest, Jesus is silent before his accusers. When asked finally by the high priest if he is "the Messiah, the Son of God" (26:63), Jesus replies "You have said so" (26:64). The high priest condemns him for blasphemy because he has claimed to be God's Son. The scribes and the elders concur with the charge and proceed to vilify Jesus, spitting in his face, striking and slapping him. The reader will remember the parable of the wicked tenants (21:33-41), a parable that implicated the religious leaders. In that story the wicked tenants had seized and killed the owner's son who had been sent to them. In their actions against Jesus, God's Son, the religious leaders are acting out the parable.

Matthew's is the only Gospel to include the story of Judas' death (27:3-10; cf. Acts 1:16-20 for a variant account). This incident highlights the innocence of Jesus, while reinforcing the guilt of Judas and the religious leaders. After Judas hangs himself, the chief priests and elders take the money they had given to Judas and buy a field in which to bury strangers. Even this act Matthew interprets as a fulfillment of the scriptures.

When describing the appearance of Jesus before Pilate, Matthew shapes the narrative in a way that downplays the culpability of Pilate and heightens the responsibility of the religious leaders and the crowds. Pilate is "greatly amazed" by Jesus (27:14) and realizes that the reason the religious leaders had turned Jesus over to him was their jealousy toward Jesus (27:18). Then in a passage unique to Matthew, Pilate's wife advises him to "have nothing to do with that innocent [or, "righteous"] man" (27:19) because of a dream she had. Pilate's wife recognizes what we as readers have known throughout the Gospel. The crowds, who have been rather ambiguous characters toward Jesus in the Gospel, now are persuaded by the chief priests and the elders to demand that Jesus be crucified. Pressured by their demands and fearing a riot, Pilate washes his hands, declaring, "I am innocent of this man's blood" (27:24). The crowds then cry out, "His blood be on us and on our children!" (27:25). The rejection and repudiation of Jesus by his own people, that is, Israel—which was seen in the negative response of the religious leaders to his ministry—has now been completed.

The soldiers take Jesus away to crucify him, mocking him by their words and actions as the "King of the Jews" (27:29). Their mockery—as well as that of the passersby, the two bandits crucified with him, and the religious leaders who taunt him as the Son of God and the King of Israel—is recognized by the reader as the deepest irony. Jesus is indeed "king," but not in the way they use the title. He is king, "not as one who restores to Israel its national splendor and not as one who foments rebellion against Rome, but as the one who saves others by willingly giving himself over to suffering and death."[12]

The crucifixion of Jesus is accompanied by strange and dramatic events: the curtain in the Temple is torn in two, an earthquake occurs, and saints are resurrected and appear to many people (27:45-54). Matthew relates these events to the magnitude of the crucifixion of Jesus. The rending of the Temple curtain, found also in Mark's Gospel, is likely to be understood by the reader both as God's judgment against the religious establishment that has rejected Jesus and a sign that a new way of access to God has been opened—through Jesus, rather than through sacrifices and the Temple rituals. Jesus' death takes on cosmic proportions and signifies that the end of the age is at hand. The earthquake and resurrections of the faithful dead are eschatological events, the latter signifying that Jesus has broken the power of death. Matthew's is the only Gospel that contains these two events. By including them he declares

> that in the earth-shattering moment of Jesus' death-and-resurrection, considered as a single complex event, God touches the universe with creative hands here at the end of ages as at the beginning and the old world with its old patterns and institutions starts to crack apart and the new world begins to emerge from the dust and ashes of the old.[13]

Seeing these events, a Roman centurion and others with him at the cross proclaim, "Truly this man was God's Son!" (27:54). They have rightly interpreted these strange events as God's identification with the dying Jesus. Their confession of Jesus matches the heavenly pronouncement at Jesus' baptism and transfiguration, as well as the confession of Peter at Caesarea Philippi.

Matthew introduces several characters into the narrative at this point who, unknown to the reader, have also been followers of Jesus. A group of women who had provided support for Jesus during his life now remain faithful to him even in his death (27:55-56). Likewise, Joseph of Arimathea demonstrates his loyalty to Jesus by procuring the body of Jesus and burying it in his own tomb (27:57-61). The actions of the women and of Joseph contrast with the abandonment of Jesus by the disciples.

The incident of the guards at the tomb is told in Matthew's Gospel only (27:62-66; 28:1-15). Matthew was aware of an attempt to discredit the resurrection of Jesus by some who claimed that his body had not been raised from the dead but had been stolen by his disciples (28:15). This story counters that claim. In his telling of the story, Matthew continues his negative portrayal of the Jewish leaders who not only conspire with Pilate, but are willing to violate their own regulations prohibiting such activity on the sabbath in order to carry out their plans. Because the reader has come to trust Jesus' claims that he will be resurrected, the reference to Jesus as "that impostor" (27:63) by the chief priests and Pharisees rings false.

When two of the women go to visit Jesus' tomb on Sunday morning (28:1-10), they are surprised by the appearance of an angel who announces to them that Jesus has been raised from the dead. The women are told to tell the news to the disciples. On their way to do so they are met by the resurrected Jesus who tells them to "tell my brothers to go to Galilee; there they will see me" (28:10). The reader will remember the prediction by Jesus on the Mount of Olives when he told his disciples, "After I am raised up, I will go ahead of you to Galilee" (26:32). When the disciples go to Galilee, they see Jesus and, as the two women had done, they fall down and worship him. Interestingly, however, Matthew adds, "but some doubted" (28:17). Even at the end of his story, Matthew portrays the disciples as wavering in their faith. Their "little faith" still needs strengthening.

Verses 18-20 form an apt conclusion to Matthew's Gospel. Jesus claims that to him had been given "all authority in heaven and on earth." The question of Jesus' authority has been a major theme in the book, throughout which Matthew has demonstrated Jesus' authority in both word and deed. Now, at the close of the Gospel, Jesus, the one authorized by God, in turn authorizes his disciples as he sends them out to "make disciples of all nations." The mission that had earlier been restricted to the people of Israel (10:5-6) is now expanded to include all people. As Jesus, the obedient Son, has taught and made disciples of them, they are to teach others to be obedient followers of Jesus. The closing words of the Gospel, "I am with you always, to the end of the age" (28:20), are a promise of the abiding presence of the resurrected Jesus with his people for all time. In a fitting *inclusio*, the one who was proclaimed Emmanuel, "God is with us," in the beginning of the Gospel (1:23) reaffirms at the end that he will always be in the midst of God's people.

Chapter 5

❖

The Gospel of Luke

As discussed earlier on pages 39-40, the person who wrote the Gospel of Luke also wrote the book of Acts in the New Testament. In fact, Luke is responsible for a larger portion of the writings in the New Testament than is any other writer. Luke and Acts combined comprise approximately a quarter of the New Testament corpus.[1] Some of the best-known information about Jesus—even among people who are not Christians—comes from the Gospel of Luke. The story of the birth of Jesus in a manger "because there was no place for them in the inn," the parable of the prodigal son, and the parable of the good Samaritan are examples of Luke's contribution to traditions about Jesus. Like the other Gospel writers, Luke selected, arranged, and shaped traditional materials to craft his narrative about Jesus of Nazareth.

Social Setting

Date of Writing

The general consensus of scholars concerning the date for the writing of the Gospel of Luke is around 80–85 CE, thus placing its composition at approximately the same time as that of the Gospel of Matthew. Scholars who believe that Luke was dependent on Mark would argue that it certainly was later than 75 CE (allowing a minimal time for the Gospel of Mark to circulate after it was composed around 70 CE). Furthermore, the Gospel of Luke appears to indicate an awareness of the fall of Jerusalem in 70 CE, as evidenced by the details given in the "predictions" of Jesus that the city would be destroyed (19:43; 21:20). In the opinion of many scholars, similarities between these details and the actual circumstances of the destruction of Jerusalem by the Roman army lead to the conclusion that Luke has incorporated this "after-the-fact" information into the sayings of Jesus.

Since the Gospel of Luke was written prior to Acts (the "first book" referred to in Acts 1:1 is almost certainly the Gospel of Luke), the dating of Acts provides the latest possible date for the Gospel. Scholars often note the lack of awareness in the book of Acts of any letter-writing activity by Paul, much less the contents of any of Paul's letters. Paul's letters were apparently circulating in the Christian churches around the end of the first century. For these reasons, the dominant opinion in New Testament scholarship is that Luke and Acts were written in the last quarter of the first century, likely between 80 and 85 CE.

Place of Writing

Neither the Gospel of Luke nor the book of Acts gives any clear indication of place of writing. Ancient writers claimed Achaia (the southern region of Greece), Boeotia (one of the cities reported to be where Luke died), Rome, or Antioch of Syria. In modern times, other arguments have been made for Caesarea, the Decapolis, or Asia Minor. Unfortunately, there is almost no evidence that can be given to support any of these conjectures. Virtually all scholars do agree that the Gospel of Luke was composed outside Palestine in a Greek-speaking area.

Intended Readers

Since Luke wrote in Greek, the intended audience of the work was obviously Greek-speaking. Most scholars have also been convinced that the intended readers were primarily gentile Christians, although the community may have contained some Jewish Christians as well. A dominant non-Jewish audience would account for the author's substitution of Greek terms for Hebrew or Aramaic names or titles found in Mark or Q. Some examples include: "Master" or "Lord" instead of "rabbi" (Luke 9:33; 18:41); "Skull" instead of "Golgotha" (Luke 23:33); and occasionally "lawyer" for "scribe" (10:25; 11:52). A gentile readership would also explain Luke's omission of material that was primarily of Jewish interest. For example, Luke eliminates the material in Mark 7:1-23 that deals with matters of Jewish ritual purity and other legal observances. The strong emphasis in the Gospel on the universal nature of the Christian message also coheres well with the idea that the intended readers were gentile Christians, or at least predominantly so. Beyond the identification of the readers as gentile Christians, little can be said about them.

One unique feature of the Gospel of Luke compared to the other New Testament Gospels is that Luke specifically identifies at least one of its intended readers. Luke 1:1-4 (cf. Acts 1:1) is a dedicatory prologue addressed to "most excellent Theophilus." Nothing is known about this person. Some commentators, even from ancient times, have suggested that the name (which means "lover of God" or "loved by God") is to be understood symbolically. According to this view, the work is dedicated not to any one person, but to all true children of God, that is, those who are lovers of God or loved by God. This view is not widely accepted. Dedication of a literary work to an individual, particularly to a wealthy patron, was an accepted literary convention in the Hellenistic world, especially in histories and biographies. Unfortunately, Luke tells us nothing about this "Theophilus." Some scholars have argued that he is an important Roman official whom Luke seeks to inform about the true nature of Jesus and Christianity in order to convince him that Christianity is not a subversive or dangerous religion. Others have suggested that Theophilus is a new Christian in need of further instruction in the Christian faith. Still others have suggested that he is the patron or benefactor of Luke's work who financially supported its publication. Unfortunately for modern readers, Theophilus must remain anonymous. Apparently he was a person of social rank and prestige ("most excellent Theophilus") and interested in, or a recent convert to, Christianity.

Literary and Stylistic Characteristics

Of the four Gospel writers, Luke is usually seen as the most gifted literary artist. He writes with skill and creativity, crafting a Gospel that is a more sophisticated work than the others. One commentator, Frederick W. Danker, writes, "What emerges from a literary analysis of Luke's work is the portrait of an artisan who is master of his material to an extraordinary degree."[2] The following sections highlight a few of Luke's stylistic and narrative techniques.

Sources

The author of Luke tells us at the outset of his writing that his was not the very first narrative written about the events of Jesus' life (1:1). Only after "investigating everything carefully from the very first" did Luke begin to write his account. By these statements Luke informs the readers that he has relied on various sources for the information contained in his Gospel. What were those sources? As we discussed in chapter 1, most scholars believe that Luke made use of the Gospel of Mark and a currently nonextant source known as Q. In addition, Luke had access to other information that he used in the writing of his Gospel (often referred to as "L"). Whereas Matthew incorporated approximately 90 percent of Mark into his Gospel, Luke used only around 50 percent of the Markan material. In organizing this varied material in his Gospel, Luke appears to have roughly alternated blocks of Markan material with blocks of material drawn from other sources (Q and L). The following outline demonstrates that pattern:[3]

Luke 1:1–2:52	L
Luke 3:1–6:19	Mark (and Q for material about John the Baptist and the Temptations)
Luke 6:20–8:3	Q and L
Luke 8:4–9:50	Mark
Luke 9:51–18:14	Q and L
Luke 18:15–24:11	Mark and L
Luke 24:12–24:53	L

As can be seen, the pattern is not exact. At times Luke combines some Q or L material with Mark.

Assuming that Luke used Mark, one can readily detect some major changes that Luke made in this source. Basically, Luke follows the Markan outline, but five major deviations from the Markan arrangement are evident:

(1) Luke adds infancy narratives, telling of the births of John the Baptist and of Jesus (chaps. 1–2).
(2) Luke adds the special material in 6:20–8:3.
(3) Luke omits the material in Mark 6:45–8:26.
(4) Luke expands the journey of Jesus to Jerusalem by adding material from Q and L (9:51–18:14).
(5) Luke adds stories of postresurrection appearances and the ascension of Jesus (24:13-53).

Style

Luke was a skillful user of the Greek language. The quality of his Greek writing is superior to that of the other Gospel writers, and in fact is considered by Greek scholars to be among the best in the New Testament. His writing, while still reflecting the Greek spoken by the common people, often approaches the level of cultured, literary Greek. Luke frequently makes grammatical and stylistic improvements on the material he borrows from Mark. An example of this literary polishing is Luke's removal of many of the occurrences of the historic present form of verbs used by Mark. Again, whereas Mark often strings together thoughts with an inelegant "and" (*kai* in Greek), Luke creates a polished sentence structure.

Another striking stylistic element in Luke is his use of Septuagint Greek style. In certain sections of the Gospel (as well as Acts), Luke shifts into a style of writing reminiscent of the Septuagint (the Greek translation of the Hebrew Bible). In the Gospel this is most pronounced in chapters 1 and 2. After the stylized prologue in 1:1-4 that utilizes elegant Greek, the narratives beginning in verse 5, which tell of the births of John the Baptist and Jesus, abruptly switch to a "biblical Greek." After chapter 2 Luke takes up his "normal" writing style. The early readers of Luke's Gospel could hardly fail to notice the change. It would be similar today to a writer shifting from modern English to a King James Bible style of writing (Elizabethan English). Why does Luke change his style in this manner? Some scholars have argued that Luke is borrowing from another source at this point. Others, however, see it as further evidence of Luke's skill as a writer: he adapts his style to fit the subject matter. Explaining this use of "biblical" style, Luke Timothy Johnson claims that in the infancy narratives Luke chooses language "evoking both specific texts and the general atmosphere of the biblical world. After the elegant Greek period of the prologue (1:1-4), the reader is immediately transported to the world of Ruth and the Judges (1:5). The story of Jesus is thus rooted in the longer story of God's people."[4]

Characters

As with the other Gospels, the central figure in Luke's Gospel is Jesus. Unlike Mark and Matthew, however, who identify and make claims about Jesus in the opening verses of their Gospels, Luke does not introduce Jesus until the middle of the first chapter. There Mary is told that she will soon conceive and bear a son who will be called Son of God (1:35) and will be a Davidic king (1:32-33). As we will see, Luke uses several other titles to identify Jesus, titles such as Lord, savior, Messiah, master, Son of Man, prophet, and teacher. Whereas Mark portrays a Jesus who suffered on behalf of others and Matthew stresses Jesus as the righteous one who called others to righteousness through his teachings, Luke emphasizes Jesus as the Savior for all humanity, especially for the lowly and the outcast.

The disciples in Luke also are portrayed somewhat differently than in Matthew and Mark. The harsh portrait of the disciples in Mark has been softened, even more so than in the Gospel of Matthew. For example, whereas in Mark two of Jesus' disciples come asking for preferential places in the final kingdom (10:35-40), Matthew makes the story less negative toward the disciples by having their mother make the request (20:20-23). Luke, however, completely omits this unflattering episode. Compare also the Lukan version of the story of the stilling of the storm (8:22-25) with the Markan account (4:35-41). Mark reports the accusatory question of the disciples, "Teacher, do you not care that we are perishing?" (v. 38). Luke changes the question into a statement. Notice also the scene in Gethsemane. Instead of the disciples falling asleep three times while Jesus is praying (as in Mark and Matthew), Luke records only one instance of their failure. Furthermore, an excuse is provided for them even there, for the narrator adds that the reason for their sleep was due to their grief (22:45). Luke also does not include the painful indictment against the disciples that they deserted Jesus at his arrest (cf. Mark 14:50; Matt 26:56).

As in the other Gospels, the religious authorities in Luke are opponents of Jesus. Their conflict with Jesus is a major element of the plot that drives the story forward. In Luke, however, this conflict is initially not as harsh as it is in the other Gospels. Luke even presents two occasions when Jesus accepts the invitation to eat a meal in the home of a Pharisee (11:37; 14:1), and another incident when some Pharisees warned Jesus that Herod Antipas wanted to kill him (13:31). Thus although the religious leaders are often presented as being Jesus' antagonists, even strongly so (11:53-54), a few positive images also occur. Toward the end of the Gospel, however, the strongly negative image of the religious leaders is clear. They look for an opportunity to kill Jesus (19:47; 22:2), send dishonest spies to entrap him by his answers to their questions (20:20), and finally arrest him and turn him over to the Romans (22:47–23:1).

Even in his negative portrayal of the religious leaders, Luke does not match the intensity of the harsh polemic of Matthew. Luke does contain some of the woes against the scribes ("lawyers" in Luke) and Pharisees that are found in Matthew (apparently derived from Q), but Luke does not have as many of them. Furthermore, in Luke these denunciations occur in two different settings, rather than grouped together in one tirade. For Luke the religious authorities epitomize those who reject Jesus and his message. They are the opposite of Jesus. Whereas he is the compassionate agent of God who opens the kingdom of God to all who would come, they through their false teachings, hypocrisy, and exclusiveness act as hindrances to those who seek the kingdom (11:52).

Structure

Luke basically follows the outline of the Gospel of Mark, with several noteworthy changes. One aspect of Luke's arrangement of his material that has caught the eye of careful readers is the geographical and theological prominence of Jerusalem for Luke. Contrary to the other Gospels, Luke's Gospel begins in Jerusalem with the announcement of the impending birth of John the Baptist. Furthermore, according to Luke, Jesus goes to the Temple in Jerusalem as a boy of twelve. The large Lukan insertion, 9:51–18:14, is likewise a journey to Jerusalem. Finally, in contrast to Matthew and John, in Luke all the resurrection appearances of Jesus occur in or around Jerusalem. In the book of Acts, Luke's second volume, the movement of action is away from Jerusalem as the gospel message is spread throughout the Mediterranean world.

Why this focus on Jerusalem? For Luke Jerusalem is the city of suffering, the place where God's prophets are killed. Jesus states that he must be on his way to Jerusalem "because it is impossible for a prophet to be killed outside of Jerusalem" (13:33). Jesus' movement toward Jerusalem for his suffering, death, and resurrection is in fulfillment of the words of the prophets (18:31). Thus, there is a divine necessity for Jesus to be focused on Jerusalem. Luke Timothy Johnson adds, "For Luke, the city and Temple stand as symbols of the people of Israel. The death of Jesus and the beginning of the church there provide the paradigmatic expression of the Jewish people's acceptance or rejection of God's visitation. Jerusalem is the pivotal place in the story of the prophet and the people."[5]

Because Jerusalem is the location of Jesus' death, resurrection, and ascension, it is primarily the place of God's act of salvation. The book of Acts describes the spread of the good news of God's salvation, beginning in Jerusalem and then going to "Judea and Samaria, and to the ends of the earth" (Acts 1:8). As the outline below demonstrates, the structure of

Luke's Gospel has been shaped by his focus on Jerusalem and his modification of the Markan structure.

Major Themes in the Gospel of Luke

Luke's abilities as a writer extend beyond the literary and stylistic characteristics noted above. He demonstrates his skill as well in the way he emphasizes particular motifs and ideas throughout his Gospel.

Fulfillment of Scriptures

As was discussed in the previous chapter, the author of Matthew utilized passages from the Hebrew scriptures to explain the significance of Jesus, presenting Jesus as a fulfillment of several scriptural texts. Luke also emphasizes Jesus as the fulfillment of the scriptures, but in a way different from Matthew. Matthew often quoted specific texts, introduced by citation formulas: "This was to fulfill what was spoken through the prophet," or "this is the one about whom it is written." Luke presents the fulfillment of scriptures in a more general, less mechanical way. Jesus fulfills "all that is written" (21:22) or the things that are "in all the scriptures" (24:27). Luke sees the events he narrates (primarily the life, death, and resurrection of Jesus) as part of the divine plan that God has previously determined. For that reason Luke often uses the expression "it must" of various events, as a way of showing that certain events must take place as fulfillment of God's plan mentioned in the scriptures (9:22; 17:25; 24:7). Charles Talbert argues that the use of this prophecy/fulfillment theme was an important legitimation device in Luke's work, verifying for the readers the truth of the Christian message.[6]

Identity of Jesus

Son of God. Luke uses many of the same titles for Jesus that are used by the other Gospel writers. The title "Son of God," though not used quite as frequently in Luke as in the other Synoptics, is still an important title for Luke. In the announcement to Mary of her impending pregnancy, the angel makes it clear that this child will be special, for he will be called "Son of God" (1:32, 35). This title points to the unique relationship between Jesus and God: "No one knows . . . who the Father is except the Son and anyone to whom the Son chooses to reveal him" (10:22). In Luke as in Matthew the story of the virginal conception of Jesus indicates that his sonship is of a different kind than any "sonship" in which his followers participate.

Messiah. The title "Messiah" appears frequently in Luke. The angels announce to the shepherds that this child who is born is "the Messiah, the Lord" (2:11). Simeon had been promised that he would not die until he had seen "the Lord's Messiah" (2:26). At the sight of the infant Jesus, Simeon knows that the promise has been fulfilled. Thus the narrator makes the identification explicit for the reader: Jesus is the long-awaited Messiah. This is information concealed from most of the characters in the story, but we as readers are privy to this identification. Luke is careful to show that Jesus is "king of the Jews" and Messiah, but not in a political sense. The repeated declarations of Jesus' innocence by Pilate and by Herod Antipas are Luke's way of showing that Jesus was not a political, militaristic Messiah (23:4, 14, 15, 22). Rather he was the Messiah who would "suffer . . . and then enter into his glory" (24:26).

Savior. Other titles are important to Luke as well, including "Lord," "Son of Man," "prophet," "servant," "master," and "savior." The last one in this list is particularly significant because Luke is the only synoptic Gospel in which that title is used. Luke applies the title "Savior" to Jesus only once, when the angels announce to the shepherds, "To you is born this day in the city of David a Savior, who is the Messiah, the Lord" (2:11). Significantly, in the previous chapter the same title is applied to God also (1:47). Even though Luke only uses the title once with Jesus, the activity of saving is associated with him on several occasions. Jesus describes his mission as "to seek out and to save the lost" (19:10), and he tells several people that their faith has saved them (7:50; 8:48; 17:19; 18:42). In fact, the theme of saving/salvation brackets the whole Gospel. In the infancy narratives not only is Jesus identified as the Savior, but both Zechariah and Simeon speak of Jesus as God's means of salvation (1:71, 77; 2:30). At the crucifixion of Jesus, three times his saving ability is ridiculed. Because the narrator has made it clear that Jesus is indeed the one who saves, the reader hears the irony in these mocking words by Jesus' opponents.

Universal Salvation

The Gospel of Luke has an inclusive understanding of the mercy of God. God's grace and salvation are extended not just to the people of Israel but to all humanity. Luke sets the birth of Jesus in the context of world history (2:1-2), implying that this event has universal significance. The announcement of the angels at Jesus' birth is that this event is "good news of great joy for all the people" (2:10). When Simeon sees the baby Jesus in the Temple, he proclaims that this child is God's salvation, which had been "prepared in the presence of all peoples,/a light for revelation to the Gentiles/and for glory to your people Israel" (2:31-32). In giving Jesus' genealogy, Luke traces his lineage back to Adam, signaling his linkage to all people and their inclusion in his saving work. In the descriptions of John the Baptist and his preparation for Jesus, only Luke among the Gospel writers adds a universal dimension by extending the quote from Isaiah 40:3 to include verses 4 and 5, the latter of which says (in the Septuagint version), "and all flesh shall see the salvation of God" (3:6). Jesus' sermon in the synagogue at Nazareth (4:16-30) pointed to God's concern for all people, including non-Israelites, a point not missed by his audience.

Concern for the Outcasts

Closely related to the theme of universal salvation is the Lukan concern for the socially and religiously marginalized. From the beginning of the Gospel story this is evident when the first announcement of the birth of Jesus is made to shepherds, who were often seen as having a despised occupation. The reason for such an unfavorable reputation was because "being away from home at night they were unable to protect their women and therefore were considered dishonorable. In addition, they often were considered thieves because they grazed their flocks on other people's property."[7] Yet these outcasts, who were not allowed to give testimony in court, were chosen to be witnesses to the birth of the Messiah. Furthermore, the circumstances of Jesus' birth—born in a manger—emphasize his connection with the poor and lowly. The Magnificat, sung by his mother Mary, celebrates the theme of reversal—the lowly and poor will be exalted, while the rich and powerful will be brought low.

In his inaugural sermon in Nazareth, Jesus reads from Isaiah 61:1-2 and identifies his ministry as being the proclamation of good news to the poor, the recovering of sight for the blind, and the setting free of those who are oppressed (4:16-20). The Lukan version of the Beatitudes pronounces blessings on those who are poor, hungry, and excluded (6:20-23). Jesus frequently associates with tax collectors, even going home with Zacchaeus, a chief tax collector (19:1-10). Luke introduces the parables of the lost sheep, the lost coin, and the lost son by saying that Jesus told these parables because the Pharisees and scribes were grumbling because he was welcoming sinners, that is, the religious and social outcasts (15:1-32). Only Luke contains the parable of the good Samaritan, in which a Samaritan, despised by the Jews, is the hero of the story (10:25-37). When Jesus heals the ten lepers, the point is emphasized that the only one who expresses gratitude to Jesus is a Samaritan (17:11-19).

Concern for Women

In first-century Palestine, women also were marginal members of society; their roles were primarily private, domestic roles rather than public ones. Social codes strictly limited what was and was not allowed for women. Jesus on several occasions breaks the boundaries of these patriarchal, societal codes. He had women followers and supporters and often used women as the central figures in the illustrations he told (15:8-10; 18:1-8). He publicly associated with women and treated them with fairness and equality. Luke's version of the birth of Jesus focuses on Mary, whereas Matthew's focuses more on Joseph. The Gospel of Luke is the only Gospel to contain the story of Jesus' visit to the home of Mary and Martha and his affirmation of Mary's choice to listen and learn from him as a disciple (10:38-42).

Recently several scholars have argued a different position on Luke's view of women. They claim that in Luke's Gospel women are intentionally marginalized and relegated to the traditional roles of women, rather than being depicted in leadership roles or given equal treatment with men. Some have even argued that part of the purpose of the Gospel of Luke is to undermine the developing leadership roles of women in his community. The comment of R. Alan Culpepper on these opposite appraisals of Luke's characterization of women appears to be fair and balanced:

> Luke remains grounded in the social context of the first century. Nevertheless, if its portrayal of Jesus' relationships with women falls short by contemporary standards, it was radical in a first-century context. Jesus permits a woman to touch his feet in public and to sit at his feet with male disciples, and he defends a woman from the scorn of Simon the Pharisee. While Luke's Jesus does not succeed in freeing women from the shackles of societal repression, he specifically includes women among those for whom the

coming of the kingdom is good news and points to the inauguration of a new community in which freedom, dignity, and equality may be realized.[8]

Discipleship

Luke paints a generally positive portrait of the disciples. They are faithful followers of Jesus, in spite of their occasional lapses and even doubts at the end (24:38, 41). They are given understanding and taught the scriptures (24:45) so that they might continue the work that Jesus has begun. Their task is to be witnesses to what they have seen and heard. In Luke the disciples are not only witnesses to his teachings, preachings, and miracles, but they are also witnesses to his crucifixion (23:49—"all his acquaintances" watched the crucifixion) and to his resurrection.

Holy Spirit

The disciples of Jesus are not left to their own resources in carrying out their task. They are empowered by the Holy Spirit to go forth from Jerusalem to all the nations. The work of the Holy Spirit, or Spirit of God, is evident throughout Luke's Gospel. From the births of Jesus and John the Baptist, to Jesus' baptism and his temptation, to the ministry of Jesus, the Holy Spirit is present to guide and empower. Jesus teaches that God will give the Holy Spirit to those who ask (11:13). The reader hears this emphasis on the gift of God's Spirit and the workings of the Spirit as encouragement and reassurance.

Prayer

Prayer is an important part of the life of Jesus in the Gospel of Luke and should be a characteristic practice of his followers as well. The Gospel depicts Jesus in prayer on several occasions (5:16; 6:12; 9:18, 28; 10:21-22; 11:1; 22:39-46). From the cross he prays that God will forgive those responsible for his death (23:34). Even his dying words are a prayer (23:46). He quotes scripture that claims that the Temple is to be a house of prayer (19:46) and becomes upset when it is not allowed to function for that purpose. He teaches his disciples how to pray, offering them a model to follow (11:1-4). He exhorts them to pray diligently (18:1) and encourages them to pray for strength (21:36) and to pray that they might be kept from times of trial (22:40, 46). Knowing of Peter's coming denial of him, he prays for a strong and resilient faith for Peter (22:32).

Outline of the Gospel of Luke

The following outline will serve as the basis for our closer examination of the Gospel of Luke. Readers are encouraged to read the text of the Gospel in conjunction with the Reading Guide that follows the outline.

  I.   Prologue (1:1-4)
 II.   The Infancy Narratives (1:5–2:52)
III.   The Period of Preparation (3:1–4:13)
 IV.   The Galilean Ministry (4:14–9:50)
  V.   The Journey to Jerusalem (9:51–19:27)
 VI.   The Jerusalem Ministry (19:28–21:38)
VII.   The Passion Narrative and the Resurrection Appearances
       (22:1–24:53)

Reading Guide to the Gospel of Luke

Prologue (1:1-4)

Unlike any of the other Gospels, the opening of the Gospel of Luke begins with a formal dedicatory prologue. This approach follows literary convention, as can be seen by comparing these verses with the opening words of other ancient writers such as Herodotus, Thucydides, Polybius, Diodorus Siculus, Philo, and Josephus. Charles Talbert has listed the major elements in the prefaces of ancient histories and biographies as follows:[9]

(1) A statement about the author's predecessors, usually mentioning their inadequacies
(2) A description of the work's subject matter
(3) A statement about the author's qualifications for writing
(4) The plan or arrangement of the work
(5) The purpose of the writing
(6) The author's name
(7) The name of the official addressee

The Lukan prologue contains six of these seven components, with only the name of the author missing. Admittedly, Luke's preface gives only a scant indication of the work's subject matter ("the events that have been fulfilled among us") and of the plan of the book ("an orderly account").

This prologue conveys several bits of information to the reader. First, Luke states that his work will not be the first attempt to tell the story that he recounts. Many others have written works before him, works that Luke obviously consulted. The Gospel of Mark and the Q document would likely be among these previous works he mentions. Second, Luke does not claim to be an eyewitness to the events he narrates. He is passing on traditions he received, which suggests that he is at least a second- or third-generation Christian. Third, the purpose of Luke's writing is so that Theophilus "may know the truth concerning the things about which you have been instructed." This Theophilus is apparently an interested observer or a recent convert to Christianity. Luke writes to give him assurance about what he had initially heard about the life and teachings of Jesus. Even though this work is addressed specifically to Theophilus, it is not a private letter, but a work intended to be read or heard by a larger audience.

The Infancy Narratives (1:5–2:52)

Luke tells not one but two birth stories, the stories of the births of John the Baptist and Jesus. More than in any other Gospel, the lives of John the Baptist and Jesus are entwined in Luke. Although Luke gives more attention to John than do the other Gospel writers, Luke still presents John in a secondary role to Jesus. The announcement of their impending births, the birth narratives, and their ministries are depicted in ways that show the superiority of Jesus to John.

Luke presents seven related scenes in this section: the annunciation of John's birth (1:5-25); the annunciation of Jesus' birth (1:26-38); the visit of Mary with Elizabeth (1:39-56); the birth, circumcision, and naming of John (1:57-80); the birth, circumcision and naming of Jesus (2:1-21); the presentation of Jesus in the Temple (2:22-40); and the visit of the child Jesus to the Temple (2:41-52). The annunciation stories closely parallel each other and follow a pattern familiar to readers of the Hebrew Bible [cf. the stories of the births of Ishmael (Gen 16:7-12), Isaac (Gen 17:1-22), Samson (Judg 13:2-25), and particularly Samuel (1 Sam 1:4-20)]. O. C. Edwards summarizes this pattern as follows:[10] (a) the appearance of an angel, (b) fear on the part of the recipient of the angel's message, (c) the announcement that the woman is or is about to become pregnant, (d) the recipient expresses doubt or objection, and (e) a sign is given to validate the message.

The story of the announcement of John's birth stresses the piety of Zechariah, the father of John, who is in the Temple performing his priestly duties when the angel makes the announcement to him. Both Zechariah and his wife, Elizabeth, are described as "righteous before God, living blamelessly according to all the commandments and regulations of the Lord" (1:6). From the beginning, then, Luke's story is firmly rooted in Judaism. The angel Gabriel announces to Zechariah that his prayer will be answered: the childless couple, advanced in age, will have a son. Even more astounding, this will be no ordinary child. He will be "great in the sight of the Lord" (1:15) and will be filled with the Holy Spirit. He will be an Elijah-like figure, sent to prepare the way for the Lord (1:17).

As wonderful as is this news, it is eclipsed by the second annunciation Luke narrates, the announcement of Jesus' birth. Even more miraculous than the birth of a child to a woman of old age, the birth of Jesus is the birth of a child to a young girl who is a virgin. We are told that at this time Mary is engaged, or betrothed, to Joseph, a more formal arrangement than engagement today. Although betrothed couples did not live together or engage in sexual relations, their relationship was a legal one, arranged by their families. Only a formal divorce or death could end the relationship. Sexual intercourse by a betrothed woman was considered adultery.[11] Mary becomes pregnant not through sexual intercourse but by an act of God. What is more, although John will be the forerunner who will prepare his way, the child of Mary [who will also be "great" (1:32)] will be the Son of God. The reader understands the message: John is great, but Jesus is greater still. Mary is not an unwilling participant in this divine drama; rather, like the prophet Isaiah in his encounter with God in the Temple (Isa 6:8), Mary responds to the news by saying, "Here am I" (1:38).

The theme of the superiority of Jesus to John is continued in the story of Mary's visit to Elizabeth, her relative. As soon as Mary speaks to Elizabeth, the unborn John leaps in his mother's womb. Elizabeth interprets this movement as a sign of recognition: the child in her womb acknowledges that Mary is the mother of the Lord. Mary then breaks forth in praise to God because of the special favor that God has bestowed on her. This passage, known as the Magnificat because of the first word in the Latin translation, emphasizes a theme that we will see throughout Luke's Gospel, that the coming of the Lord is good news for the outcast and the powerless. The rich and powerful are overthrown, while the lowly are lifted up and the hungry are filled. Mary identifies herself as one of the lowly who has been especially favored by God.

The fourth scene in this section describes in the barest of words the birth of John, mentioning the joy that accompanied his arrival. The note of joy is found throughout the Lukan infancy narratives. The activity of the Holy Spirit also is emphasized in these narratives. As Elizabeth had been filled with the Holy Spirit upon her meeting with Mary, now Zechariah is filled with the Holy Spirit and bursts forth in a song of praise, the so-called "Benedictus" (1:68-79). His song is a celebration of God's mercy shown in the fulfillment of the promise to send a savior to the people. The reader will understand that the savior who is sent is not John, but Jesus, whose birth has only been foretold and has not yet occurred. This child whose birth has taken place is called the "prophet of the Most High," the one who "will go before the Lord to prepare his ways" (1:76). The narrator then tells us that the child John grew and was "in the wilderness until the day he appeared publicly to Israel" (1:80). As O. C. Edwards notes, this is "a smooth transition that gets John offstage until his ministry but places him on the spot where he will next appear."[12]

In Christian history, the Lukan story of the birth of Jesus has been the best-known and most liked of the Gospel birth stories. In Luke's narrative, Mary and Joseph live in Nazareth. As a result of a census for taxation purposes, the couple has to go to Bethlehem, the ancestral home of Joseph, who is of the line of David. While there, Mary gives birth to Jesus (apparently in a stable or area of the house with animals, although the reader must infer this information) and places him in a manger.[13] Shepherds, alerted by angels to this wondrous birth of "a Savior, who is the Messiah, the Lord" (2:11), visit the newborn child and his family. The birth of Jesus in a lowly manger and the visit by shepherds, who were social and religious outcasts, reinforce the Lukan emphasis on the marginalized. The angels announce that this birth is "good news of great joy for all the people" (2:10), providing hints to the reader of a theme that will be important in Luke's Gospel—Jesus brings salvation not just for the people of Israel, but for all people.

This theme of universal salvation is present as well in the scene of Jesus' presentation in the Temple. Simeon, a man who "was righteous and devout, looking forward to the consolation of Israel" (2:25), recognizes that Jesus is the long-awaited Messiah and offers a song of praise (2:29-32; the "Nunc Dimittis") in which he declares that Jesus is "a light for revelation to the Gentiles/and for glory to your people Israel" (2:32). The reader hears the words of Simeon to Mary as an ominous prediction that all will not go smoothly for this Messiah. Simeon says, "This child is destined for the falling and the rising of many in Israel, and to be a sign that will be opposed so that the inner thoughts of many will be revealed—and a sword will pierce your own soul too" (2:34-35). The reaction of the prophet Anna in the Temple is further confirmation of the special status of this child.

The episode in Luke 2:41-52 is the only story in any of the New Testament Gospels about the childhood of Jesus. Later Christian tradition created numerous stories of the boy Jesus and the miraculous deeds he performed. By comparison, Luke's story is very subdued. The child performs no miracles, but demonstrates his wisdom and insight in his dialogues with the Jewish teachers in the Temple. The point of the story is found in Jesus' question to his distraught parents who have been looking for their missing son, "Did you not know that I must be in my Father's house?" Already, Luke shows us that Jesus was aware of his intimate relationship with God. In spite of this knowledge, Jesus is the dutiful child who returns home with his parents and is obedient to them.

After the Temple incident (and earlier after the shepherds appeared at the birth of Jesus; 2:19), the narrator informs us that Mary "treasured all these things in her heart" (2:51). The reader is likely to be puzzled by her reaction later in the Gospel when she seems to show no awareness of anything special about Jesus. Commenting on this oddity, O. C. Edwards Jr. writes:

> How can she be surprised by the unusual nature of her son after the annunciation, the visitation, the homage of the shepherds who had received an angelic revelation, and the prophecies of Simeon and Anna? Was she Our Lady of Invincible Ignorance? No. Part of the answer lies in the Lukan prose style, which creates individual edifying scenes without asking how consistent they are with one another. Part of it lies in Mary's role as the only person who is a faithful member of the household of God in (a) the infancy, (b) the ministry of Jesus, and (c) the postresurrection community (Acts 1:14). In order to act appropriately at each stage, she cannot carry over too much insight from previous stages.[14]

The Period of Preparation (3:1–4:13)

The narrator introduces this section with specific historical references, informing us that a new phase of the story has begun. Luke not only sets the story of Jesus within Palestine, but he places it in a world context ("In the fifteenth year of the reign of Emperor Tiberius," 3:1), thus subtly reminding the reader that the events of Jesus' life have universal significance.

Onto this world stage steps John the Baptist, to play his part as the one who will prepare the way for Jesus. In Luke's version of John's preaching and baptizing, the theme of repentance is strongly emphasized. Luke includes John's ethical admonitions to those who came out to hear him: true repentance results in a changed lifestyle. The reader who is familiar with the Markan and Matthean accounts of Jesus' baptism will be surprised by Luke's version. Luke does not explicitly say that Jesus was baptized by John. Between the account of John's activity and the baptism of Jesus, Luke narrates the arrest and imprisonment of John by Herod, leaving the reader with the ambiguous impression that John is not present at the baptism of Jesus. Why has Luke altered the tradition in this manner? John's baptism of Jesus could be interpreted as implying that John was superior to Jesus. To avoid that idea, Luke describes Jesus' baptism in the passive voice, thus avoiding any indication of the details of his baptism. Luke makes the relationship between John and Jesus clear in the words of John to the crowds in 3:16, "I baptize you with water; but one who is more powerful than I is coming. . . . He [Jesus] will baptize you with the Holy Spirit and fire." John has now played his part, and he departs from the stage.

The brief description of Jesus' baptism highlights two themes important to Luke: the praying of Jesus and the Holy Spirit. The Holy Spirit has been active in the lives of Elizabeth (1:41) and Zechariah (1:67), with John the Baptist (1:15), in the conception of Jesus (1:35), and with Simeon (2:25-26). Now it descends upon Jesus, and he is ready to begin his ministry.

Like Matthew, Luke provides a genealogy for Jesus (3:23-38). Unlike Matthew, however, Luke does not begin his Gospel with a listing of Jesus' ancestry. Luke places the genealogy between the baptism of Jesus and the story of his temptations. This placement is likely significant for Luke. The divine announcement at Jesus' baptism declares him to be God's Son, whereas the taunting challenge of the devil to Jesus in the temptations is, "If you are the Son of God. . . ." Sandwiched between these two episodes, then, is the genealogy of Jesus, which traces his ancestry to "Adam, son of

God." This is Jesus' true identity. He is the one who is truly the "Son of God."[15]

Not only is the placement of the genealogy different in Matthew and Luke, but the contents are vastly different as well. The numerous inconsistencies between the two lists should be a clue that these genealogies should not be taken as historically accurate. The authors have rearranged and otherwise altered traditional materials to highlight specific themes important to them. By tracing Jesus' ancestry all the way back to Adam (the supposed source of all humanity), instead of only to Abraham, Luke signals to the reader the importance of Jesus—he is the savior for all humanity.

Likewise, in Luke the temptation of Jesus (4:1-13) is not connected with his baptism as it is in Matthew and Mark. In Luke the temptation episode serves as a prelude to the beginning of the ministry of Jesus. The temptations are struggles for Jesus concerning his identity as Son of God and consequently the shape and course his ministry will take. In faithfully resisting the temptations to use his power and authority as Son of God for personal gain, Jesus demonstrates his solidarity with God and his fidelity to the will of God.

The Galilean Ministry (4:14–9:50)

The Holy Spirit came upon Jesus at his baptism, was present with him during his temptations, and now empowers him as he begins his ministry in Galilee (4:14). All three synoptic Gospels tell of Jesus' activity in his hometown of Nazareth. Only Luke, however, places it at the very outset of his ministry. This arrangement in Luke creates a slight problem for the reader when Jesus anticipates the thoughts of the people: "Do here also in your hometown the things that we have heard you did at Capernaum" (4:23). In contrast to Matthew and Mark, who have already told us of Jesus' activity in Capernaum, Luke has not described any episodes yet in Capernaum. By placing this pericope at the beginning of Jesus' ministry, Luke intends to provide the interpretive key for understanding all of Jesus' ministry. Only Luke gives the content of Jesus' inaugural sermon in his hometown. The text from Isaiah that Jesus reads (Isa 61:1-2) is a summation of Jesus' own ministry. That is what is meant when Jesus says, "Today this scripture has been fulfilled in your hearing" (4:21). The reader should note the appropriateness of the Isaianic text to Luke's portrayal of Jesus with its emphasis on "the Spirit of the Lord" and the work of God that brings good news to the poor, release to the captives, sight to the blind, and freedom for the oppressed. As we will see in the remainder of the Gospel, the Lukan Jesus is greatly concerned for the poor, the oppressed, and all the marginalized of society. Jesus' fulfillment of the words of this text were foreshadowed in Mary's song of praise in chapter 1.

Initially impressed and amazed by the teachings of Jesus, the crowd turns against him when he interprets his mission in universal terms. The point of his statements about the widow in Sidon and Naaman the Syrian, characters from the Hebrew Bible, is that God's grace was extended to non-Israelites. Jesus has just announced that the time for the fulfillment of God's promises was now. Expecting that they will be the recipients of these blessings, the people are incensed when Jesus declares that God's promises are open to people who are not Israelites. In fact, many of them will be excluded. In rejecting Jesus, they have proven true the proverb he quotes to them, "No prophet is accepted in the prophet's hometown" (4:24).

Luke presents four scenes in the remainder of chapter 4 that depict Jesus' activity in Capernaum in which he teaches, casts out demons, heals Simon's mother-in-law, cures various diseases, and preaches. These reports can be seen as examples of the fulfillment of the passage from Isaiah that Jesus read in the synagogue at Capernaum. In telling about the call of Simon Peter, James, and John, only Luke includes the story of the miraculous catch of fish (5:1-11). In the context of Luke's Gospel this narrative perhaps explains why Peter and the others were so willing to follow Jesus: they had been convinced by his mighty deeds. That understanding does not seem to do justice to the story in Luke, however. The key to the incident is likely the climactic declaration of Jesus, "From now on you will be catching people" (5:10). As their obedience to Jesus led them to be successful in catching fish, likewise their obedience in following him will yield a great catch of people for the kingdom of God.

The other Lukan scenes in Jesus' Galilean ministry reinforce the portrait of Jesus as healer and proclaimer of good news. The two themes are combined in the story of the healing of the paralyzed man (5:17-26), for not only does Jesus cure him of his paralysis but he also declares that the man's sins are forgiven. Conflict with the Pharisees over Jesus' association with tax collectors and the religiously outcast (5:29-32) and over his fasting (5:33-39) and sabbath laws (6:1-11) brings to mind the words of Simeon, "This child is destined for the falling and the rising of many in Israel, and to be a sign that will be opposed" (2:34).

After the calling of the disciples (6:12-16), Luke gives his version of the Sermon on the Mount (6:17-49), much shorter than in Matthew. (The Lukan version is sometimes called the Sermon on the Plain due to the locale mentioned in 6:17.) Some of the sayings collected in Matthew 5–7 are found elsewhere in Luke. The Lukan concern for the poor and marginalized is evident in his version of the Beatitudes, where the ones who are blessed are the poor, the hungry, those who weep, and those who are hated and defamed. Contrast these with the more spiritualized versions in Matthew 5:3-12. Luke also adds corresponding woes aimed at those who are rich, full, laughing, and held in high regard (6:24-26). The remainder of the Sermon on the Plain provides instructions for disciples, stressing the importance of loving others, of refraining from being judgmental, and of bearing spiritual fruit.

The story of the healing of the centurion's slave (7:1-10) provides another example of Jesus' ability to heal, but it also reinforces the Lukan emphasis on outsiders. The centurion, a Roman soldier, is a non-Israelite. His actions lead Jesus to exclaim, "Not even in Israel have I found such faith" (7:9). The following scene highlights Jesus' power even more (7:11-17). Not only can he heal, he can also raise the dead. The similarities between the acts of Jesus and those of the prophets are clear (cf. this episode with the activity of Elijah in 1 Kgs 17:8-24), leading the people to identify Jesus as a great prophet (7:16). In Luke he is a prophet, but also much more! Simon the Pharisee, who invited Jesus to eat with him, denies that Jesus is a prophet (7:39). The reader recognizes the blindness of Simon, partially because of what we have already encountered, but also because in the scene with Simon, the woman who anoints Jesus is the one who is praised by Jesus (7:36-50).

These episodes, along with others in the Gospel, provide the background for Jesus' reply to John's question about whether he is the "one who is to come" (7:20). Jesus answers by pointing to what he has done: "the blind receive their sight, the lame walk, the lepers are cleansed, the deaf hear, the dead are raised, the poor have good news brought to them" (7:22). The healing of the Gerasene demoniac (8:26-39) and the healing of Jairus' daughter (8:40-56) are further confirmations that in Jesus the words of the prophets are indeed fulfilled.

The question of the identity of Jesus arises on other occasions in the latter part of this section. Herod, hearing about the activities of Jesus, asks, "Who is this about whom I hear such things?" (9:9). Later, Jesus raises the question with his disciples about his identity (9:18-20). Peter replies that Jesus is "the Messiah of God," an identification that Jesus apparently accepts but then corrects: He is the Son of Man who must suffer, be rejected, killed, and then be raised from the dead (9:22). In the context of the Gospel, Jesus' statement is directed not only to the disciples but also to the question of Herod. The transfiguration scene that follows continues to raise the question of the identity of Jesus (9:28-36). Here the divine sonship of Jesus is stressed. The heavenly voice declares, "This is my Son, my Chosen; listen to him!" (9:35). The one thus identified as Messiah, Son of Man, and Son of God speaks and acts with divine authorization. Those who would be disciples are to listen and learn from him.

After these clear indications of the significance of Jesus, this section of the Gospel closes with several brief episodes. The first two are good examples of how Luke softens the negative portrayal of the disciples found in Mark. The healing of the boy with seizures is in Mark and Matthew a story about faith, particularly the disciples' lack of faith. If their faith had been stronger, they would have been able to heal the child. In Luke nothing is said about the inadequate faith of the disciples. The point of the story for Luke is not to teach about faith, but rather to demonstrate the power of God at work in Jesus, who has just been declared to be God's Son. Note the final words of the scene: "And all were astounded at the greatness of God" (9:43).

The next episode contains Jesus' second prediction of his fate (9:44). In contrast to the other Gospels, Luke includes here only the words that Jesus will be betrayed, not that he will be killed and resurrected. Whereas all three synoptic writers mention the disciples' failure to understand this saying, only Luke excuses them for their lack of understanding by explaining that "its meaning was concealed from them, so that they could not perceive it" (9:45). Luke thus softens the negative image of the disciples. But he does not completely remove it, as is seen in the next pericope of this section in which the disciples argue over which of them will be the greatest (9:46-48). The disciples are still in need of insight and teaching. They have failed to understand the significance of the transfiguration and the meaning of the passion predictions of Jesus. They still do not understand what discipleship involves, thinking only of themselves. John's misguided attempt to stop someone from casting out demons in the name of Jesus (9:49) is additional evidence of their lack of understanding. This need for further understanding prepares for the next major section of the

Gospel, the journey to Jerusalem, during which Jesus gives additional instructions to the struggling disciples.

The Journey to Jerusalem (9:51–19:27)

In this section of the Gospel, Luke diverges from both Matthew and Mark. All three present Jesus traveling from Galilee to Jerusalem, but only Luke gives such an extensive treatment of the journey. The section is composed of several parables, sayings of Jesus, episodes of healings, and other stories, often rather loosely strung together. The overarching theme of this entire section is the further teaching of the disciples. Jesus is preparing them not only for what awaits in Jerusalem but also for their eventual tasks to be "witnesses" to all the world (24:48; Acts 1:8).

The reader is apt to be puzzled by several aspects of this Lukan "travelogue." First, with the exception of a few notations of movement, very little progress seems to be made on this journey. The trip motif at times seems to be forgotten. Second, travel from Galilee to Jerusalem was normally a three-day trip. Luke's Gospel gives the impression of a much longer journey. [Note that there is sufficient time for the seventy followers who are sent out to complete a mission in "every town and place where he himself intended to go" (10:1).] Third, the geographical references in Luke are confusing. In 13:31-33 Jesus is warned to leave because Herod Antipas wants to kill him. Herod Antipas had control over Galilee and Perea; yet according to the narrative (9:52) Jesus is out of Galilee and into Samaria and perhaps even Judea, neither of which was under the jurisdiction of Herod Antipas. This scene would make sense prior to Jesus' departure from Galilee, but not afterwards. Also puzzling is the statement in 17:11 that Jesus was passing "between Samaria and Galilee." Commentators have struggled to understand what Luke meant, since Samaria abuts Galilee and Jesus has already moved into Samaria anyway. Luke's knowledge of Palestinian geography apparently was inaccurate.

All of this suggests that Luke's travelogue is a literary construction, rather than a historical account of Jesus' journey to Jerusalem. As mentioned above, Jerusalem has theological and symbolic importance for Luke. It is the place where God's prophets are killed (13:33), and because it is the place of Jesus' death and resurrection, it is the place of salvation. There is a divine necessity for Jesus to be on his way to Jerusalem. That is why at the beginning of the journey, Luke tells us, "When the days drew near for him to be taken up, he set his face to go to Jerusalem" (9:51). That statement provides more than just geographical direction. It sets the tone for the travelogue and indeed the remainder of the Gospel. Because of Jesus' earlier pronouncements of his fate, the reader understands the seriousness of these words. "To be taken up" has an ominous sound. Jesus "set his face to go to Jerusalem" in order to fulfill his role as the Son of God who must suffer.

As Luke began Jesus' Galilean ministry with a story of Jesus' rejection (4:16-30), he likewise begins this section of the Gospel with a story of rejection, this time by some Samaritans (9:51-56). The response of James and John to this rejection—they want to command fire to come down and consume the Samaritans—echoes the activity of the prophet Elijah in 2 Kings 1:9-16. Jesus does not accept their response, however, for he is not Elijah; he is much more. Misunderstanding of the way of Jesus is clear in the episodes of three persons who make tentative commitments to being disciples of Jesus (9:57-62). These stories signify that the road to Jerusalem—the way of discipleship—is tough and demanding. Halfhearted or partial commitments will not suffice.

The mission of the seventy (10:1-20), which seems to be a variation of the sending out of the disciples in 9:1-6, sounds a positive note in the story. The mission is a rousing success, which Jesus interprets as a major defeat for Satan (10:18). This incident foreshadows the later success of the followers of Jesus as they spread the Christian message throughout the Mediterranean world, particularly if the use of the number seventy is intended, as some scholars have suggested, to symbolize all the nations of the world (compare the table of nations in Gen 10:2-31).

What is required to be a faithful disciple? Luke groups together several episodes that provide three answers to this question. First, love of God and love of neighbor are the primary responsibilities of one who would be a disciple (10:27). A specific example of this teaching is found in the parable of the good Samaritan (10:29-37), in which Luke's concern for outcasts is reinforced by the presentation of the Samaritan as the hero of the story. Second, unwavering commitment characterizes the true disciple. During a visit to the home of Mary and Martha (10:38-42), found only in Luke, Jesus praises Mary because she has demonstrated undivided loyalty to Jesus as she has listened to his teaching. In her devotion, she demonstrates the commitment of the true disciple, as opposed to Martha who is "worried and distracted by many things" (10:41). Third, prayer, an activity important to

Jesus in Luke, should also be important to disciples. At the request of the disciples, Jesus teaches them how to pray, offering them a model prayer (11:1-4).

The journey to Jerusalem is not without controversy. Some opponents claim that Jesus' power is from Satan (Beelzebul) rather than from God (11:14-23). Such people are a part of this "evil generation" (11:29) that asks for a sign as proof of Jesus' identity. They do not recognize the sign that is in their midst already, the sign of the Son of Man (11:30). Because they refuse to "hear the word of God and obey it" (11:28), they are like someone with an unhealthy eye: they live in darkness (11:33-36). The reader encounters additional scenes of conflict and controversy in the denunciations of the Pharisees and the lawyers (11:37-54) who "neglect justice and the love of God" (11:42) and who have kept others from entering the kingdom of God (11:52). The response of the scribes and Pharisees (they are "hostile toward him . . . lying in wait for him"; 11:53-54) foreshadows for the reader what lies ahead for Jesus at the end of his journey.

Luke presents an assortment of teachings of Jesus in chapter 12, all of which are further instructions on the life of discipleship. In this section Jesus offers encouragement and reassurance to his disciples (12:1-12), teaches that "life does not consist in the abundance of possessions" (12:15), and tells them that they should not be overly anxious about material needs but should trust in God (12:22-31). The true disciple is not concerned with worldly goods and possessions but with performing deeds (such as giving alms) that build up "treasure in heaven" (12:33). The theme of the final judgment is woven throughout this section and is obvious in the teaching that a faithful disciple should always be ready for the Lord's return (12:35-48; the end time is in mind here). The reader will likely be surprised by Jesus' saying that he has come not to bring peace but division (12:51). At first glance this seems to run counter to the joyous proclamations of peace in 1:79 and 2:14. But the reader should remember the words of Simeon, "This child is destined for the falling and the rising of many in Israel" (2:34). Furthermore the peace that the angels proclaimed was peace for those whom God favors (2:14). As we have seen already in the Gospel, many do not accept the way of Jesus and thus do not share in this promised peace.

Jesus calls the people to repentance (13:1-9) and warns that many will try to enter the kingdom of God but will not be able (13:22-30). An episode sandwiched between these two tells of the controversy over a woman who is healed on the sabbath (13:10-17). Jesus' opponents in this story will strike the reader as examples of those who need to repent (but do not) and will not be able to enter the kingdom of God. The reader is reminded of the ominous direction in which Luke's story is moving by the words that Jesus says in 13:33: "I must be on my way, because it is impossible for a prophet to be killed outside of Jerusalem."

As Luke presents the material, a meal in the house of a Pharisee provides the setting for the teachings of Jesus in chapter 14. The scrambling of the guests for the places of honor leads Jesus to tell a parable that teaches the importance of humility (14:7-11). A second parable, about the great dinner, is a parable of reversal (14:15-24). Those who think they are a part of God's kingdom are actually turning down invitations to enter the kingdom. This rejection of the invitation (i.e., by the religious leaders and others who presume to be a part of God's kingdom) means that the kingdom will go to the outcasts. Continuing his instructions, Jesus warns that the requirements of discipleship are hard. Anyone who would be a disciple should carefully consider the cost (14:25-33).

The three parables of chapter 15 are given in response to the grumbling by the Pharisees and scribes about Jesus' inclusion of outcasts. The parables of the lost sheep, the lost coin, and the lost son all point to the graciousness of God, who extends forgiveness and mercy to those who are lost. The reader should note the contrast between the attitude of the opponents of Jesus and the attitude of God: whereas the opponents grumble and complain, God rejoices at the inclusion of the outcasts.

The dominant theme of the teachings in chapter 16, addressed specifically to the disciples, is the proper use of wealth, a theme Luke has dealt with previously (12:13-21). The reader is apt to be shocked by the hero of the opening parable, a dishonest steward, or manager (16:1-13). The point of the parable, modified by the appended sayings in verses 10-13, is that disciples must be as shrewd as the dishonest steward in the way they manage their possessions. Material goods can become one's master if one does not use them wisely (16:13). In light of Luke's concern for the poor, the wise use of money would be giving money to help meet the needs of the poor. The parable of the rich man and Lazarus (16:19-31) provides a vivid example of a person who does not use riches wisely and shows no mercy to the poor. The reader will hear in the closing sentence of the parable a reference to the resurrection of Jesus and the rejection of the gospel as it is proclaimed by the postresurrection community. This last statement claims,

"If they do not listen to Moses and the prophets, neither will they be convinced even if someone rises from the dead" (16:31).

On the journey to Jerusalem additional teachings are given to the disciples concerning the need to forgive those who have offended them (17:1-4), about the power of faith (17:5-6), about one's duty to serve God without expectation of reward (17:7-10), and concerning the eschatological coming of the Son of Man (17:22-37). The emphases in the teaching on the last days are that the Son of Man will come unexpectedly and that the disciple must always be prepared. The statement of Jesus to the Pharisees in verse 21—"the kingdom of God is among you"—indicates that the kingdom of God is a present reality. There is still a future aspect—the coming of the Son of Man will bring to completion the kingdom—but the kingdom (God's rule) has already begun in the lives of those who are responsive to God's authority. In Luke the kingdom is both present and future. It is present in Jesus and in those who accept him; yet, it is also future and the faithful await its coming. The sayings in 17:20-37 hold in tension the present and future aspects of the kingdom.

The story of the cleansing of the ten lepers (17:11-19) shows the power of Jesus to heal and stresses the importance of faith, but it also fits Luke's attempt to portray outsiders in a positive light. Of all ten lepers who are healed only one expresses thanks to Jesus. That one is a Samaritan, specifically identified in the story as a foreigner (17:18).

Instructions for the disciples continue as Jesus tells two more parables, both of which are unique to Luke. According to the interpretation given by Luke, the first parable, about an unscrupulous judge and a powerless but persistent widow (18:1-8), stresses the need to be persistent in prayer. The second parable features a Pharisee and a tax collector, both of whom come to the Temple to pray (18:9-14). In the Lukan setting this parable is directed to "some who trusted in themselves that they were righteous and regarded others with contempt" (18:9). This story is another parable of reversal—the truly righteous man is the social and religious outcast (the tax collector) and not the "righteous" Pharisee. If the first parable teaches the need for persistence in prayer, the second teaches the need for humility in prayer and reliance upon God's mercy.

The episode in which the disciples try to prevent the children from coming to Jesus (18:15-17) demonstrates that they have still not completely grasped the nature of the kingdom. When the radical demands of the kingdom are made clear to the rich ruler who comes to Jesus (18:18-25), the demands are too severe for him, prompting Jesus to exclaim, "How hard it is for those who have wealth to enter the kingdom of God!" (18:24). In answer to the disciples' concern that no one, then, could enter God's kingdom, Jesus tells them, "What is impossible for mortals is possible for God" (18:27).

For the third time in the Gospel, Jesus tells the disciples about the fate awaiting him in Jerusalem (18:31-34). As before, the disciples do not understand because the message is hidden from them. Approaching Jericho, Jesus meets a blind man who cries out to be healed (18:35-43). Responding to the man's faith, Jesus restores his sight. The man then becomes a follower of Jesus. The placement of this story is a key to its interpretation. The reader should detect in this story a contrast to the "blindness" of the disciples and perhaps also a contrast with the actions of the rich ruler. As R. Alan Culpepper explains, "The blind beggar, therefore, is an antitype of both the disciples and the rich ruler. He gains his sight (which the disciples will not do until after the resurrection; see 24:31: 'Then their eyes were opened') and follows Jesus (which the rich ruler was unable to do)."[16]

Two final pericopes bring the journey to Jerusalem to an end. In one episode Jesus enters Jericho and meets Zacchaeus, described as "a chief tax collector" and a rich man (19:1-10). He is identified later in the story as a "sinner" probably because he was considered ritually unclean by the ultra pious. As a tax collector, he would have to handle a large quantity and variety of objects and thus be rendered ritually unclean.[17] Jesus invites himself to the home of Zacchaeus, and as a result of his visit, Zacchaeus promises to give half of his possessions to the poor and to restore fourfold anything he has defrauded from anyone. As a chief tax collector, he was perhaps guilty of cheating or extortion and through such means gained his wealth. The actions of Zacchaeus are evidence of true repentance, recalling for the reader the demands for repentance expressed by John the Baptist in chapter 3. Repentance, the proper use of wealth, love of neighbor, and concern for the socially and religiously outcasts are all themes that are woven together in this story.

The final pericope of the travelogue (19:11-27) is a parable, told "because he was near Jerusalem, and because they supposed that the kingdom of God was to appear immediately" (19:11). This parable is similar to the Matthean parable of the talents (the two are likely variants of the same story) but it takes on a completely different meaning in Luke. Most New

Testament scholars are reticent to apply allegorical interpretations to the parables of Jesus, arguing that Jesus told parables rather than allegories. Allegorical interpretations attached to the parables in the New Testament are usually seen as having been added by the later Christian community or the Gospel writers themselves. We are not concerned here with the meaning of the parable as Jesus might have told it. Our task is to understand the parable as it appears in Luke, taking into consideration the Lukan context and shape of the parable. As Luke uses the parable it becomes an allegory, teaching that the fulfillment of God's kingdom will not come with the death of Jesus but will occur upon his eschatological return. In the interim period, the followers of Jesus must be faithful to the ministry entrusted to them, in spite of the rejection of Jesus and his message by the people of Israel ("the citizens of his country" 19:14). The parable thus contains a call to faithfulness for the disciples and a word of judgment against those who reject Jesus. The latter group will become particularly prominent in the closing chapters of Luke's Gospel.

The Jerusalem Ministry (19:28–21:38)

A transition in the Gospel occurs at 19:28. The journey to Jerusalem has ended; Jesus now enters the city of destiny. In this section Luke will present examples of Jesus engaged in teaching, all set within the confines of the Temple, and the growing opposition and rejection by the religious leaders. In contrast to Mark, Luke does not fit the ministry of Jesus into a one-week scheme ("Holy Week"). In Luke these events occur over an indeterminate period of time. The first episode in this section describes the preparation for Jesus' entry into Jerusalem and then the entry itself (19:29-44). The manner of Jesus' entry has royal and military overtones, similar to the entrance into cities by conquering generals or visiting kings. Luke makes the kingship theme explicit by having "the whole multitude of the disciples" greet Jesus as he rides into the city with the words, "Blessed is the king/who comes in the name of the Lord!" (19:38). Drawn from Psalm 118:26, this blessing was a typical greeting of Jewish pilgrims on the way to Jerusalem for Passover. Jesus, however, is not an ordinary pilgrim. He is the king, the "one who comes" (cf. 7:19), the Davidic Messiah (cf. 1:32-33; 18:38-39). Luke alone adds to the acclamation of the crowd the words, "Peace in heaven,/and glory in the highest heaven!" (19:38). The reader will remember the similar announcement of the angels at the birth of Jesus,

"Glory to God in the highest heaven,/and on earth peace among those whom he favors!" (2:14).

This joyous, exuberant scene is tempered by the reaction of some of the Pharisees present, who ask Jesus to tell his disciples to be quiet (19:39). This response signifies that the peace that Jesus brings is not universal. He continues to create division and conflict as the Pharisees, and ultimately Jerusalem, reject him. The Lukan Jesus even interprets the people's rejection of him as being responsible for the coming destruction of Jerusalem (19:42-44). Like the prophets of the Hebrew Bible who announced God's impending judgment on Jerusalem and its people (cf. Jer 6:15; Mic 3:12; Ezekiel 4–5), Jesus pronounces judgment on a Jerusalem that rejects God's message and God's messenger. Jesus weeps over the city that refuses to recognize and accept him as God's emissary of peace.

When he arrives in Jerusalem, Jesus goes to the Temple and drives out those who by selling items in the Temple are profaning it as a place of worship (19:45-46). For Jesus this is his "Father's house" (2:49). He now cleanses it and claims it as a place for his teaching. In this section of the Gospel the remainder of Jesus' time is spent in the Temple "teaching the people" and "telling the good news" (20:1). Luke presents several episodes here that demonstrate the growing opposition to Jesus by the religious leaders and their determination to rid themselves of him. They question his authority (20:1-8), are eager "to lay hands on him" (20:19), and send spies to entrap him (20:20).

Jesus then tells a parable directed against those who oppose him, comparing them to wicked tenants leasing a vineyard (20:9-19). The tenants mistreat the slaves sent to them by the owner of the vineyard and finally kill the owner's beloved son. Understanding that the parable is an indictment of their rejection of Jesus, the scribes and chief priests try to trap Jesus by asking him about paying taxes to the Romans (20:20-26). Jesus outsmarts his opponents, however, and silences them by telling them that since the coinage bears the image of the emperor, it belongs to him. In light of this, they are to "give to the emperor the things that are the emperor's, and to God the things that are God's" (20:25). Because of the negative ways in which the religious leaders have been presented throughout the Gospel, the reader understands the last part of this statement to be a further indictment of the leaders. They have consistently failed to give "to God the things that are God's."

The Sadducees also try to ensnare Jesus by asking him a question about the resurrection, a doctrine the Sadducees did not accept (20:27-40). Again, Jesus silences his questioners, answering their question and proving from scripture the validity of the doctrine of the resurrection. Jesus then becomes the questioner, asking about the nature of the Messiah as the Son of David (20:41-44). In the answer he gives to his own question, the point seems to be that the Messiah is the Son of David, but he is much more (i.e., the role of Jesus as Messiah is more than the traditional expectation of a person who will liberate the nation and establish his political kingdom).

Jesus continues his attack on the religious leaders by warning his disciples about the leaders' ostentatious displays of ego and pride coupled with their greed and injustice (20:45-47). The sight of a poor widow giving her offering in the Temple alongside the larger gifts of the wealthy prompts Jesus to praise her generosity, which is greater proportionately than that of the rich (21:1-4).

The final episode of Jesus' teaching in the Temple is an extended eschatological discourse (21:5-36). Jesus deals with the coming destruction of the Temple and Jerusalem, as well as the end-time coming of the Son of Man. By means of warnings about coming persecutions, imprisonments, and family divisions, Jesus prepares his disciples for the future they will face as faithful disciples. As his coming has brought about divisions and opposition, the same result will occur as they go out as his witnesses. The reader will recognize the accuracy of these statements. Jerusalem did fall, and as the book of Acts reports, the followers of Jesus did face many imprisonments and arrests. In spite of all that happens, the disciples of Jesus are to be ready at all times for the coming of the Son of Man (21:34-36).

The Passion Narrative and the Resurrection Appearances (22:1–24:53)

The last section of Luke's Gospel opens on a foreboding note: "The chief priests and the scribes were looking for a way to put Jesus to death" (22:2). Satan, who has been "off-stage" since the end of the temptations of Jesus when "he departed from him until an opportune time" (4:13), now reappears to lead Judas to find a way to betray Jesus. The reader senses a heightening of the dramatic tension.

In the setting of the Passover meal, Jesus points forward to the time when he will share a meal with the disciples when the kingdom of God is fulfilled (22:16). The reference to his impending suffering, the interpretation of the bread and wine, and the statement that his betrayer is at the table impose a somber mood on this scene. (One peculiarity of the Lukan last supper scene, compared to the other Gospels, is that Luke mentions two cups of wine instead of one. Because several cups of wine were consumed at a Passover meal, Luke's account is historically plausible.)

The next scene (22:24-38) would be shocking to the reader, if the narrator had not already portrayed the disciples as still in need of further instruction. In the midst of Jesus' table talk about his impending death, the disciples erupt into an argument over which of them is the greatest. Jesus tells them that they are to follow his example and demonstrate true greatness through service. Because they have stood by Jesus in his times of difficulty, the disciples are promised a place at the messianic banquet when Jesus returns and a role as judges (or better, "rulers," as the judges in ancient Israel were) over the reconstituted Israel, the new people of God.

In comparison to Matthew and Mark, Luke reduces the negative portrayal of the disciples throughout this section. He omits the statement by Jesus that all the disciples will desert him (cf. Mark 14:27-31; Matt 26:31-32); he softens the prediction of Peter's denial by attributing it to Satan and giving an assurance that Peter will return to faithfulness (22:31-34); he reports only once instead of three times the disciples' failure to stay awake on the Mount of Olives as Jesus agonizes in prayer (22:39-46); furthermore he provides an excuse for their sleep ("because of grief," 22:45); and he omits the statement that all the disciples fled when he was arrested.

The reader should note the prevalence of prayer in this section. Jesus tells Peter that he has already prayed for Peter's endurance in faith (22:32); Jesus prays earnestly before his arrest on the Mount of Olives (22:41, 45); twice while on the Mount of Olives Jesus encourages the disciples to pray "that you may not come into the time of trial" (22:40, 46). In Luke prayer is an important activity of Jesus and should be an important part of the life of his followers.

The story of Peter's denial (22:54-62) contains several differences from the other Gospel accounts, most notably that Jesus is present at Peter's denial. Luke's skill as a storyteller is evident in his including the detail that after Peter's denial, Jesus "turned and looked at Peter" (22:61), a look that pierces the heart of Peter and causes him to weep bitterly. Jesus is then taken before the Jewish council of elders, chief priests, and scribes (the Sanhedrin), where he is interrogated about his identity (22:63-71). Is he the Messiah? The Son of God? They interpret his response as affirmative, but do not accept his claims. As readers, we know the truth of these claims, for from the beginning of the Gospel we have been told that Jesus would reign from "the throne of his ancestor David" (1:32), a messianic identification, and that he would "be called Son of God" (1:35). Even these titles are not sufficient, for Jesus implies that he is also the Son of Man who "will be seated at the right hand of the power of God" (22:69).

Luke has shaped the story of Jesus' trial before Pilate to emphasize the innocence of Jesus (23:1-25). The charges that the religious leaders lay before Pilate are political charges—Jesus has been perverting the nation by forbidding the payment of taxes and claiming to be a king. The first charge is clearly false, as Luke has carefully shown in an earlier episode (20:20-26). The second charge is also false, at least in the way they intend it. Jesus was a king, but not a political king. On three occasions Pilate declares Jesus innocent (23:4, 14, 22). Luke even enumerates them so the reader will not miss the point: Pilate, the Roman governor, does not see Jesus as a threat, as a revolutionary. Even Herod Antipas (in Jerusalem likely because it was Passover), to whom Jesus is sent, finds Jesus innocent (23:6-12). (The story of Jesus being sent to Herod occurs only in Luke.) Finally, at the insistence of the crowds that Jesus be crucified, Pilate gives in and turns Jesus over to be executed.

Taken out to the place of crucifixion, Jesus is crucified between two criminals (23:26-49). The religious leaders and the soldiers mock Jesus with taunts about his being the Messiah of God and the King of the Jews. The latter identification is used as an inscription over his cross. In those taunts the reader recognizes the truth that the opponents of Jesus refuse to see. Even in his dying, Jesus responds with forgiveness as he prays, "Father, forgive them; for they do not know what they are doing" (23:34). One of the crucified criminals joins in the mockery, saying "Are you not the Messiah? Save yourself and us!" (23:39). The other criminal rebukes him, points to Jesus' innocence, and asks to be remembered by Jesus when he comes into his kingdom. In reply Jesus promises the man that he will be with Jesus in paradise, the place reserved for the righteous. The responses of these two men to Jesus typify the reactions seen throughout the Gospel—some reject Jesus while others follow.

The death of Jesus is presented in Luke as a hero's death: Jesus dies as the ideal martyr.[18] He is innocent, yet goes to his death bravely and with dignity. At the moment of death, the Lukan Jesus utters no cry of forsakenness as in Mark. Rather, like a noble and faithful martyr, Jesus prays,

"Father, into your hands I commend my spirit" (23:46). Notice that Luke contains no saying like that found in Mark that Jesus' death was a ransom for many (22:25-27; cf. Mark 10:42-45). For Luke the death of Jesus is not explicitly a saving event, an atonement for sin. On the other hand, one cannot completely rule out any salvific significance for Jesus' death in Luke. The concentration of references to Jesus' saving himself or others found in the crucifixion scene (23:35, 37, 39) suggests to the reader an association between the death of Jesus and his role as savior (2:11, 30). Luke hints, but does not make this connection explicit. For Luke, Jesus' faithful confrontation with death as a martyr provides a model for his followers when they too are faced with death for being faithful witnesses. A comparison of the parallels between the death of Jesus in the Gospel and the stoning of Stephen in Acts (6:8-8:1) demonstrates how Luke has used the martyr death of Jesus as a model.

At Jesus' death the centurion standing by exclaims, "Certainly this man was innocent" (23:47), reinforcing the Lukan theme of the innocence of Jesus. The response of the crowds is to return home, "beating their breasts" (23:48). They too apparently recognize the innocence of Jesus and possibly their complicity in his death. After Jesus is dead, Joseph of Arimathea, "a good and righteous man" who "was waiting expectantly for the kingdom of God" (23:50-51), takes the body of Jesus and buries it in an unused tomb as the sabbath approaches.

After the sabbath is over, some women go to the tomb to prepare the body with spices for a proper burial (23:54-56). Upon arrival they find the stone rolled away from the entrance and the body of Jesus missing. At the tomb "two men in dazzling clothes" (24:4) appear beside them and tell them that Jesus has risen and remind them that while in Galilee Jesus had predicted his resurrection. The women return to the disciples to tell them the news. The disciples do not believe the women's story, but think it is only "an idle tale" (24:11). Peter, however, goes to the tomb to see for himself.

Luke narrates two postresurrection appearances of Jesus, neither of which is found in any other Gospel. Both of these appearances in Luke occur in or near Jerusalem, in contrast to Matthew and John, each of which contains an appearance in Galilee. [Note that Luke omits Jesus' prediction that he would meet the disciples in Galilee (cf. Luke 22:1-39 with Mark 14:28 and Matt 26:32) and changes the wording of the message to the women at the tomb to reflect this omission (cf. Luke 24:6 with Mark 16:7

and Matt 28:7)]. As mentioned before, the geographical location of Jerusalem is important to Luke. It is the city of destiny, the city of God's redemptive activity. Furthermore Luke wants the disciples to remain in Jerusalem because that is the place where they will receive the Holy Spirit ("power from on high"; 24:49) and from which they will be sent out on mission (24:47).

The first Lukan postresurrection appearance occurs to two followers of Jesus, Cleopas and an unnamed individual, as they are on their way to Emmaus, a village close to Jerusalem (24:13-35). At first these two do not recognize Jesus as he joins them on their trip. They explain to him why they are so downcast, telling him the things that have happened to "Jesus of Nazareth, who was a prophet mighty in deed and word before God and all the people" (24:19). The reader recognizes by now that this identification of Jesus is only partially correct. Jesus is a prophet, but he is much more than that in Luke. The irony of the dejected statement of the two men is clear to the reader: "We had hoped that he was the one to redeem Israel" (24:21). Jesus then upbraids them for their lack of understanding about the necessity of the Messiah's suffering and begins to teach them from the scriptures. When they arrive in Emmaus Jesus stays and eats with them. Luke tells us that when Jesus "took bread, blessed and broke, and gave it to them" (24:30) they recognized who he was. The reader should notice the obvious similarities between this scene and the last supper account. By means of this pericope Luke is assuring his readers that Jesus is not dead but is alive and continues to make his presence felt among his followers. In the reading of scripture (24:27) and in the eucharistic meal (24:30) Jesus is particularly present with his community. Upon returning to Jerusalem the two men find that Jesus had also appeared to Peter, the details of which Luke does not recount.

The second appearance pericope (24:36-53), an appearance to the eleven disciples (Judas vanishes in Luke after his betrayal; but see Acts 1:16-20), stresses the bodily nature of Jesus' resurrection, a point made in the first pericope as well. He is not a ghost or an angel but the resurrected Jesus with a body that can be seen and touched and with which he can eat with them. Luke has in mind some new type of bodily existence, not just a resuscitated corpse, for in his resurrected state Jesus is able to appear and disappear at will (24:31, 36).

Jesus' final words to his disciples remind them that his death and resurrection are a fulfillment of the scriptures. Furthermore, they are given a task: "repentance and forgiveness of sins is to be proclaimed in his name to all nations, beginning from Jerusalem" (24:47). The fulfillment of this task is described in Luke's second volume, the book of Acts, which also narrates the coming upon them of "the power from on high" (Luke 24:49) as the Holy Spirit empowers them to carry out their commission as witnesses for Jesus (Acts 2:1-4).

After leading the disciples out to Bethany, Jesus is carried up into heaven and the disciples return to Jerusalem. The Gospel then ends where it began—in the Temple—with the disciples filled with the "great joy" that the angels had announced at Jesus' birth (2:10).

Chapter 6

❖

The Gospel of John

Robert Kysar entitled his introduction to the fourth canonical Gospel, *John, the Maverick Gospel*. That title is an appropriate description for this book that is strikingly distinctive from the synoptic Gospels. As noted in the first chapter, much of the material common to the Synoptics is missing from the Gospel of John, and much of John is not found in the Synoptics. Furthermore, the chronology, structure, and vocabulary of the book, as well as its presentation of Jesus, is vastly different compared to the first three Gospels. In spite of these differences—or perhaps because of them—the Gospel of John has endeared itself to readers who have savored the stories of Nicodemus, of the woman at the well, and of the raising of Lazarus. Readers have been intrigued by the picturesque imagery of the fourth Gospel, in which Jesus is described as the good shepherd, the light of the world, the bread of life, the gate, and the vine. This Gospel may appear last in the canonical ordering, but it is certainly not last in popularity among readers of the New Testament.

Social and Historical Origins

Date of Writing

The earliest extant copy of any portion of the New Testament is a small fragment of a papyrus manuscript of the Gospel of John. Known as P^{52}, this tiny scrap measures approximately 3½ inches by 2½ inches and contains portions of John 18:31-33, 37-38. This manuscript, found in Egypt, dates to the early second century, sometime around 125 CE. The significance of this fragment is certainly out of proportion to its size. It is important not only because it is the earliest New Testament text, but also because it provides us with the latest possible date for the writing of the fourth Gospel. Allowing time for the Gospel to circulate and become known in Egypt (assuming it did not originate there) pushes back that date to around 100–110 CE.

As for the earliest possible date for the writing of John, several passages in the Gospel (9:22; 12:42; 16:2) reflect extreme tensions, perhaps even a decisive break, between Judaism and Jewish Christianity. This setting matches the post-70 CE situation when Jewish leadership was trying to redefine and restructure Judaism after the destruction of Jerusalem. The meetings of Jewish scholars at Jamnia (Yahvneh) between 70 and 135 CE dealt with these issues. The so-called "Benediction Against Heretics" (*Birkat ha-Minim*), the twelfth benediction among nineteen in later Jewish prayer books, is often cited as evidence of the critical tensions between synagogue and church at this time.[1] Much uncertainty exists about the original form of this benediction (actually more of a curse or malediction), the date of its composition, and its original intention. In the opinion of many scholars, this curse on heretics was likely formulated (or revised) in the last quarter of the first century CE and was directed at several variant (and from a Pharisaic viewpoint, heretical) Jewish groups, including but not limited to Jewish Christians. If so, a date for the writing of the Gospel of John around 90–95 CE seems to fit the evidence.

As mentioned in chapter 1 above, the history of the composition of the Gospel of John is complex. Most scholars posit a multistage process in which the Gospel was revised, enlarged, and reorganized before it reached the form in which we know it today. The earliest stages of this process could have taken place even before 70 CE. The dates given here for the writing of John (90–95 CE), as well as the following discussion of its origin, refer to the latest stage of its development.

Intended Readers

What was the historical and social situation that prompted the writing of the fourth Gospel? Who were its intended readers? The conflict between the synagogue and the church that is present within the Gospel reflects the situation when the Gospel was being written and not the actual situation during the time of Jesus. Thus during the period of the writing of the fourth Gospel, John and his intended readers were in an environment in which they felt excluded from the synagogue (even if no official banishment of Jewish Christians from synagogue worship had taken place, expulsion had apparently occurred in some instances; cf. 9:22, 34; 16:2). Possibly some

Jewish people in John's community who were believers in Jesus were afraid to make this known publicly (cf. 12:42-43). Perhaps part of the purpose of the fourth Gospel was to encourage these "secret" Christians to publicly acknowledge their faith in Jesus.

That John's intended readers were Jewish Christians is suggested not only by the references to synagogue exclusion but also by the Gospel's use of images and motifs from the Hebrew Bible (Moses, the Exodus tradition, Wisdom traditions) and Jewish practices (the Passover and other Jewish feasts). Some aspects of the Gospel, however, point to a wider intended readership than Jewish Christians alone. In several places in the Gospel, John explains Hebrew terms or Jewish practices, unnecessary asides if the readership was totally composed of Jewish Christians. These explanatory comments probably indicate a mixed (Jewish and gentile) Christian audience for the Gospel. As some scholars have suggested, this may indicate that the Gospel originally was addressed primarily to Jewish Christians but as it was revised in subsequent editions explanatory comments were added to make it appropriate for gentile Christians as well.

Place of Writing

Due to certain concepts and terminology in the Gospel that scholars once considered to be non-Palestinian and non-Jewish (light/darkness dualism, spirit/flesh dualism, emphasis on knowledge, the concept of the *logos*), scholars earlier attempted to locate the religious and intellectual milieu of the Gospel of John within Hellenistic philosophy (particularly Platonism and Stoicism) or Gnosticism. John was considered to be the most Hellenistic and least Jewish of the four Gospels. Due in large part to the discovery of the Dead Sea Scrolls at Qumran beginning in 1947, the setting from which the Gospel of John originated has been reassessed. We now have a better understanding of the diversity of Palestinian Judaism. Many of the terms and concepts found in the Gospel of John also appear in the Qumran writings. For example, the emphases in John on the contrasts between light/darkness and truth/falsehood are also emphases of the Dead Sea Scrolls. This similarity between the Gospel of John and the Dead Sea Scrolls does not necessarily indicate that the Gospel of John was dependent on the Scrolls, but that John was at least familiar with these ideas and terms that were popular among this group of Palestinian Jews of the first century.

Whether these ideas came to John directly (or indirectly) from the Dead Sea Scrolls or the Qumran community is debatable.

Most scholars now are inclined to argue for a Palestinian Jewish background for the Gospel of John. The diversity within first-century Judaism helps explain the variety of terms, ideas, and issues that one encounters in the fourth Gospel. Scholars have noted the parallels between the Gospel of John and the Jewish scriptures, Jewish wisdom traditions, rabbinic Judaism, and the Qumran writings. To claim that the primary background for the Gospel is Palestinian Judaism is not to deny the influence of other streams of thought. Palestine, including Palestinian Judaism, was not immune to Hellenistic ideas, terms, and thought patterns. Because of the complicated multistage process of composition of the Gospel of John, more than one locale or milieu may have helped shape the traditions and versions of the Gospel before it reached its final form. In regard to the Palestinian background of the Gospel, we should perhaps think of that setting as the scene for the development of the early traditions and some revisions of the Gospel. The final form may have taken shape outside Palestine.

The traditional location for the writing of the Gospel (that is, for the final form of the Gospel) is Ephesus in Asia Minor. That is the location most often cited in the writings of the early church leaders. Toward the end of the second century, Irenaeus, bishop of Lyons, wrote, "John, the disciple of the Lord . . . did himself publish a Gospel during his residence at Ephesus in Asia."[2] The possible connection of the Gospel of John with the book of Revelation would lend support to the Ephesian hypothesis because Revelation certainly comes from the general area of Ephesus. The book of Revelation also attests to strained, even hostile, relationships between Christians and Jews in Ephesus, which would cohere with the synagogue/church conflict in the Gospel of John. Furthermore, some passages in the Gospel of John appear to be directed at followers of John the Baptist, who after his death continued as his disciples and likely saw him as superior to Jesus (cf. 1:6-9, 19-36). The book of Acts reports that disciples of John the Baptist were present in Ephesus upon Paul's arrival there (19:1-7). More recently, arguments have been made for Alexandria in Egypt and Antioch in Syria as the place where the fourth Gospel was completed. As with the other Gospels, the final determination of the location of the writing of the Gospel of John remains unsettled.

Literary and Stylistic Characteristics

The distinctiveness of the fourth Gospel lies not only in the differences between its contents and those of the synoptic Gospels but also in the way John tells his story of Jesus. From the opening words, "In the beginning was the Word," the reader senses that he or she has entered a different world in the Gospel of John. John uses different vocabulary, writing style, and symbols from those of the other evangelists. His characterization of Jesus is unlike that of the Synoptics, both in terms of Jesus' own self-awareness and in terms of his characteristic speech and language. Note, for example, that the Johannine Jesus tells no extended parables and only twice uses the expression "the kingdom of God" (3:3, 5). These distinctive literary and stylistic characteristics of the fourth Gospel contribute significantly to the richness of this narrative.

Style

As almost any student of New Testament Greek can attest, the Gospel of John is written in some of the easiest Greek to read in the New Testament. It uses simple grammatical constructions and a limited vocabulary. C. K. Barrett comments,

> His Greek moves slowly and within narrow limits, which clearly distinguish it from the other gospels; but it must be acknowledged to be an adequate instrument for the author's purpose. In spite of the small vocabulary the reader never receives the impression of an ill-equipped writer at a loss for the right word; rather that of a teacher who is confident that his message can be summed up in a few fundamental propositions which he has learnt to express with studied economy of diction.[3]

John's writing has often been described as having a poetic or at least quasi-poetic character due to the solemn dignity of the work and the presence in the Gospel of parallelisms and rhythmic patterns. The language of the fourth Gospel seems strongly influenced by a Semitic background, which should be expected if the proposed origin for the Johannine traditions is correct.

Irony and Misunderstanding

The Gospel of John exhibits a degree of playfulness not found in the other Gospels. The author at times "winks" at his readers, letting them know that they know something that others do not. Ironic statements and situations abound in the Gospel in which the reader recognizes a truth that is obscured or misunderstood by the characters in the story. As the reader becomes aware of and appreciative of the author's use of irony, the message of the Gospel becomes clearer and the reader is drawn into the inner circle of those who know the truth.

A few examples of the many instances of irony in John are 1:46; 4:12; 7:27, 35-36; 8:22; 9:40; 11:50-51. John also uses terms or sayings that have double or ambiguous meanings, often providing opportunities for Jesus to explain his meaning and to provide further teaching. For example, in his conversation with Nicodemus, Jesus says that in order to enter the kingdom of God one must be born "from above" (3:3). The Greek term translated as "from above" can also carry the meaning "anew" or "again." Whereas Jesus intends the first meaning, Nicodemus understands the latter meaning. This misunderstanding opens the door for Jesus to elaborate on his message. Another example is the encounter between Jesus and the Samaritan woman at the well (4:1-42). Jesus offers her "living water," meaning the gift of true life from God. The woman, however, understands "living water" to mean actual water that is flowing or "living" and not stagnant (an important distinction in Jewish ritual use of water). The use of irony and misunderstanding in the fourth Gospel enlivens the text and adds a touch of playfulness to the Gospel. More than that, however, these characteristics of John create an intimate bond between the author and the reader, making the reader feel privy to "inside" information and challenging the reader to look for the deeper meaning of John's Gospel.

Figurative and Symbolic Language

Closely related to, and sometimes even a part of, the irony and misunderstandings in the fourth Gospel is the use of figurative and symbolic language. Metaphors abound in the Gospel of John, particularly metaphors for Jesus. Jesus describes himself or is described by others as the Lamb of God, the bread of life, the light of the world, the gate for the sheep, the good shepherd, the resurrection, the way, the truth, the life, and the vine. Dualistic symbols also add to the richness of the language and style of the fourth Gospel. These dualistic symbols point to the two possibilities that confront every person (including the reader); one chooses either for God or against God, a life of faith or one of unbelief. Examples of these contrasts in the Gospel of John would include light/darkness, above/below, spirit/flesh, life/death, truth/falsehood, heaven/earth, and God/Satan.

Characters

The Jesus of the fourth Gospel stands apart from the Jesus depicted in the synoptic Gospels. One of the most obvious differences comes at the very beginning of the Gospel where the prologue implies that Jesus is the preexistent *logos*. The divine sonship of Jesus is not something announced at his baptism or his birth, but is moved back even earlier, back to "the beginning" (1:1). There is definitely no "messianic secrecy" motif in John; all the way through the Gospel various characters proclaim the identity of Jesus. Jesus himself readily claims messianic status and divine sonship, and throughout the Gospel closely identifies his will and his works with those of God. We will examine John's view of Jesus, that is, his Christology, in further detail when we explore some of the major themes in the Gospel of John.

A variety of other characters appears in the fourth Gospel, including the disciples, "the Jews," and several minor characters, some of whom are not found in the other Gospels. The disciples are relatively positive models in the Gospel of John. They recognize the identity of Jesus and become faithful followers. They are not perfect models, though, for they sometimes misunderstand and doubt. The anonymous "Beloved Disciple" is an exception to the previous statement, however. He is the ideal disciple who never misunderstands or doubts and who serves as a model for true discipleship.

In the Gospel of John "the Jews" are for the most part the opponents of Jesus. They represent unbelief, the ones who reject the light for the darkness. The harsh portrayal of the Jews in this Gospel should not be seen as an accurate description of the reaction of the Jewish people to Jesus during his lifetime. Several points need to be remembered: (1) John gives a stereotyped presentation of the Jewish people. Little distinction is made among the variety of Jewish groups and individuals of the first century. No mention is made of Sadducees, Herodians, scribes, or elders. Instead, all the leaders are grouped together as Pharisees. (2) "The Jews" serve a literary rather than a historical function in the Gospel of John. "The Jews" represent the negative side of John's dualistic understanding. They are "from below"; they reject the light; they do not know God; they reject Jesus. "The Jews" are a caricature in John of the unbelieving world. For this reason, the Johannine Jesus can speak about "their law" or "your law," as if he himself were not Jewish (7:19; 8:17; 10:34). (3) This stereotypical and sometimes pejorative presentation of the Jewish people was likely occasioned by the historical circumstances during the composition of the Gospel. The conflict between church and synagogue of the last quarter of the first century has been read back into the story of Jesus. The reader should understand the polemics of John's Gospel as a struggle, a rivalry, between two related groups—Judaism and Jewish Christianity—rather than as an accurate historical description of the situation of Jesus. All the earliest followers of Jesus, as well as Jesus himself, were Jewish. Thus Jesus was not rejected by "the Jews" but by a certain segment of the Jewish people. The modern reader must be careful not to allow the polemics of the fourth Gospel to contribute to contemporary attitudes of anti-Judaism or anti-Semitism.

Sources

As discussed in chapter 1, most scholars believe the Gospel of John developed independently of the synoptic Gospels. If John were aware of the existence of Matthew, Mark, and Luke, he apparently did not use them as sources for the composition of the fourth Gospel. Many of the traditions that underlie the Synoptics apparently came to John through other means. Scholars attempting to isolate John's sources have not reached agreement on what those sources might have been. One widely held suggestion is that John made use of a "signs source," that is, a collection of miracles or signs that Jesus performed. They claim that this signs source was a written document that circulated in John's community and was partially incorporated into the Gospel in chapters 1–12. Support for this concept is found in the special use of the term "signs" in John and the role of these wonder stories (usually thought to be seven in number) in promoting faith in John's Gospel. In 2:11 and 4:54 specific numbering is assigned to the first two miracles, seemingly pointing to the remains of an earlier system of numbering the miracles of Jesus.

Some scholars have suggested a "passion source" from which John drew his story of the arrest and crucifixion of Jesus. A third suggestion has been the existence and use of a "sayings source" upon which the discourses of Jesus in the fourth Gospel were based. Of these three proposed sources, the "signs source" has received the most support by modern scholars. The "signs source" is still a much debated issue in Johannine studies, however, and one should be cautious about basing any interpretations on this hypothetical source. John definitely relied on various traditions, oral and possibly written, in composing the fourth Gospel. What those traditions were we may never be able to ascertain.

Structure

Whereas Matthew, Mark, and Luke follow a somewhat similar structure for their stories of Jesus, John has a different arrangement of the material. In the Synoptics, Jesus' primary ministry is in Galilee, followed by a climactic movement toward Jerusalem. Jesus visits Jerusalem only once (excluding his visit as a child, which only Luke mentions), at the end of his life when the so-called "cleansing of the Temple" occurs. On the basis of information from the Synoptics, one could conclude that Jesus' ministry lasted approximately one year. John, on the other hand, situates a major portion of Jesus' ministry in Jerusalem, which Jesus visits several times. Since John mentions three different Passovers (2:13; 6:4; 11:55), at the very least a two- or three-year ministry is required in John's presentation. Furthermore, in contrast to the Synoptics John places the cleansing of the Temple episode at the beginning rather than at the end of Jesus' ministry.

Scholars generally agree that a major divide occurs in John's Gospel at 13:1. The material prior to 13:1 is anticipatory: Jesus' "hour" had not yet come. In 13:1, however, we are told that now "Jesus knew that his hour had come to depart from this world." The first part of the Gospel moves toward the "hour," the moment of Jesus' glory. The last part of his Gospel focuses on this climactic moment. During the first half, Jesus addresses his message to a wider audience, the "world." In the latter half, he concentrates on teaching and preparing his disciples. The first few verses of the Gospel, 1:1-18, serve as a prologue, whereas chapter 21 is almost universally seen as a later appendix to the Gospel. The structure, then, falls readily into four major parts, as is indicated in the outline given below.

Major Themes in the Gospel of John

Emphasis on certain themes is one of the ways in which the fourth Gospel paints a different portrait of Jesus from those contained in the synoptic Gospels. An examination of some of the major themes in John will help sharpen our understanding and appreciation of John's meaning and message.

Identity of Jesus

Who is Jesus? That question lies at the heart of the fourth Gospel. Certainly all the Gospel writers were interested in answering that question. What is different about John's answer? For one thing, no other Gospel holds before its readers as dazzling an array of answers to that question as does the Gospel of John. Jesus is presented as the Word made flesh, the Son of God, the Lamb of God, the Messiah, the King of Israel, a teacher come from God, the one sent from God, the Son of Man, rabbi, the bread of life, the Holy One of God, the light of the world, the gate for the sheep, the good shepherd, the resurrection and the life, the way, the truth, and the life, the King of the Jews, the true vine, Lord, and God. Several of these ascriptions we have encountered earlier in our examination of the synoptic Gospels; others are unique to John.

Another difference in the way John answers the question about Jesus is the explicit and forthright manner in which the identity of Jesus is proclaimed in the fourth Gospel. By means of the "messianic secrecy" motif, Mark mutes the public identification of Jesus. Matthew and Luke, although not emphasizing the secrecy motif to the extent of Mark, still present Jesus as reticent to accept or claim messianic or divine status. Such is not the case in John, however. Nothing is secret or hidden about Jesus. In chapter 1 alone, various characters proclaim Jesus as "the Lamb of God who takes away the sin of the world," the Son of God, the Messiah, rabbi, and the King of Israel. The Johannine Jesus makes no effort to deny or correct these identifications. In fact, Jesus himself speaks freely and often about his identity, claiming to be the Son of God, the Messiah, and the one sent from God. He claims a unique relationship with God and a unity between himself and God.

The Christology of John is a "higher" Christology than that found in the Synoptics. In Mark, Jesus is proclaimed Son of God at his baptism; in Matthew and Luke this occurs at his birth. In John, however, Jesus is given preexistent status. As "the Word," he "was in the beginning with God" (1:2). He is the one who descends from God to reveal God to the world and then ascends to return to God. Furthermore, John ascribes divine status to Jesus. Not only was the Word with God, "the Word was God" (1:1). This divine identification at the beginning of the Gospel is matched by the words of Thomas addressed to the risen Jesus at the end of the Gospel: "My Lord and my God" (20:28). The Johannine Jesus is seemingly aware of his divine status, claiming, "Whoever has seen me has seen the Father" (14:9). His use of the "I am" sayings (particularly the absolute "I am" sayings with no predicate) also suggests an identification with God, for these sayings seem to be an intentional adaptation of the divine name in Exodus 3:14.

While the fourth Gospel identifies Jesus with God, at the same time it also makes a distinction between the two. The Word "was God," but on the other hand was "with God." Jesus refers to God as "Father"; he is the Son who has been sent by the Father. Jesus is thoroughly dependent upon the Father, prays to the Father, and does the will of the Father. This paradoxical depiction of Jesus as being identical to/separate from God is the fourth Gospel's means of emphasizing the oneness of Jesus and God. Jesus is not a second God. The Gospel of John is thoroughly monotheistic. Jesus so fully reveals God and does the will of God that to accept Jesus is to accept God; to reject Jesus is to reject God. This understanding lies behind the fourth Gospel's exclusive claims for Jesus—"No one comes to the Father except through me" (14:6). One who sees and knows Jesus sees and knows God.

The Death of Jesus

The death of Jesus in John is not a defeat but a victory. This is Jesus' "hour" toward which Jesus and the whole Gospel story have been moving. Through his death he reveals the nature and heart of God who "so loved the world that he gave his only Son, so that everyone who believes in him may not perish but may have eternal life" (3:16). His death is his enthronement as king, his glorification, his exaltation. There is a double meaning in John's description of Jesus' death as his being "lifted up" (3:14; 8:28; 12:32, 34). He is literally lifted up as he is hung on the cross, but he is "lifted up" as well in exaltation and glorification. His death, resurrection, and ascension are all part of one dramatic movement in the Gospel of John.

The crucifixion of Jesus is part of the process whereby he returns to his heavenly origin.

Miracles as Signs

All four Gospels portray Jesus as one who performs miracles or mighty deeds during his ministry. He heals the sick, feeds the hungry, raises the dead, casts out demons (only in the Synoptics), and has power over the natural world. The fourth Gospel views these acts of Jesus in a different manner from the way the Synoptics view them. In the Synoptics, Jesus' mighty acts are seen as pointers to the arrival of God's kingdom, or God's power. Luke 11:20 expresses this belief: "But if it is by the finger of God that I cast out the demons, then the kingdom of God has come to you." In the teaching, preaching, and activities of Jesus, the kingdom of God is breaking into human history. When John the Baptist sends his disciples to Jesus to ask if Jesus is "the one who is to come," that is, the expected eschatological figure, Jesus answers John by pointing to his deeds of healing and raising the dead (Matt 11:2-6; Luke 7:18-23). His actions are evidence of the arrival of God's kingdom and of himself as God's agent.

In the Gospel of John, on the other hand, the miracles of Jesus are not eschatological pointers. Rather they are "signs," as the fourth Gospel often calls them, signs that point toward the identity of Jesus and lead to faith in him. In the Synoptics faith is often a prerequisite for a miracle to occur (Mark 2:5; 5:34; 6:5-6); for John these signs, when properly understood, lead to faith. The problem with "the world" is that it is not able to interpret these signs and believe in the one who performs them. The fourth Gospel, however, expresses an ambivalent attitude towards these signs. Although the signs are said to be performed for the purpose of leading people to faith (cf. 20:30-31), faith based on signs is depicted as inferior or even suspect faith (2:23-24; 4:48). The fourth Gospel is aware of the ambiguity of signs. Signs do not always lead to adequate faith. Some people want the signs because of the physical benefit they provide, not because they lead to faith (6:26). Some people see the signs, but never see beyond them to the truth to which they point (12:37). Other people, however, see the signs and believe in the one who has the power to perform them (2:11; 4:53; 6:14; 7:31; 11:45; 12:11). For those in the last category, the signs are important aids to faith. Even so, faith that is dependent on signs is preliminary, or immature, faith. Ultimately, those who "see" must move beyond a "signs" faith, for "blessed are those who have not seen and yet have come to believe" (20:29).

Realized Eschatology

Eschatology refers to beliefs about the end time, or the last things. The synoptic Gospels emphasize an apocalyptic eschatology. Jesus (the Son of Man) will return at the end of time to bring to fulfillment the kingdom of God. At the last judgment all will be judged on the basis of their faithfulness to God. The righteous will be rewarded with eternal life; the wicked will be punished. Some elements of this traditional eschatological outlook can be found in the fourth Gospel (5:28-29; 6:39-40, 44, 54; 12:48; 14:3). Along with this traditional future eschatology, John includes several passages that speak of the future acts and promises as occurring in the present. Judgment is not something that occurs only at the end of time, but is already taking place now (3:17-21). Eternal life is a present reality, not just an experience that begins after death or the last judgment (3:36; 5:24). Even resurrection is a present experience for the believer (5:21; 24). Because Jesus is the bearer of salvation, the "Word made flesh," the future is already realized in the present.

How can these two contradictory eschatological views—future and realized—be held together in one Gospel? Robert Kysar provides a cogent interpretation:

> The evangelist seemed to want to say that these eschatological realities are present in the life of the believer, although there is still a future and unfulfilled quality to them. The result of the evangelist's view is that believers are invited to turn their attention from the future to appreciate the quality of Christian existence in the present. But part of that Christian life style is to stand suspended between the present and the future. The evangelist may have wanted to correct an excessively future orientation without dispensing with the value of the future for the believer.[4]

Spirit/Paraclete

The fourth Gospel embodies a rich pneumatology, or doctrine of the Spirit. The Greek term used in John for the Spirit of God that is sent into the world is *parakletos*—"Paraclete." A paraclete is literally someone who is "called alongside" someone else. The word can mean "advocate," such as a lawyer who stands alongside a client to assist, defend, and guide. Or it can mean "comforter" or "counselor." Jesus tells his followers that after he leaves them he will send the Paraclete to them (15:26; or at his request the Father will send the Paraclete; 14:16, 26). Thus they will not be left alone following his departure. The tasks of the Paraclete will be to testify on Jesus' behalf, to teach and guide Jesus' followers, to remind them of what Jesus has said, to be with them, to declare what is to come, and to glorify Jesus. The Paraclete will function as the presence of Jesus with his believers. In relation to the unbelieving world, the Paraclete will judge and convict them for their unbelief.

The Paraclete functions as the presence of Jesus during his absence from the disciples. It is the Spirit of Jesus. The promise of the coming of the Paraclete is fulfilled in chapter 20 when the resurrected Jesus appears to his disciples. Jesus "breathed on them and said to them, 'Receive the Holy Spirit' " (20:22). As Genesis 2:7 says that God breathed the breath of life into the first human at creation, John has Jesus breathe new life into his followers by sending the Holy Spirit to be with them. (In Hebrew and Greek the words for "breath" and "spirit" are the same.) The reader hears the promise of the Spirit/Paraclete as a promise for all believers and not just for the first generation of disciples. Succeeding generations of believers share in this gift of God's Spirit.

Outline of the Gospel of John

The following outline will serve as the basis for our closer examination of the Gospel of John. Readers are encouraged to read the text of the Gospel in conjunction with the Reading Guide that follows the outline.

   I.   Prologue 1:1-18
  II.   Jesus' Revelation to the World (1:19–12:50)
      A. Testimonies to Jesus (1:19-51)
      B. From Cana to Cana (2:1–4:54)
      C. Jesus at the Festivals (5:1–10:42)
      D. Intimations of Jesus' Death (11:1–12:50)
 III.   Jesus' Revelation to his Disciples (13:1–20:31)
      A. Farewell Discourse (13:1–17:26)
      B. Death and Resurrection of Jesus (18:1–20:31)
 IV.   Epilogue (21:1-25)

Reading Guide to the Gospel of John

Prologue (1:1-18)

The Gospel of John has the most memorable opening lines of any of the Gospels: "In the beginning was the Word, and the Word was with God, and the Word was God." The Greek term translated here as "Word" is *logos*. The concept of the *logos* had a rich heritage, both in Judaism and in the Hellenistic world. In Judaism, the word of God was powerful, for through God's word the world came into existence (Genesis 1). The Hebrew prophets spoke of God's word: "The word of the Lord came to me" and "Hear this word of the Lord." The "word" of God was more than just information; it conveyed the presence and power of God as well.

Jewish wisdom literature also contributed to the idea of the *logos*. In such works as Proverbs, Sirach, and the Wisdom of Solomon, the authors personify wisdom and talk of it being present at creation and even being the means of creation. The Hellenistic Jewish philosopher Philo also spoke of the *logos* as being the divine agent of creation. The Stoic philosophers used the term *logos* to describe the aspect of God that permeated the entire universe, ordering, guiding, and controlling all things. All of these ideas likely lie in the background of John's use of *logos*. John has taken a term that would have been well-known in his day and infused it with new meaning. "This *logos* that everyone is talking about," John says, "has entered human history and 'become flesh' in Jesus of Nazareth."

In summarizing his discussion of John's use of *logos*, G. R. Beasley-Murray writes:

> The attempt should never be made to explain it on the basis of Hellenism or Judaism alone. Its roots are in the ancient religions of the nearer Orient in which ancient Israel was set, and from which the Greeks themselves learned. The powerful and creative Word of Marduk, Ellil, Ptah, Re is to be compared with the mighty and creative Word of Yahweh in the OT, which merged with the Wisdom of ancient tradition, blossomed in later Judaism, and was fused with the Torah. Yet Greek readers would not have read the prologue without recalling some of the primary elements of the Logos concept in their own traditions, even though they had never read a philosophical book or heard a lecture on philosophy (how many moderns who use the word "evolution" have read Darwin?). Its use in Hellenistic religion was, as we have seen, widespread, popularized through Philo, the forerunners of Gnosticism, and the Hermetica. . . . John's employment of the concept to

introduce the story of Jesus was a master-stroke of communication to the world of his day.[5]

The prologue introduces the reader to several ideas that will be filled out in the remainder of the Gospel. Jesus is the light of the world, the one who reveals most clearly the nature and attributes of God. The appearance of Jesus will cause a division: some will accept him, while others will reject him. Jesus is the giver and source of life. The prologue also introduces John (the Baptist), "a man sent from God" (1:6), who came to testify about Jesus and to point others to him.

Jesus' Revelation to the World (1:19–12:50)

The major portion of the first half of the Gospel focuses on Jesus presenting the revelation of God to his contemporaries. Through his teaching and miracles, Jesus reveals "his glory" (2:11), that is, the presence and activity of God. The purpose of this revelation is to elicit faith from those whom Jesus encounters. As we shall see, response to Jesus' revelation is mixed.

Testimonies to Jesus (1:19-51). Four short scenes comprise this section, all of which contain testimonies to the identification and significance of Jesus. John the Baptist, mentioned already in the prologue, plays a central role in the first three scenes. In the first scene (1:19-28) religious leaders from Jerusalem interrogate John about his identity. John emphatically denies that he is the Messiah, Elijah, or "the prophet" (apparently meaning an eschatological prophet who was believed to precede the Messiah). Rather he is the voice who announces and testifies to Jesus, "the one who is coming after me" (1:27). In the second scene (1:29-34), Jesus appears and is identified by John as "the Lamb of God who takes away the sin of the world" (1:29), likely a blending of images from the Passover lamb and the lamb in the "servant songs" of Second Isaiah (cf. especially Isa 53:4-9).

The reader who is familiar with the story of Jesus' baptism will be surprised at its absence in the fourth Gospel. Obviously that event is in the background here, but it is never explicitly mentioned as it is in the Synoptics. The omission of the baptism of Jesus by John (which could imply Jesus' submission to John) is likely for the same reason that the fourth Gospel repeatedly emphasizes that John is not the light or the Messiah (1:8, 20, 27, 30): the author wants to make clear that John is of lower status than

Jesus. This idea, perceptible in the other Gospels, is unmistakable in the fourth Gospel. As many scholars have argued, this emphasis possibly indicates the presence in the Johannine community of a group of disciples of John the Baptist who were claiming that John was superior to Jesus, perhaps that John was the Messiah.

In these scenes John performs the role assigned to him in 1:7. John "came as a witness to testify to the light, so that all might believe through him." John even sends two of his disciples to become followers of Jesus (1:35-42). John then fades from view (he will reappear briefly later in the Gospel), as Jesus takes center stage and calls his first disciples. The real focus of these last two scenes (1:35-42, 43-51) is not the calling of the disciples but their testimony about Jesus. John the Baptist has already described Jesus as the Lamb of God and the Son of God. Now Andrew, Philip, and Nathanael describe him as the Messiah (1:41), as "him about whom Moses in the law and also the prophets wrote" (1:45), rabbi, Son of God, and the King of Israel (1:49). There is certainly no "messianic secret" in the Gospel of John!

This John the Baptist pattern (testifying to Jesus' identity and then leading others to become followers of Jesus) is repeated by Andrew, who brings his brother Simon Peter to Jesus, and by Philip, who brings Nathanael to Jesus. This is the paradigm for all followers of Jesus—bearing witness to Jesus and making disciples of others. The reader can appreciate the irony of Nathanael's initially skeptical response to Philip—"Can anything good come out of Nazareth?" (1:46). Nathanael is eventually convinced to become a follower of Jesus based on Jesus' apparently superhuman knowledge of Nathanael. Jesus' reply to Nathanael—"Do you believe because I told you that I saw you under the fig tree?" (1:50)—introduces a motif that will become prominent in the fourth Gospel, the relationship between miracles (or "signs") and faith.

From Cana to Cana (2:1–4:54). A geographical *inclusio* characterizes this section of the Gospel. Jesus begins in Cana, a small village in Galilee (2:1), travels to Capernaum (also in Galilee), down to Jerusalem in Judea, up through Samaria to Galilee, and ends in Cana (4:46). The miracles of Jesus, which John calls "signs," are important in the fourth Gospel. They are signs because they are pointers to the identity and significance of Jesus; they lead people to faith.

The first of Jesus' signs occurs at a wedding in Cana (2:1-12). During the wedding the supply of wine is exhausted. Jesus' mother mentions the problem to him, apparently assuming that he will be able to remedy the situation. Jesus' response seems to be a refusal of her request, yet he acts to resolve the problem by turning water into wine. Because of the Johannine affinity for symbolism, the reader is justified in looking for a symbolic meaning to this rather mundane act of Jesus. The clue to the story is in the narrator's note that the water jars were for water for Jewish purification rituals (2:6). The changing of water to wine represents a change from the former rituals, institutions, and practices to the new way of Jesus. This first sign achieved its purpose: the sign revealed Jesus' glory and as a result the disciples believed in him (2:11).

John places the episode of the cleansing of the Temple (2:13-22) adjacent to the miracle at Cana. The messages of the two episodes are similar in that both point to a radical change that was needed in the existing religious order. Jesus' actions in the Temple were a challenge to Temple authority and Temple practices. He represents a new voice from God, a new authority. The significance of Jesus' dramatic actions and his strong words are not missed by the Temple authorities who ask for a sign that will confirm Jesus' authority to act as he did. Jesus' response—"Destroy this temple, and in three days I will raise it up" (2:19)—leads to a misunderstanding by the religious leaders who understand Jesus to be referring to the actual Jerusalem Temple. The narrator, however, explains that Jesus was referring to "the temple of his body" (2:21), a reference that the disciples remember after his resurrection.

One of the classic cases of misunderstanding in the Gospel of John occurs in the next episode, featuring Nicodemus (3:1-21), a Pharisaic leader who comes to Jesus "by night" (3:2). (Notice the double meaning of "night" for John. Nicodemus comes to Jesus not only when it is physically dark, but also when he is spiritually "in the dark.") Jesus tells Nicodemus that in order to see the kingdom of God one must be born from above, meaning a spiritual rebirth. Nicodemus understands Jesus to mean born "again," which is another possible meaning for the Greek word *anōthen*. This misunderstanding opens the way for Jesus to pursue the conversation further. Two additional instances of double meanings occur in this episode: Jesus plays on the double meaning of the Greek word *pneuma*, which means both "wind" and "spirit," and talks about the Son of Man being "lifted up," which in John refers in a literal way to Jesus' death (being lifted up on the cross) and in a figurative way to his exaltation and ascension.

The dialogue with Nicodemus shifts to a monologue in which Jesus emphasizes that God sent his Son to bring eternal life to the world (some interpreters, however, consider verses 16-21 to be the voice of the narrator rather than the words of Jesus). Contrary to God's desire, the coming of the light also brings condemnation to those who "loved darkness rather than light" (3:19).

The Gospel does not tell us what happens to Nicodemus. Does he accept Jesus' teaching? Does he leave unchanged by this encounter? Or, in Johannine terminology, does Nicodemus come out of darkness to the light, but never comprehend the light? Nicodemus appears on two other occasions in the fourth Gospel (7:50; 19:39), neither of which provides solid evidence for knowing whether Nicodemus became a follower of Jesus. In the fourth Gospel Nicodemus appears to represent persons with partial or hidden faith in Jesus. He expresses strong interest in Jesus and his teachings but is hesitant to make an explicit confession of faith. (We will return to Nicodemus at the end of the Gospel.)

At the end of chapter 3 John the Baptist reappears for the last time in the Gospel (3:22-30). As he did earlier, John again points away from himself to the one who is to come after him. John recognizes that he himself must fade into the background as Jesus becomes prominent. The words of 3:31-36, whether from John the Baptist or from the narrator, bear witness to the status and mission of Jesus. Jesus is "the one who comes from above" (3:31) and was sent by God. God "has placed all things in his hands" (3:35) and he is "above all" (3:31). Those who believe in Jesus ("the Son") have eternal life; those who disobey face God's wrath, or judgment.

Throughout this section of the Gospel, Jesus reveals himself to the people and they respond in various ways. The people in Jerusalem who witness his miracles believe in him on that basis, but the narrator leads the reader to question the depth of their belief (2:23-24). Nicodemus comes to Jesus full of questions, but never makes an explicit confession. In chapter 4 Jesus engages a Samaritan woman in dialogue. Their discussion is filled with double meanings and misunderstandings. Even after Jesus explicitly claims to be the expected Messiah (4:26), the woman is not totally convinced. Yet her testimony about Jesus leads others to Jesus. After hearing him themselves, they proclaim that he "is truly the Savior of the world" (4:42). Returning to Galilee, Jesus meets a royal official who begs Jesus to heal his son (4:46-54). As a result of Jesus' healing the child, the man and all his household become believers in Jesus. For the narrator, the purpose of the signs is accomplished: they are intended to lead to faith.

Jesus at the Festivals (5:1–10:42). The Jewish religious festivals, which serve as a backdrop for the events of this section, provide a unifying structure to the various incidents narrated here. The text mentions an unnamed festival (5:1), the Feast of Passover (6:4), the Festival of Booths (7:2), and the Festival of Dedication (10:22). Themes and imagery related to these festivals permeate the narratives and related dialogues. Jesus, whose identity is a major issue in this section, encounters intense opposition from those who do not believe in him, especially from the religious leaders.

The first episode of this section describes Jesus healing a man on the sabbath (5:1-18). The reader will understand this event as another sign that Jesus performs, a sign pointing toward his identity as God's Son and calling for a response of faith. The response of the healed man is unclear. Does he demonstrate ingratitude by pointing Jesus out to the authorities (5:15)? Is he spiritually blind as well as physically lame (5:13)? Or does his announcement in verse 15 that Jesus was the one who healed him represent a statement of faith? Regardless of the response of the healed man, the response of the religious authorities to Jesus' action is clear. Instead of faith, the sign evokes opposition (5:16). Angered over the violation of the laws prohibiting work on the sabbath, as well as over Jesus' identification of his work with that of God's, the religious leaders begin to persecute Jesus. Jesus then launches into a lengthy monologue in which he claims that as the Son of God, he does the work of God ("the Father") and has received authority from God (5:19-29). Jesus points to three kinds of evidence that support his claims: the testimony of John the Baptist, the works (signs) that he performs, and the testimony of the Jewish scriptures (5:30-40). Yet in spite of these witnesses, the people still do not accept Jesus.

In chapter 6 Jesus is inexplicably back in the Galilean region where he miraculously feeds over five thousand people with a boy's lunch of five barley loaves and two fish (6:1-15). In response to this sign, the people proclaim Jesus to be the eschatological prophet who was expected to appear. This identification and the subsequent attempt by the people to force Jesus to become king (a messianic king) are misguided (6:14-15). He is more than a prophet, and his kingship is of a different nature.

As elsewhere in the fourth Gospel (2:23-25), a faith response based on signs is at best shallow faith. The inadequacy of the people's response to Jesus is highlighted later when the crowds come looking for Jesus (6:22-24). Recognizing that they are following him only because he provides food for them, he chastises them for their lack of understanding (6:26). Jesus encourages them to seek bread from heaven, "the food that endures for eternal life" (6:27). Jesus proclaims that he himself is the bread of life that they need, the "living bread that came down from heaven" (6:51).

Jesus' remarks prompt misunderstandings. The people ask, "Is not this Jesus, the son of Joseph, whose father and mother we know? How can he now say, 'I have come down from heaven'?" (6:42). The origin of Jesus is an important theme in the Gospel of John. As readers, we know his true origin—he is from God. The crowds, however, do not grasp that truth. They see only his human origins. Likewise, they do not understand Jesus' sayings about bread. In a statement that is ripe with eucharistic overtones, Jesus says, "The bread that I will give for the life of the world is my flesh" (6:51). Because they remain in spiritual darkness, the people hear only the literal meaning of Jesus' words. As often happens in the fourth Gospel, the misunderstanding by the people provides the opportunity for Jesus to expound on his statements as he tells the people, "Those who eat my flesh and drink my blood have eternal life, and I will raise them up on the last day; for my flesh is true food and my blood is true drink" (6:54-55). To eat and drink means to believe in Jesus, to follow him. The reader cannot help hearing echoes of the church's celebration of Communion. These strong eucharistic overtones are somewhat surprising, for as we shall see, John is the only New Testament Gospel that does not include a reference to bread and wine at the last supper of Jesus with his disciples.

The reader should also note the chronological setting of this incident—when the Passover was near (6:4). The Passover commemorates the Hebrews' exodus from Egypt and their wilderness wandering, during which time God through Moses provided bread from heaven (manna) to sustain the people. Jesus, greater than Moses, now offers them true bread from heaven that provides not physical life but spiritual life.

Not only the crowds but even some of Jesus' followers find his teachings too hard to accept and turn away from following him (6:60-71). Whereas the crowds and these former followers depict rejection of Jesus, Simon Peter represents true faith, one who has seen, and heard, and believed. In a poignant scene, Jesus turns to the twelve and asks, "Do you also wish to go away?" Peter replies, "Lord, to whom can we go? You have the words of eternal life. We have come to believe and know that you are the Holy One of God" (6:67-69). The reader recognizes that Peter has indeed grasped the true identity and mission of Jesus.

The Jewish Festival of Booths (or Tabernacles) provides the setting for the events that follow in the next chapters. Rejection of and opposition to Jesus increase as he teaches and debates in Jerusalem, although some people do believe in him (7:31). The question of Jesus' identity arises several times. Some accuse him of being a deceiver (7:12) or of having a demon (7:20) and seek to arrest him (7:30). As earlier, some claim that he is the eschatological prophet (7:40), while others think he may be the Messiah (7:41). Others deny that he is the Messiah on the basis of his origin—he is from Galilee, not from Bethlehem, the hometown of David and thus the place from which the Davidic Messiah would arise (7:41-42). Earlier in this same chapter some disputed Jesus' identity as the Messiah because his origins were known, in contrast to a popular tradition that the origins of the Messiah would be a secret (7:27). The claim of the people to know the origin of Jesus is one of the supreme ironies in the Gospel. They know only his earthly origin, not his heavenly one. Those who indeed know where Jesus comes from—from God—believe in him and follow him.

(The episode in 7:53–8:11, the story of the woman caught in adultery, is not found in the earliest and best manuscripts of John. Furthermore, the style and vocabulary of the passage differ significantly from the rest of the Gospel. Most scholars, therefore, are convinced that these verses are not an original part of the fourth Gospel. Instead of its placement here, some manuscripts that include the text place it elsewhere in the Gospel of John. A few manuscripts place it in Luke's Gospel. Even though the story is not originally a part of the fourth Gospel, most scholars consider it an authentic story from the life of Jesus that circulated orally and was eventually preserved by its incorporation into the Gospel of John.)

Jesus' claim, "I am the light of the world" (8:12), is one of the famous "I am" sayings of the Gospel. The phrase "I am" (see particularly 8:58) is of great importance in John because the use of this phrase by the Johannine Jesus is a form of divine identification. In Exodus 3:14 "I am" is given to Moses as the name of God. Thus when Jesus applies the phrase to himself in the fourth Gospel the reader should hear another way in which the author of John makes clear the true identity of Jesus. Jesus is one with God. He was sent by God ("the Father"), he knows God, and he reveals God to those who are receptive. Most of his audience reject him, however, because they "are not from God" (8:47). Rather they are those who walk in darkness instead of in the light (8:12). The setting of the Feast of Booths for this discourse likely explains the use of light/darkness imagery. During the festival, four large golden lamps were lit as the people celebrated with dancing and singing. With this setting as background, Jesus proclaims, "I am the light of the world" (8:12).

Chapter 9 continues the use of the light/darkness imagery in a masterful way. On a surface reading this chapter tells a story of a man blind since birth whom Jesus heals. The metaphorical significance of sight and blindness in the fourth Gospel, however, causes the reader to suspect a deeper meaning in the story. Sight represents not just physical sight but spiritual insight; blindness represents spiritual blindness as well as physical blindness. The man not only gains physical sight, but he also gains the ability to "see" who Jesus really is. His spiritual eyes are progressively opened in the story as he initially identifies Jesus simply as "the man called Jesus" (9:11). Later, he says Jesus is a prophet (9:17); then, a man from God (9:33). Finally, in the climax of the scene, the healed man worships Jesus and cries out, "Lord, I believe" (9:38).

The author has crafted this story in such a way that there is an upward movement of the healed man as he gains spiritual sight and a downward movement of the opponents of Jesus who slide further and further into spiritual darkness. Their opposition and hostility to Jesus continue to mount as they close their eyes to the light that is before them. As religious leaders, the Pharisees believe that they already "see the light." The reader knows the answer to the question asked by these opponents, "Surely we are not blind, are we?" (9:40).

The imagery shifts from light/darkness to sheep and shepherds in chapter 10. In two additional "I am" sayings, Jesus proclaims that he is the gate for the sheep (10:7) and that he is the good shepherd (10:11). Jesus expounds on these metaphors, declaring that he is the one who provides sustenance, life, and protection for the sheep (the believers) in contrast to the religious leaders, who are more like hired hands who really do not care for the people, or even worse, like thieves and bandits who take advantage of the people. As before, the words of Jesus bring a mixed reaction from the people (10:19-21).

The final episode in this section occurs at the Festival of Dedication (Hanukkah) in the Temple in Jerusalem (10:22-39). The question of Jesus' identity is still the primary issue. The people ask Jesus explicitly if he is the Messiah. He replies, "I have told you, and you do not believe" (10:25). Jesus claims that he and the Father are one (10:30), meaning their work and mission are the same. For this reason, he can say, "The Father is in me and I am in the Father" (10:38). The response of the people to Jesus turns violent as they take up stones to stone him (10:31) and then try to arrest him (10:39). Jesus escapes and goes to the other side of the Jordan River, where some who had heard the preaching of John the Baptist believe in Jesus (10:40-42).

Intimations of Jesus' Death (11:1–12:50). The events of chapters 11 and 12 bring the second section of the Gospel (1:19–12:50) to a close. Jesus performs his last and greatest sign, and the religious leaders harden their resolve to rid themselves of Jesus. In addition to serving as a climax to this section of the Gospel, these chapters also act as a bridge to the next part of the Gospel, which focuses on the death of Jesus. Chapter 11 introduces new characters into the narrative, the family of Mary, Martha, and Lazarus. The illness and subsequent death of Lazarus provide the opportunity for Jesus to demonstrate graphically what the Gospel has been proclaiming— Jesus is the source of life.

The reader is apt to be puzzled by Jesus' response to the news of the illness of Lazarus: "This illness does not lead to death; rather it is for God's glory, so that the Son of God may be glorified through it" (11:4). Jesus then waits two more days until setting out to visit this family of friends. Jesus' reaction seems callous and self-serving. Jesus' comments, however, are interpretive comments that help prepare the reader to understand the significance of the death and raising of Lazarus. The illness will lead to a death that is only temporary, because Jesus will bring new life. Furthermore, in John the glorification of Jesus is his death, resurrection, and ascension. Thus the illness and eventual death of Lazarus (whose purpose is that "the Son of God may be glorified") point forward to the death of Jesus. The death and raising of Lazarus are a sign, pointing not to Lazarus but to Jesus, who is himself "the resurrection and the life" (11:25).

By stating that when Jesus arrived Lazarus had been dead for four days (11:17), the narrator makes sure the reader does not mistakenly believe that Lazarus is not really dead. Popular Jewish belief of the day held that a person's soul or spirit stayed around the tomb for three days after death and then departed. By noting that Lazarus has already been dead for four days, the narrator confirms beyond any doubt the reality of Lazarus' death. In the conversation between Martha and Jesus, Martha expresses faith in Jesus and the belief that on the last day her brother will be resurrected (11:24). Jesus claims, however, that *he* is the resurrection and the life. For those who believe in him, death has already lost its power. Eternal life is not just a future hope but a present reality.

When he is taken to Lazarus' tomb, Jesus issues a command to Lazarus, "Come out!" (11:43). Still wrapped in burial cloths, Lazarus emerges, a dramatic sign that Jesus is indeed the giver of life. Even this sign, however, is not convincing to all. Although some of the people believe in Jesus because of the raising of Lazarus, the religious leaders grow increasingly concerned (11:45-53). Knowing the fate of the nation of Israel and its Temple, the reader detects the irony in the leaders' statement, "If we let him go on like this, everyone will believe in him, and the Romans will come and destroy both our holy place and our nation" (11:48). Even more ironic are the words of Caiaphas the high priest, "It is better for you to have one man die for the people than to have the whole nation destroyed" (11:50). As the narrator makes clear, Jesus will indeed die not just for the nation, but for all the "dispersed children of God" (11:52). In the synoptic Gospels Jesus' cleansing of the Temple is the event that solidifies the religious leaders' determination to put Jesus to death. In contrast, in the Gospel of John the raising of Lazarus is the "last straw" that brings about the eventual death of Jesus.

The impending death of Jesus continues to dominate the narrative. A few days later when Jesus is again in Bethany, Mary anoints his feet with perfume, an act Jesus interprets as an act of faith and devotion, an anticipatory anointing of his body for burial (12:1-8). The complaint of Judas about Mary's action prepares the reader for the disastrous role that he will play in the story of Jesus. The reader should see Mary and Judas as contrasting characters in this episode—Mary represents faithful discipleship, whereas Judas represents failure and unbelief.

The raising of Lazarus continues to evoke reactions from the people. On the one hand, many of the crowd believe in Jesus and proclaim him "King of Israel" when he rides into Jerusalem (12:12-19; John is the only Gospel to mention that the people greeted Jesus with palm branches, which explains the name "Palm Sunday" for the Sunday prior to Easter). As readers, we should be cautious about faith that is "signs" faith, for in the fourth Gospel such faith is often very tenuous. On the other hand, the religious leaders not only continue to reject Jesus but now decide that they must eliminate Lazarus, who is a walking testimony to the power of Jesus (12:10-11).

The attempt of some Greeks to come to Jesus (12:20-22) prefigures, and is an example of, Jesus' ability to "draw all people to myself " (12:32). Jesus has come not only for the Jewish people but for all the world. Already he has begun to draw them to him. In their complaint against Jesus—"the world has gone after him" (12:19)—the Pharisees speak more truth than they realize, for as the reader knows, after the death of Jesus his message did spread throughout the world.

In several places earlier in the Gospel, reference is made to Jesus' "hour" not having come yet (2:4; 7:30; 8:20). Jesus' "hour" is his time of glorification—his death, resurrection, and ascension. In the fourth Gospel Jesus is in charge of his own destiny. No one forces his hand. He operates on a divine timetable. At the end of his public ministry, however, the "hour" has come (12:23). In John, even though Jesus states that his "soul is troubled" (12:27), he does not agonize over what lies ahead as he does in the Synoptics. He accepts the events of this "hour," knowing that the path to glory includes his death.

Jesus ends his public ministry in John by summarizing his call for the people to believe in him and receive eternal life (12:27-36, 44-50). He speaks with the authority of the Father, for he is the emissary from God who speaks the message God has given him. For the most part, the people prefer to remain in darkness rather than come to the light that is with them for only a short time longer (12:37). Even some who do believe, do so only secretly (12:42-43). In the story world of the Gospel, these secret believers would include Nicodemus and Joseph of Arimathea. In the world of the author, this reference likely points to Jews who were attracted to the Christian faith but were afraid to make their commitment known and thus remained "secret" Christians.

Jesus' Revelation to His Disciples (13:1–20:31)

In contrast to the Synoptics, which portray Jesus teaching his disciples as well as the crowd throughout his ministry, John presents Jesus concentrating almost exclusively on "the world," those outside the circle of disciples, during the first part of his ministry. Starting in chapter 13, however, the fourth Gospel portrays Jesus as focusing on the disciples. He instructs them and prepares them for his imminent departure from them. Another way of viewing the Gospel of John is to see the first half of the Gospel presenting the descent of Jesus ("the word became flesh"), whereas the last half prepares for his ascent, his glorification.

Farewell Discourse (13:1–17:26). John places this entire section, from 13:1–17:26, in the setting of the last meal that Jesus shares with his disciples. The reader who is familiar with the Synoptics will be surprised, possibly puzzled, by John's description of the last supper. The chronological setting is different in John and the Synoptics. Whereas the Synoptics plainly state that the last meal that Jesus ate with his disciples was a Passover meal (Mark 14:12-16), John just as clearly notes that it was not a Passover meal but the day of Preparation for Passover (19:14; according to Jewish custom, a day began and ended at sunset). According to both schemes, Jesus ate his last meal with his disciples on a Thursday evening and was crucified on a Friday. On that year did Passover begin on Thursday at sundown (according to the Synoptics) or on Friday at sundown (according to John)? Did the Synoptics alter the chronology to make a theological statement, that is, that Jesus' death is God's new act of deliverance and redemption, a new "exodus" from the slavery of sin and death? Or did John alter the chronology in order to have the death of Jesus ("the Lamb of God who takes away the sin of the world"; 1:29) coincide chronologically with the slaughter of the Passover lambs in the Temple, which occurred each year on the day before Passover? Since we do not know the exact year in which Jesus died and thus do not know when Passover began during that year, no certain conclusion can be reached and scholars disagree. Both traditions seem to be theological interpretations.

Also in sharp contrast to the Synoptic presentation of the Last Supper is the absence of any mention of bread and wine in the fourth Gospel. For John the focus of the last meal is not the bread and wine and the origin of the church's celebration of the Eucharist (the Eucharist was important to the Johannine community, however, as chapter 6 demonstrates). The central element of the Last Supper in John is a foot-washing scene. This activity is an acted-out parable of Jesus' humility, service, and love for his disciples and is a model for Jesus' disciples to follow in their relationships with others. The shadow of the cross falls across the scene through Jesus' comment to Simon Peter, "You do not know now what I am doing, but later you will understand" (13:7). This statement "is John's way of showing us that this symbolic act of love presages the meaning of the cross where Jesus' supreme act of love will be affirmed as the glory of God present in this world."[6]

Two examples of failed discipleship intrude into this intimate moment between Jesus and his disciples. Jesus quietly singles out Judas as the one who will betray him (13:21-30) and then predicts that Peter will soon deny him three times (13:36-38). Because the narrator has presented Jesus as a reliable figure throughout the Gospel, the reader trusts that these predictions will come true as well. By now the reader has come to appreciate the dual meaning inherent in the narrator's comment about Judas' departure from the group in order to carry out his planned betrayal—"and it was night" (13:30). In addition to the literal meaning, the statement also points out the spiritual reality of the situation. Judas leaves the light of Jesus and enters the darkness of evil to carry out his misdeed.

Chapters 14–16 comprise a lengthy discourse by Jesus. This farewell discourse has sometimes been called Jesus' last will and testament, for it consists of his final teachings, encouragement, and exhortations to his disciples. This type of writing—a farewell or testament of an individual—was common in the ancient world. Several themes intertwine in Jesus' words to his disciples. Jesus speaks of his imminent departure from the world, but assures the disciples that they are not to worry. He leaves in order to prepare a place for them where they can abide with him forever (14:1-7). Even during the interim before Jesus returns, the disciples will not be alone. Jesus will not leave them as orphans but will continue to abide with the disciples in the same way that the Father has dwelled in him. Furthermore, after his ascension the Spirit of God (the Holy Spirit, the Advocate) will come and dwell with them to teach and guide them and to remind them of what Jesus has told them (14:18-31).

The task of the disciples is to obey the commandments or teachings of Jesus, supremely his commandment that they love one another (15:1-17). By continuing in their relationship with Jesus ("abiding in him"), the disciples will be able to draw strength from him and "bear much fruit" (15:5, 16). The intimate relationship that Jesus shares with the Father is the paradigm for the relationship that the disciples are to have with Jesus.

Jesus warns the disciples that just as the world rejected him, so it will also reject those who belong to him (15:18-25; 16:1-4). Their persecutors, even those who think that such persecution is an act of devotion to God, demonstrate by their actions that they really do not know God. The disciples should not be discouraged, however, for Jesus has forewarned them of the hatred the world will feel toward them. Even more important, they are to take courage because Jesus has conquered the world (16:33).

In chapter 17 Jesus ends his discourse to his disciples and offers a prayer to God, asking first that God would glorify him now that his "hour" has come (17:1-5). Note that in John there is no agony scene in which Jesus wrestles with his fate. In the fourth Gospel Jesus willingly lays down his life (15:13) because this supreme act of love is the means of bringing eternal life to his followers. Jesus prays for his disciples also, asking God to protect them as they are sent out into the world and to make them one in the same way that Jesus and the Father are one (17:6-19). Through their unity with each other and their intimate relationship with Jesus and the Father, the disciples will bear witness to the world that Jesus is indeed from God (17:20-24).

Jesus' prayer extends beyond a concern for his present disciples to "those who will believe in me through their word" (17:20). The readers will hear a reference to themselves in this verse. The original readers of the Gospel (as well as all subsequent followers) believed in Jesus not on the basis of having seen firsthand the signs that Jesus performed nor having heard his words themselves. Rather they became believers on the basis of the faithful witness of the first disciples of Jesus as it was passed on by tradition.

Death and Resurrection of Jesus (18:1–20:31). In chapters 13–17 time moves slowly. The entirety of those five chapters is set during the meal shared by Jesus and his disciples. The lengthy discourse allows Jesus to interpret his death and ascension and to offer comfort and assurance to the disciples. As soon as Jesus' prayer is finished, the pace quickens and the events of Jesus' arrest, trial, and crucifixion happen quickly. Now that Jesus' "hour" has arrived, there is no delay. Even in his arrest, Jesus is not a victim in the fourth Gospel. He knows in advance all that is going to happen (18:4). When the soldiers and Temple police come to arrest him, Jesus takes the initiative and asks them whom they are seeking. In a statement ripe with theological meaning, Jesus replies to their search for him by saying, "I am" (18:5). When Peter tries to defend Jesus with violence, Jesus rebukes him, saying, "Am I not to drink the cup that the Father has given me?" (18:11). The disciples do not run away and abandon Jesus; rather, he is in control and orders the soldiers to take him and let his disciples go free (18:8).

John is the only Gospel that mentions that Jesus was taken to the house of Annas (former high priest and father-in-law of Caiaphas, the current high priest) in addition to the house of Caiaphas for questioning (18:12-14). John intertwines the account of Peter's denial of Jesus with the story of Jesus' questioning before the religious authorities (18:15-27). This intertwining sharpens the contrast between the faithful testimony of Jesus and the failure of Peter. As Robert Kysar comments,

> It is Peter who is on trial here, not Jesus. More accurately, it is humanity on trial, humanity represented by the religious leaders and by poor Peter. The antiphonal telling of the two trials—Jesus' *and* Peter's—makes it clear that humanity is being charged and tried. While the innocent Jesus is being tried, it is Peter who is found guilty. . . . Humanity is found guilty, but without even so much as a sigh of regret.[7]

The irony of the actions of the religious leaders when they take Jesus to Pilate is clear. They seek to put to death the one who has been sent from God, yet they refuse to enter Pilate's headquarters for fear of ritual defilement (18:28). In Johannine terms, they stumble in the darkness even though the light is in their presence. Scholars have often noted the literary skill with which the author has crafted this story of Jesus before Pilate. Raymond Brown, for instance, finds here seven episodes (18:28-32, 33-38a, 38b-40; 19:1-3, 4-8, 9-11, 12-16a), each balanced "in setting, content, and even in length."[8] The setting of the episodes alternates between the inside and the outside of the praetorium (the residence of Pilate; NRSV: "headquarters"). Because the religious leaders will not enter the gentile residence, Pilate must go out to meet with them.

The theme of kingship dominates the trial before Pilate. In answer to Pilate's question to Jesus asking him if he is the King of the Jews, Jesus responds that his kingdom is not from this world (18:36). Throughout the fourth Gospel, the question of Jesus' origins has been raised. That issue surfaces again here in Jesus' reply and even more explicitly in Pilate's later question to Jesus, "Where are you from?" (19:9). Pilate, like the other characters in the Gospel of John who fail to believe in Jesus, never understands or accepts where Jesus is really from—he is the one sent from God. When Jesus explains that he came into the world in order to testify to the truth, Pilate asks, "What is truth?" (18:38). The reader detects the irony in this question, for standing in front of Pilate at that very moment is the one who in the fourth Gospel proclaims, "I am the truth" (14:6).

Pilate mocks Jesus as king, but finds him not guilty of criminal charges (19:1-6). Pilate's boasting of power over Jesus (19:10) is proved false by his fear and powerlessness to release Jesus when he is warned of the consequences of such action (19:12). Pilate is powerless, as well, to make the right decision. He chooses for darkness, rather than for light. The religious leaders make that same choice. Pilate sarcastically asks them, "Shall I crucify your King?" To which the chief priests reply, "We have no king but the emperor" (19:15). This statement is even more jarring when one notes that in the Hebrew Bible, God is often described as king. In claiming that they have no king but the Roman emperor, the religious leaders have indicated their true allegiance. Their words confirm what their actions have already shown: they belong to the world and not to God.

In keeping with the Johannine portrait of Jesus who is in control and who goes valiantly to his death, Jesus carries his own cross to Golgotha (19:17), rather than needing the assistance of Simon of Cyrene as in the Synoptics. Neither is there a cry of abandonment from the cross. The dying Jesus, in charge to the end, finally exclaims, "It is finished" and "gave up" his spirit (19:30).

The piercing of Jesus' side and the information that because he was already dead his legs were not broken on the cross (a common practice to hasten death) are the author's means of emphasizing the reality of the death of Jesus (19:33-34). The one who "became flesh" has now died. The flow of blood and water from Jesus' pierced side perhaps has deeper significance, as well, reminding the reader of the Gospel's use of water imagery in connection with Jesus (4:10-15; and possibly 7:37-39).

Nicodemus reappears in the story and assists Joseph of Arimathea in preparing Jesus' body and burying it (19:38-42). Both men represent, at best, hidden faith—Nicodemus never having acknowledged his belief in Jesus, and Joseph described as a secret disciple. Their actions here at the end of the Gospel are ambiguous. Should the reader understand that by coming to take care of Jesus' body the two men have finally "come 'out of the closet' with their faith"[9] and thus proclaim their commitment to Jesus? Or do they remain "secret disciples," representatives of those who believe but "did not confess it, for fear that they would be put out of the synagogue" (12:42) thereby remaining outside the kingdom of God?[10] Whereas both readings are possible, both Nicodemus and Joseph of Arimathea seem to be sympathetic characters who finally at the cross are emboldened to make public their loyalty to Jesus. They serve as models for other "secret Christians" who are hesitant to confess their faith in Jesus.

The resurrection appearance stories in chapter 20 are vastly different from any stories told by the Synoptic writers. In a statement laden with theological symbolism, the fourth Gospel notes that "it was still dark" (20:1) when Mary Magdalene goes to the tomb on Sunday morning. Seeing that the stone had been rolled away from the tomb, Mary runs and tells Simon Peter and the disciple "whom Jesus loved." Mary assumes that the body of Jesus has been stolen. When Peter and the other disciple arrive at the tomb, however, what they find indicates that the body of Jesus has not been stolen: his grave cloths are left behind in the tomb. The empty tomb and the grave cloths lead the Beloved Disciple to belief, although not to complete faith yet. Gail R. O'Day comments on this scene:

> The beloved disciple's faith is as complete as faith in the evidence of the empty tomb can be. To say that the beloved disciple believes in the resurrection is to rush the story, however, as v. 9 reminds the reader. Jesus' glorification is not yet over; the disciples have not yet experienced Jesus' resurrection, nor has Jesus ascended to the Father (cf. 20:17). Only after Jesus is glorified, when the Paraclete is given to the community, will the disciples understand and remember the Scriptures (2:22; 12:12; cf. 14:26).[11]

After the two disciples return home, Mary remains at the tomb (20:11-18). Peering inside she sees two angels who ask her why she is weeping. When the resurrected Jesus appears to her, at first she fails to recognize him. When he calls her name, Mary realizes that this person is Jesus (20:16). Her attempt to cling to Jesus perhaps represents her failure to realize that after his resurrection Jesus has entered into a new relationship with his followers. Obedient to Jesus' instructions, Mary becomes a model for future believers as she returns and spreads the news of her encounter with the risen Jesus (20:18).

On that same evening Jesus appears to the disciples who are gathered together in fear (20:19-25). Through his words and his presence Jesus transforms their fear into rejoicing and imparts the Spirit of God to them. Empowered by the Spirit, the disciples are sent forth by Jesus and charged with the task of forgiving sins, which is a continuation of the work that the earthly Jesus has begun. When Thomas, who had not been present when Jesus appeared to the other disciples, hears about the appearance, he refuses to believe. This original "doubting Thomas" demands proof before he will believe. He receives the needed proof a week later when Jesus appears to them a second time, showing Thomas the wounds in his hands and side (20:26-29). Thomas responds with a confession of faith in the risen Jesus: "My Lord and my God!" (20:28). The one who "was with God . . . and was God" (1:1) receives the proper worship and confession.

The reader will certainly hear in Jesus' response to Thomas a message directed to all future believers: "Blessed are those who have not seen and yet have come to believe" (20:29). The faith of future generations is not inferior because they were not eyewitnesses of the "signs" of Jesus. Indeed those who believe without having seen are blessed. Chapter 20 ends with a statement of the purpose of the Gospel: "that you may come to believe that Jesus is the Messiah, the Son of God, and that through believing you may have life in his name" (20:31).

Epilogue (21:1-25)

Majority scholarly opinion holds that the final chapter in the fourth Gospel belongs to a later stage of the Gospel's composition than do the earlier chapters.[12] Some consider that the same person responsible for the remainder of the Gospel wrote chapter 21 at a later date. Other scholars argue that the author of this final chapter was a later editor, or redactor. As it stands now, chapter 21 offers an additional appearance story of the risen Jesus to his disciples. The setting is the Sea of Galilee (or Tiberias) where one night several of the disciples have gone fishing. Early in the morning Jesus appears on the lake shore and instructs the unsuccessful fishermen to cast their net on the right side of the boat. Following his instructions, they catch a net full of fish. At this point, the Beloved Disciple recognizes Jesus, which leads Peter to jump overboard and head to shore. When the disciples arrive, Jesus invites them to eat the bread and fish that he has prepared for them. This story has similarities with the feeding of the multitude in chapter 6. Both stories have eucharistic overtones. Perhaps, like the appearance story in Luke 24:28-35, this episode functions to proclaim that the resurrected Jesus is present with his followers in the eucharistic meal.

After the meal Jesus questions Peter about his love for Jesus (21:15-19). The threefold repetition of the question serves as a counterbalance to Peter's threefold denial of Jesus at his trial. For this reason, this scene is sometimes viewed as Peter's reinstatement by Jesus. Jesus emphasizes to

Peter that Peter must put into practice his love by caring for Jesus' sheep, which means to serve and minister to others in the way that Jesus has cared for the disciples. These words are an echo of Jesus' teachings to the disciples at the last supper. For Peter, faithfulness to Jesus' call to "follow me" will include following Jesus even in martyrdom (21:18-19).

Whereas Peter would die a martyr's death, such would not be the fate of the Beloved Disciple (21:20-23). He served as a faithful witness to Jesus in another way, by being the one whose testimony was the source for the fourth Gospel (21:20-24). The faith of the Beloved Disciple bore much fruit, not only in the Gospel but also in the countless believers who join with the "we" in verse 24 to proclaim, "We know that his testimony is true."

Chapter 7

❖

The Other Gospels

The previous four chapters have examined the understanding of Jesus conveyed by the four New Testament Gospels. As we have seen, each of these works presents a different portrait of Jesus, based on the individual author's historical and social setting and theological outlook. Because these four presentations of Jesus are the versions of the Jesus story that are most widely known, many students assume that these Gospels contain all the stories about Jesus of which we are aware. As we shall see, however, in the early centuries of the church many Jesus traditions circulated outside the New Testament.

Beyond the Canonical Gospels

As we discussed in chapter 1, the earliest traditions about Jesus were oral traditions. These sayings of Jesus and stories about him functioned in a variety of ways in the early church as this new Jesus movement spread out into the Mediterranean world. Eventually some of these traditions were gathered into collections, some were incorporated into the four canonical Gospels, while still other traditions were eventually lost. Obviously all the earliest stories about Jesus were not included in the Gospels of Matthew, Mark, Luke, and John. The fourth Gospel explicitly says, "But there are also many other things that Jesus did; if every one of them were written down, I suppose that the world itself could not contain the books that would be written" (21:25).

As the church grew and expanded, individuals created additional stories about Jesus, some rooted in historical happenings, but most were the products of pious imaginations. Various collections of materials related to Jesus circulated in different Christian communities. These works, like the canonical Gospels, claimed to contain the sayings and deeds of Jesus. Some of these literary works are roughly similar to the New Testament Gospels, even though all of them were not known as "gospels." Fortunately, some of these writings have been preserved and are extant today, although in some cases only fragments of the works remain. In other cases, copies of the gospels themselves have not survived, but quotations from them can be found in other early Christian writings. For example, the *Gospel of the Ebionites* is known today primarily by seven quotations from it by the fourth-century bishop, Epiphanius. These noncanonical gospels are often called "apocryphal gospels" in order to distinguish them from the four Gospels that are contained in the New Testament. (The word "apocryphal" means "hidden," apparently indicating that in antiquity certain works were "hidden" from the general public because they were deemed to contain material either too advanced and esoteric or too heretical.)

As mentioned in chapter 1 of this study, the application of the term "gospel" to these noncanonical works is controversial. Do these apocryphal works really belong to the same literary genre as do the Gospels of Matthew, Mark, Luke, and John? Are there enough similarities between the apocryphal and canonical gospels to justify using the same term to describe them all? Some scholars, while recognizing that these apocryphal gospels are examples of Jesus literature produced in the early church, argue that the differences between the canonical and apocryphal gospels are too great for them to be grouped together. John P. Meier, for example, defines a gospel narrowly as "a narrative of the words and deeds of Jesus of Nazareth, necessarily culminating in his death and resurrection, which narrative is meant to communicate to the believing audience the saving effects of the events narrated."[1] This definition would exclude almost all the noncanonical gospels.

Other scholars, such as Helmut Koester, argue for a broad definition of the term "gospel." The term "gospel literature," Koester states, "should include all those writings which are constituted by the transmission, use, and interpretation of materials and traditions from and about Jesus of Nazareth."[2] On the basis of this definition, virtually any work that claims to transmit the words and/or deeds of Jesus would warrant classification as a gospel. The problem with such a broad definition, which Koester recognizes, is that it lumps together works that in actuality belong to a variety of literary genres. Some are narratives, some are collections of sayings, and some are dialogues or discourses. In response to this criticism, Koester and others argue that the term "gospel" should not be used as a name for a specific literary genre. Rather, as Stephen Patterson states, the term "gospel" should be applied broadly "to a larger body of literature, which itself encompasses a multiplicity of forms and genres."[3]

A reading of both the apocryphal and canonical literature reveals that the four canonical Gospels are more closely related to each other than they are to any of the other so-called gospels. Each of the canonical Gospels tells the story of the life of Jesus, concluding with an account of his death and resurrection. Furthermore, each of them contains sayings of Jesus as well as reports of his activities. The apocryphal gospels, however, lack one or more of these characteristics. Some of them, while narrative in form, concentrate only on one aspect of the life of Jesus (his birth or his death). Others are a collection of sayings or dialogues, with little or no narrative of the deeds of Jesus. Whether one opts for a broad definition and calls all of these works—canonical and apocryphal—gospels, or whether one uses a narrower definition that includes only the canonical Gospels, one must recognize that the canonical Gospels are distinctively different in form and content from the apocryphal works.

The canonical and apocryphal gospels should not be pitted against each other, however, on the assumption that the canonical works are historically reliable whereas the apocryphal gospels are totally fictitious. As we have mentioned already, the canonical Gospels cannot be read as strict historical accounts. They are literary works, shaped by literary, theological, and sociological factors, as well as by historical facts. Thus some of the information in the canonical Gospels would not stand up under historical scrutiny. On the other hand, reliable historical traditions may be contained in some of the apocryphal gospels. For instance, several scholars have argued that the *Gospel of Thomas* contains authentic sayings of Jesus or in some cases versions of his sayings closer to the original than those found in the canonical Gospels. Thus historical reliability is not the distinguishing feature between the canonical and apocryphal gospels. Granted, most scholars would readily admit that any one of the canonical Gospels contains far more reliable historical information about Jesus of Nazareth than do all the apocryphal gospels combined. In fact, the apocryphal gospels provide very little additional reliable information about the teachings or the activities of Jesus (some scholars would say none). That conclusion, however, must be reached only after a study of each tradition, not assumed prior to beginning one's study.

Likewise, one should not make the mistake of assuming that the apocryphal works were from the outset blatantly theologically inferior to the canonical works. Certainly from the perspective of the Christian church today these apocryphal gospels are outside the bounds of acceptable theological traditions (that is the reason they are called "apocryphal"). Many of these works originally, however, were quite popular with certain Christian groups. Only gradually were they excluded and deemed "heretical" or nonorthodox. We will examine that process later when we discuss canonization of the Gospels.

The presence or absence of the term "gospel" in the title of a work is not a true indication of whether the work should be considered a gospel. Some works that were not called gospels actually deserve that designation, such as the *Dialogue of the Savior*. On the other hand, some works that were called "gospels" do not belong in that category, even on the basis of the broader definition of that term given above, because they do not purport to relate words or deeds of Jesus. Included in this category of inappropriately labeled "gospels" would be the *(Coptic) Gospel of the Egyptians* and the *Gospel of Truth*.

Scholars frequently divide the collection of apocryphal gospels into three categories: narrative gospels, revelation dialogues and discourses, and sayings gospels. In the following sections we will discuss several of the more important or more interesting apocryphal gospels that circulated in the early Christian communities according to these three categories.

Narrative Gospels

In form the narrative gospels are rather similar to the canonical Gospels because they claim to tell the story of Jesus, although they usually deal with a limited portion of the life of Jesus. In many cases they give evidence of the pious imagination of the early Christians who expanded canonical traditions or created new stories to fill out the gaps in information about Jesus.

Gospel of the Ebionites. This work, written around the middle of the second century, is known today only through quotations of the document by Epiphanius in the fourth century. The work was given its current title by modern scholars because this gospel was claimed to be used by the Ebionites, a Jewish-Christian group of the second through the fourth centuries. The Ebionites adhered to many tenets of the Jewish law, rejected the teachings of Paul, and apparently denied the doctrine of Jesus' virgin birth.

The *Gospel of the Ebionites* seems to be a harmonized account of the synoptic Gospels, particularly the Gospels of Matthew and Luke. Like Mark, the *Gospel of the Ebionites* began with John the Baptist and the baptism of Jesus, likely omitting the birth stories of Jesus because they were unacceptable. The other excerpts quoted by Epiphanius describe Jesus calling his disciples, report a saying of Jesus in which he says that he has come to do away with sacrifices, present a version of the synoptic saying of Jesus in which he redefines his family (Mark 3:31-35), and give the disciples' question and Jesus' answer concerning where they would eat the Passover meal. The contents of these fragments point to a belief in vegetarianism and a struggle against Jewish ritual and worship practices.

Gospel of the Hebrews. Like the *Gospel of the Ebionites*, the *Gospel of the Hebrews* is an early Jewish-Christian writing. Originally written in Greek, this work was probably written in Egypt during the latter part of the first century or the first half of the second century. The only surviving texts of the *Gospel of the Hebrews* are quotations of the work by early Christian writers. Scholars have collected seven such fragments of the text. If the work of Nicephorus, patriarch of Constantinople in the ninth century, is correct, the original version of this writing was rather long. Nicephorus claims that the *Gospel of the Hebrews* contained 2200 lines, only 300 fewer than the Gospel of Matthew.[4]

The extant fragments, which show no evidence of dependence on the New Testament Gospels, describe Jesus' preexistence, his coming into the world, his baptism, some otherwise unknown sayings of Jesus, and a report of the resurrected Jesus' appearance to his brother James. An appearance to James (here apparently the first appearance of the risen Jesus) is unknown in the canonical Gospels, although the apostle Paul does mention an appearance to James (1 Cor 15:7). Likewise absent from the canonical Gospels is the tradition found in the *Gospel of the Hebrews* that James was present at the last supper with Jesus.

Gospel of the Nazoraeans. This work is the third of the apocryphal gospels that is classified as a Jewish-Christian work. The title is not original but was given to the work by scholars on the basis of remarks made by early Christian writers who referred to a gospel in use by the Jewish-Christian group called the Nazoraeans who were located in Syria. No copy of this gospel has survived to the present. It is known only through twenty-three excerpts gathered from early church writings, most of them given in the ancient sources as variants to the Gospel of Matthew. This gospel, written probably in the first half of the second century, was closely related to the Gospel of Matthew and was perhaps an expansion of Matthew.

The extant quotations of the *Gospel of the Nazoraeans* do not present any religious ideas that would have been unacceptable to mainstream Christian belief. The excerpts do, however, present some interesting elaborations of stories found in the canonical Gospels. The *Gospel of the Nazoraeans* describes Jesus' mother suggesting to Jesus that they go to John the Baptist to be baptized. Jesus objects on the basis that he is sinless. The synoptic story of the rich man who comes and questions Jesus (Matt 19:16-24) becomes in the *Gospel of the Nazoraeans* a story of two rich men who come to Jesus. In contrast to the Synoptics, the *Gospel of the Nazoraeans* says that at the death of Jesus the lintel of the Temple collapsed, not that the curtain was torn in two.

Gospel of Peter. This work claims to be written by Simon Peter, one of the disciples of Jesus. Two early copies of this manuscript have been discovered. A portion of the text was found in a late eighth-century papyrus manuscript in Akhmim, Egypt, at the end of the nineteenth century. In addition, two fragments (containing only about three verses) from a second- or third-century manuscript of the text were discovered among the papyrus documents found in Oxyrhynchus, Egypt. The Akhmim text, by far the larger of the two copies, is only a partial text of the *Gospel of Peter*, beginning with the appearance of Jesus before Pilate and ending with the resurrection of Jesus. The text breaks off before reporting any resurrection appearances of Jesus.

The date of the original *Gospel of Peter* and its relationship to the canonical Gospels have been strongly debated. Until recently, consensus held that the *Gospel of Peter* was written after the canonical Gospels (probably in the first half of the second century) and was dependent on them. More recently, some scholars have argued for an earlier dating of the *Gospel of Peter*, some claiming that its composition preceded that of the four New Testament Gospels and was even used as a source by the canonical Gospels. John Dominic Crossan fine tunes the theory of the gospel's composition by claiming that behind the present *Gospel of Peter* was an earlier version of it, what he calls the *Cross Gospel*.[5] The four canonical Gospels used the *Cross Gospel* as their source for the passion narrative of Jesus. Later, the *Cross Gospel* was expanded and adapted to become the *Gospel of Peter*. Whereas Crossan and others have developed a plausible argument for an early dating of the traditions in the *Gospel of Peter*, they have failed to convince the majority of New Testament scholars.

One of the noticeable characteristics of the existing text of the *Gospel of Peter* is the exoneration of Pilate for any guilt in the death of Jesus. Instead, the Jewish people are presented as completely at fault. This polemic against the Jews likely reflects the late-first-century or early-second-century conflict between Judaism and Christianity. The most intriguing passage in this work is the account of Jesus' resurrection. The canonical Gospels do not describe the resurrection; they simply report that it happened. The *Gospel of Peter*, on the other hand, describes the events in this manner:

> Now in the night in which the Lord's day dawned, when the soldiers, two by two in every watch, were keeping guard, there rang out a loud voice in heaven, and they saw the heavens opened and two men come down from there in a great brightness and draw nigh to the sepulchre. That stone which had been laid against the entrance to the sepulchre started of itself to roll and gave way to the side, and the sepulchre was opened, and both the young men entered in.
>
> When now those soldiers saw this, they awakened the centurion and the elders—for they also were there to assist at the watch. And whilst they were relating what they had seen, they saw again three men come out from the sepulchre, and two of them sustaining the other, and a cross following them, and the heads of the two reaching to heaven, but that of him who was led of them by the hand overpassing the heavens. And they heard a voice out of the heavens crying, "Hast thou preached to them that sleep?", and from the cross there was heard the answer, "Yea".
>
> Those men therefore took counsel with one another to report this to Pilate. And whilst they were still deliberating, the heavens were again seen to open, and a man descended and entered into the sepulchre (vv. 35-44).[6]

Egerton Papyrus 2. Sometimes called the "Unknown Gospel," this work consists of a few small papyrus fragments that contain several episodes from the ministry of Jesus, some of which have parallels in the canonical Gospels. This work is important primarily from the questions that are raised about its relationship to the canonical gospels and the development of oral and written traditions about Jesus. In some places the stories in the "Unknown Gospel" are similar to the synoptic Gospel accounts; in other places they are similar to traditions in the Gospel of John. A variety of opinions are held by scholars concerning the relationship of this document to the canonical Gospels. Some have argued that the "Unknown Gospel" was dependent upon the New Testament Gospels; others have suggested that the New Testament Gospels were dependent upon the "Unknown Gospel"; whereas, still others have argued that the "Unknown Gospel" is dependent on a mixture of canonical Gospels and oral tradition. The proposed date for its composition has ranged from mid-first century to mid-second century.

Infancy Gospel of Thomas. This collection of stories about the boy Jesus was extremely popular in antiquity, as evidenced by the numerous versions and translations of the work that have survived. The oldest extant copy of the text dates to around the fifth or sixth century. The work is certainly much older than that, however. Irenaeus (a church leader at the end of the second century) quotes two stories that are found in the *Infancy Gospel of Thomas* (one of which is also in the Gospel of Luke), likely indicating that he knew this collection of stories. (On the other hand, Irenaeus could have been citing oral tradition along with the Gospel of Luke.) Assuming that Irenaeus was quoting from the *Infancy Gospel of Thomas*, then the work is at least as early as the middle of the second century, possibly written in Syria. Its attribution of authorship to the disciple Thomas is perhaps as late as the Middle Ages.

This gospel contains miracle tales of the child Jesus from age five to age twelve years. The last story in the collection is the account in Luke 2:41-52 of Jesus as a twelve-year-old in the Temple of Jerusalem. This story in Luke is the only information provided by the canonical Gospels about the childhood of Jesus. The *Infancy Gospel of Thomas* is evidence of the interest of the early church in these "unknown" years of Jesus' life and the extent to which pious imaginations would create tales to fill this void. The Jesus depicted in these tales is a precocious, arrogant, stubborn, and at times mean-spirited wonder-child who performs miracles not only to do good but also out of spite or vengeance. In addition to stressing the miracle-working ability of the child Jesus, these stories also stress his precocious knowledge, showing that his wisdom exceeded that of the teachers who tried to instruct him. Two examples of these tales are given here.

After this again he went through the village, and a lad ran and knocked against his shoulder. Jesus was exasperated and said to him: "You shall not go further on your way," and the child immediately fell down and died. But some, who saw what took place, said: "From where does this child spring, since his every word is an accomplished deed?"

And the parents of the dead child came to Joseph and blamed him and said: "Since you have such a child, you cannot dwell with us in the village; or else teach him to bless and not to curse. For he is slaying our children." (4.1-2)

His father was a carpenter and made at that time ploughs and yokes. And he received an order from a rich man to make a bed for him. But when one beam was shorter than its corresponding one and they did not know what to do, the child Jesus said to his father Joseph: "Put down the two pieces of wood and make them even from the middle to one end."

And Joseph did as the child told him. And Jesus stood at the other end and took hold of the shorter piece of wood, and stretching it made it equal with the other. And his father Joseph saw it and was amazed, and he embraced the child and kissed him, saying: "Happy am I that God has given me this child." (13.1-2)[7]

Protevangelium of James. This work is another infancy gospel, although the focus of this work is on the birth of Jesus rather than on his childhood. Originally written during the latter half of the second century, the *Protevangelium of James* became extremely popular. "Protevangelium" means "prior to the Gospel," so named because the work describes events prior to those found in the New Testament Gospels. The work claims to be written by James, presumably James the brother of Jesus. The purpose of the work was apparently to defend the doctrine of the virgin birth of Jesus. It does this by presenting stories about the wondrous birth of Mary, her piety as a child and later as a young woman, and her perpetual virginity.

In many ways the *Protevangelium of James* is more about the veneration and glorification of Mary than it is about Jesus. Several ideas that became prominent in popular adoration of Mary are present already in this work. Included here are the special circumstances of Mary's own birth, her piety and devotion to God, and her virginity that remains intact even through the birth of Jesus and throughout her marriage to Joseph. The document supplies information not contained in the canonical Gospels: the names of Mary's parents (Anna and Joachim), Mary's being dedicated to God and raised in the Temple from age three to age twelve, Joseph's being chosen by lot to take Mary as his wife when she was only twelve years old, Joseph's situation as a widower with children prior to his marriage to Mary, and Jesus' birth in a cave. That Joseph had children from a prior marriage serves to explain how Mary could have maintained her virginity throughout her life whereas the Gospels mention that Jesus had brothers and sisters; they were his stepbrothers and stepsisters.

The *Protevangelium of James* is dependent on the Matthean and Lukan birth narratives, supplemented by legendary materials, some modeled after birth stories in the Hebrew Bible. Although the *Protevangelium of James* offers interesting stories and provides insight into the developing venera-tion of Mary in the church, it contains no new reliable historical informa-tion.

In addition to the narrative gospels discussed here, others also circulated in ancient Christian communities. Those would include the *Gospel of Nicodemus* (or the *Acts of Pilate*), the *Secret Gospel of Mark*, Papyrus Oxyrhynchus 840, and possibly the *Epistula Apostolorum*.

Revelation Dialogues and Discourses

A popular subject for certain literature in the early church was suppos-edly new teachings or revelations from Jesus given to his disciples or other important persons. These teachings or revelations would be cast in the form of dialogues between Jesus and his followers or lengthy discourses by Jesus. Many of the gospels of this type belong to the collection of Gnostic literature discovered in Nag Hammadi, Egypt, in 1945.

The term "Gnosticism" refers to a variety of religious systems in the ancient world that offered salvation through knowledge (the Greek word for "knowledge" is *gnōsis*). Gnostic systems usually viewed the physical world as evil. At death, the "enlightened" ones were able to escape this evil, material world as their spirits or souls were freed from their bodies and returned to their true, heavenly home. Since the physical world was evil, the world could not have been created by the supreme, good god. The world, therefore, was created by a lesser god, a demiurge. Gnostic versions of Christianity arose, certainly by the second century and perhaps even earlier. In these systems Jesus was viewed as the heavenly redeemer, the revealer of supernatural, saving knowledge (*gnōsis*).

Dialogue of the Savior. This work, one of the writings found among the Nag Hammadi documents, is a complex compilation of materials from various sources. The work was likely composed during the second century. Many of the sayings in the work resemble material in the canonical Gospels of Matthew, Luke, and John and especially in the apocryphal *Gospel of Thomas*. Several scholars argue, however, that the *Dialogue with the Savior* was not dependent on any of these written works. Rather, they insist its sources for these sayings were oral traditions or earlier collections of the sayings of Jesus. Unfortunately, the only extant copy of this text is rather fragmentary.

The format of the majority of the work is a dialogue between Jesus and three of his followers—Matthew, Judas, and Mariam. Much of its content deals with eschatology. The opening words of the Savior refer to the eschatological rest:[8] "Already the time has come, brothers, for us to abandon our labor and stand at rest. For whoever stands at rest will rest forever" (120.3-8). The three followers make such requests as, "Lord, I want [to see] that place of life [. . .] where there is no wickedness, [but rather] there is pure [light]!" (132.6-9); "Tell me, Lord, how the dead die, [and] how the living live" (139.21-23); "How will [our] garments [i.e., eschatological garments] be brought to us?" (138.21); "[Why] do we not rest [at once]?" (141.3-4); "We [want] to understand the sort of garments we are to be [clothed] with [when] we depart the decay of the [flesh]" (143.11-15). Jesus' responses to his disciples reflect a mixture of both realized and future eschatology, interpreted through Gnostic thought and ideas.

The Apocryphon of James. The *Apocryphon of James* is another of the writings found at Nag Hammadi. The proposed dates for the writing of the work range from the end of the first to the beginning of the third century. The external framework of the writing is in the form of a letter from James (likely James the Just, the brother of Jesus). The letter introduces a secret writing that was revealed to James and Peter. This secret writing claims that Jesus appeared to the disciples 550 days after his resurrection. The majority of the remainder of the *Apocryphon of James* describes dialogues between Jesus and Peter and James, whom Jesus takes aside for private instruction on the occasion of this postresurrection appearance. The sayings of Jesus are a mixture of parables, admonitions, beatitudes, and wisdom sayings. Many of these sayings are reminiscent of sayings in the canonical Gospels (particularly in the Gospel of John) and in the *Gospel of Thomas*, although there is no evidence of literary dependence. The *Apocryphon of*

James may have used independent oral traditions as sources for the sayings. The excerpt that follows has echoes of the Gospel of John.

> Behold, I shall depart from you and go away, and do not wish to remain with you any longer, just as you yourselves have not wished it. Now, therefore, follow me quickly. This is why I say unto you, "for your sakes I came down." You are the beloved; you are they who will be the cause of life in many. Invoke the Father, implore God often, and he will give to you. Blessed is he who has seen you with Him when He was proclaimed among the angels, and glorified among the saints; yours (pl.) is life. Rejoice and be glad as sons of God. Keep his will that you may be saved; accept reproof from me and save yourselves. I intercede on your behalf with the Father, and he will forgive you much. (10.22–11.6)[9]

The Gospel of Mary. The *Gospel of Mary* was likely written in the second century, originally in Greek. It is known today from three partial texts, which represent two different versions of the work. Although this work was not one of the texts found at Nag Hammadi, it is a Gnostic writing.

The *Gospel of Mary* falls into two sections. In the first part, the Savior (apparently the risen Jesus) is involved in a dialogue with his disciples over the different natures of which the world is composed. Those who possess a material root are subject to sin, sickness, and death. Whereas now all natures are intermixed, ultimately all things will be resolved into their own roots. At the end of the dialogue the Savior commissions his disciples to go forth and preach the gospel of the kingdom. When the disciples grieve and despair after his departure from them, Mary Magdalene encourages and exhorts them. (The text does not specifically identify this Mary as Mary Magdalene, but that is almost certainly who is intended.)

In the second part of the work, Mary recounts to the disciples a vision that she had in which the Savior appeared to her and taught her. A large portion of this part of the text is missing. The majority of the remaining text describes the ascent of the soul as it passes the four cosmic powers and its triumph over the bondage of the world. When Mary finishes her report to the disciples, she is challenged by Andrew and Peter:

> But Andrew answered and said to the brethren, "Say what you (wish to) say about what she has said. I at least do not believe that the Savior said this. For certainly these teachings are strange ideas." Peter answered and spoke concerning these same things. He questioned them about the Savior: "Did he really speak with a woman without our knowledge (and) not openly? Are we to turn about and all listen to her? Did he prefer her to us?" (17.10-22)

Levi, another disciple, comes to Mary's defense, saying, "Peter, you have always been hot-tempered. Now I see you contending against the woman like the adversaries. But if the Savior made her worthy, who are you indeed to reject her? Surely the Savior knows her very well. That is why he loved her more than us" (18.7-15).[10]

Women seemed to have enjoyed a prominent role in Gnostic circles; Mary (or Mariam) was one of the three individuals to receive the revelation from Jesus in the *Dialogue of the Savior*. The attitude of Peter and Andrew in the *Gospel of Mary* represents the position of mainstream Christian churches of the second century, who denied teaching and leadership to women (cf. 1 Tim 2:8-15). The *Gospel of Mary* affirms women as teachers and recipients of divine revelation.

Gospel of the Egyptians. The *Gospel of the Egyptians* was a popular work during the second and third centuries, especially in Egypt. Originally written possibly in the late first or early second-century, it survives today only in a few quotations in the writings of Clement of Alexandria from the end of the second century. This work must not be confused with the *(Gnostic) Gospel of the Egyptians* found at Nag Hammadi that is inappropriately labeled a gospel. Origen (third century) listed the *Gospel of the Egyptians* as an example of a heretical gospel.

Clement's quotations of the *Gospel of the Egyptians* indicate that the work was apparently a dialogue between Jesus and Salome. The gospel promoted asceticism, particularly in regard to sexuality, and repudiated marriage and procreation. The work apparently taught that the ultimate goal of humanity would be "when the two shall be one, and the male with the female, and there is neither male nor female,"[11] that is, the total elimination of sexual differences. Such ideas are similar to ones found in various Gnostic writings, particularly the *Gospel of Thomas*. In fact, a variant of this saying is found in the *Gospel of Thomas*, suggesting that the *Gospel of the Egyptians* may be directly dependent on the *Gospel of Thomas* (Salome also appears in the *Gospel of Thomas*).

Sayings Gospels

One method of passing on the Jesus traditions was to collect and preserve the sayings attributed to him. The two clearest examples of this gospel type are Q and the *Gospel of Thomas*. As discussed in chapter 1, the letter "Q" is used to designate the hypothetical sayings source that was used by Matthew and Luke when they wrote their Gospels. Although no copy of Q has survived, most New Testament scholars today are convinced that such a collection of the sayings of Jesus circulated soon after the death of Jesus and was an important resource for early Christianity. For scholars' proposals concerning the contents of this work, see the discussion in chapter 1.

Gospel of Thomas. For modern scholars, the *Gospel of Thomas* is probably the most important of all the apocryphal gospels. Consisting of 114 sayings or small groups of sayings, this work bears a stronger resemblance to the canonical Gospels than do any of the other apocryphal gospels. This affinity lies not in its format (it contains no narratives) but in its content. Many of the sayings in the *Gospel of Thomas* are extremely similar to sayings found in the New Testament Gospels. In the opinion of many scholars, the versions of the sayings in the *Gospel of Thomas* are in many cases earlier versions than are the parallel sayings in the canonical Gospels. They base this conclusion on claims that the Thomas versions display fewer theological developments of the later church, contain less allegorical elements, or are closer to a Palestinian Jewish milieu than the canonical versions.

In addition to preserving possibly earlier versions of sayings that are in the canonical Gospels, the *Gospel of Thomas* also contains some otherwise unknown sayings of Jesus. Even scholars who are hesitant to admit any authentic Jesus traditions in the other apocryphal gospels are sometimes willing to accept that the *Gospel of Thomas* possibly contains authentic sayings of Jesus.

A Coptic version (Coptic was the ancient language of Egypt) of the text of the *Gospel of Thomas* was discovered in Nag Hammadi, Egypt, in 1945. Several decades earlier, three fragments of a Greek version of this work had been discovered in Oxyrhynchus, Egypt, although the identity of these fragments was not known until the Nag Hammadi documents were found. The *Gospel of Thomas* was likely originally written in the Greek language, probably in Syria. The Greek fragments found at Oxyrhynchus have been dated to the third century. Hippolytus, a church leader in Rome, quotes a saying from the *Gospel of Thomas* early in the third century. The latest date for the composition of the gospel would be the end of the second century. How early the gospel was actually written is strongly debated. Some scholars are convinced that the *Gospel of Thomas*, or at least an earlier version of it, was produced during the latter half of the first century (perhaps as early as the 60s or 70s), making the work a contemporary of the canonical Gospels, possibly even a contemporary of Q. Other scholars argue that it is a second-century work, later than the canonical Gospels.

The date of the *Gospel of Thomas* is tightly intertwined with the most vexing problem of this work, its literary relationship to the canonical Gospels. Was the *Gospel of Thomas* dependent on the canonical Gospels as sources? Were the canonical Gospels dependent on the *Gospel of Thomas*? Or do the New Testament Gospels and the *Gospel of Thomas* draw upon separate, independent traditions? Obviously if the *Gospel of Thomas* was not composed until the second century, the New Testament Gospels could not have used it as a source. Many scholars would argue for the late dating of the work and see it as a compilation and reworking of sayings from the New Testament, supplemented with additional sayings from Gnostic circles. John P. Meier, for instance, concludes that "the more probable hypothesis is that the *Gospel of Thomas* knew and used at least some of the canonical Gospels, notably Matthew and Luke."[12]

Few, if any scholars would insist that the canonical Gospels were directly dependent on the *Gospel of Thomas*. Some would, however, argue that the *Gospel of Thomas* is independent of the canonical Gospels and preserves early, independent (and sometimes closer to the original) traditions of Jesus. Ron Cameron, for example, is representative of several scholars who are convinced that

> the sayings in the *Gospel of Thomas* are either preserved in forms more primitive than those in the parallel sayings in the New Testament or are developments of more primitive forms of such sayings. . . . All of this suggests that the *Gospel of Thomas* is based on a tradition of sayings which is closely related to that of the canonical gospels but which has experienced a separate process of transmission. The composition of the *Gospel of Thomas*, therefore, is parallel to that of the canonical gospels.[13]

At the present time these questions about the date, sources, and reliability of the *Gospel of Thomas* remain unresolved.

The sayings in the *Gospel of Thomas* are of several types, including parables, beatitudes, community rules, proverbs, and prophetic sayings. These do not appear to be organized on the basis of any overall structure, other than some grouped by similar type or similar content. Scarcely any narrative joins the sayings together; rather, the sayings follow one after the other, introduced usually by "Jesus said." The *Gospel of Thomas* contains no traditions about Jesus' death or resurrection. Neither does it present any future eschatological sayings. The Jesus of the *Gospel of Thomas* is a teacher of esoteric wisdom.

Among the sayings that parallel New Testament traditions are the following:[14]

> Jesus said, "Now the sower went out, took a handful (of seeds), and scattered them. Some fell on the road; the birds came and gathered them up. Others fell on rock, did not take root in the soil, and did not produce ears. And others fell on thorns; they choked the seed(s) and worms ate them. And others fell on the good soil and it produced good fruit: it bore sixty per measure and a hundred and twenty per measure. (Saying 9; cf. Mark 4:1-9; Matt 13:3-9; Luke 8:4-8)
>
> Jesus said, "You (sg.) see the mote in your brother's eye, but you do not see the beam in your own eye. When you cast the beam out of your own eye, then you will see clearly to cast the mote from your brother's eye. (Saying 26; cf. Matt 7:1-5; Luke 6:41-42)
>
> Jesus said, "Blessed are the poor, for yours is the kingdom of heaven." (Saying 54; cf. Matt 5:3; Luke 6:20)
>
> They showed Jesus a gold coin and said to him, "Caesar's men demand taxes from us." He said to them, "Give Caesar what belongs to Caesar, give God what belongs to God, and give me what is mine." (Saying 100; cf. Mark 12:13-17; Matt 22:15-22; Luke 20:20-26)

A significant portion of the sayings in the *Gospel of Thomas* have no New Testament parallel. Several of these sayings appear to have a Gnostic flavoring (yet some scholars deny any Gnostic elements in the *Gospel of Thomas*). Examples of these would include:

> Jesus said, "Blessed are the solitary and elect, for you will find the kingdom. For you are from it, and to it you will return. (Saying 49; Gnosticism taught that humanity, or some persons at least, possessed a special, divine substance, called a "soul," a "spirit," or a "spark." Through correct knowledge one could be set free from the physical world and return to one's heavenly home.)
>
> Jesus said, "If they say to you, 'Where did you come from?', say to them, 'We came from the light, the place where the light came into being on its own accord and established [itself] and became manifest through their image.' If they say to you, 'Is it you?', say, 'We are its children, and we are the elect of the living father.' If they ask you, 'What is the sign of your father in you?', say to them, 'It is movement and repose' " (Saying 50).

Simon Peter said to them, "Let Mary leave us, for women are not worthy of life."

Jesus said, "I myself shall lead her in order to make her male, so that she too may become a living spirit resembling you males. For every woman who will make herself male will enter the kingdom of heaven. (Saying 114. "To make herself male" perhaps means metaphorically to renounce the physical world, especially sensuality and sexuality, including childbearing, since procreation continued the evil, material world. Also sexual differentiation was seen in Gnosticism as a product of the evil creator demiurge.)

Among the remaining sayings that have no parallel in the New Testament, a few of them sound like they could have come from Jesus. It is plausible that some of these sayings do in fact go back to the historical Jesus, but we have no way of knowing which, if any, actually are authentic. Some examples of authentic-sounding sayings are the following:

Jesus said, "He who is near me is near the fire, and he who is far from me is far from the kingdom." (Saying 82)

Jesus said, "The kingdom of the [father] is like a certain woman who was carrying a [jar] full of meal. While she was walking [on the] road, still some distance from home, the handle of the jar broke and the meal emptied out behind her [on] the road. She did not realize it; she had noticed no accident. When she reached her house, she set the jar down and found it empty. (Saying 97)

Jesus said, "The kingdom of the father is like a certain man who wanted to kill a powerful man. In his own house he drew his sword and stuck it into the wall in order to find out whether his hand could carry through. Then he slew the powerful man. (Saying 98)

The Process of Canonization

How did the Christian church move from a myriad of "gospels" to officially recognizing only four works as authentically preserving the traditions about Jesus? The term "canonization" refers to this process of selecting which writings are considered to be authoritative for a religious community. (The Greek word *kanōn* means "rule" or "standard." The word "canon" came to mean a standard list or an authoritative guide.) As we have seen, by the beginning of the second century all four New Testament Gospels were in circulation in various Christian communities in the Mediterranean world. The sayings collection Q had been in use as early as the middle of the first century, as had possibly the *Gospel of Thomas*. During the second century, several other works were in use that claimed to present traditions about Jesus. Various Christian groups and Christian leaders accepted as authoritative and quoted from some of these apocryphal gospels. For example, Eusebius, the fourth-century church historian, describes how Serapion, the bishop of Antioch, in order to resolve disagreements in the church of Rhossus once gave permission to the members to read in church from the *Gospel of Peter* (*Ecclesiastical History* 6.12). This occurred around 200 CE. At the time, Serapion had not read the *Gospel of Peter*. Later, after learning the contents of this work, Serapion wrote to the church and rescinded his earlier permission.

This proliferation of gospels was counterbalanced by the attempt of some individuals to have only one authoritative gospel. The multiplicity of gospels in the church was viewed as a theological as well as a practical problem. If there was only one true "gospel" (that is, the message about Jesus), then how could there be many "gospels"? Furthermore, which gospel was the correct one? The attempts to have a single gospel were efforts to solve these problems. Marcion with his acceptance of only the Gospel of Luke, as well as Tatian with his harmony of the four Gospels (the *Diatessaron*), are the clearest examples of this trend. Neither of these two single gospels ultimately succeeded, as we discussed in chapter 1, but the *Diatessaron* did remain popular among Christians in Syria until the fifth century.

One of the earliest references we have to the use of the Gospels in the church comes from the second-century Christian leader Justin Martyr. In his writings Justin refers to the "memoirs of the apostles," which on the basis of the quotations he gives, seems to be a reference to the synoptic Gospels.[15] These memoirs were read in public worship and served as instructions and guides for the life of the church. Apparently Justin did not include the Gospel of John as a part of the "memoirs of the apostles," either because he was not aware of it or because he did not consider it on the same level as the Synoptics.

This exclusion of the Gospel of John was not limited to Justin. Other Christians also viewed the fourth Gospel with suspicion. Even as late as the fourth century, there were some Christians who did not accept the Gospel of John. The reason for its rejection by some Christian groups was that it was popular in Gnostic and Montanist circles, leading others to view it as tainted or suspect. (Montanism was a late-second-century movement that emphasized prophecy and the workings of the Holy Spirit. It was soon condemned as heretical.) Harry Gamble has suggested that another reason for the early unpopularity of the Gospel of John may have been the "recognition of its extensive differences in outline, substance, and style from other, more popular gospels. Rather than try to reconcile these, it was easier to neglect John altogether."[16]

By the end of the second century the church was moving to a recognition of only four gospels as authoritative, although this restriction to a fourfold Gospel canon was not yet uniform. Irenaeus, writing around 180, argued extensively for four, and only four, Gospels. The arguments of Irenaeus seem rather far-fetched, perhaps as much to ancient readers as to us today. Irenaeus says,

> It is not possible that the Gospels can be either more or fewer in number than they are. For, since there are four zones of the world in which we live, and four principal winds, while the Church has been scattered throughout all the world, and the "pillar and ground" of the church is the Gospel and the spirit of life; it is fitting that she should have four pillars. . . . From which fact, it is evident that the Word . . . has given us the Gospel under four aspects but bound together by one Spirit.[17]

The arguments by Irenaeus are directed both against those who would restrict the Gospels to fewer than four and against those who would include more than four Gospels as authoritative. Marcion's attempt to limit the Gospels to the Gospel of Luke only, as well as the use of numerous other gospels by various individuals and groups, was probably an important factor in Christianity's affirming a fourfold Gospel canon.

Although there continued to be some minor variations in practice, the recognition of the Gospels of Matthew, Mark, Luke, and John as the only Gospels that were authoritative for the belief and practices of the church quickly established itself as the norm from approximately the middle of the third century onward. This is evident in the various canonical lists that began to appear, as well as in the writings of early church leaders.

What factors were at work in the choosing of the four canonical Gospels? Why were these works chosen and others rejected? It is important to realize that no church council or committee met to decide which gospels should be deemed acceptable. Rather, as the church struggled to define the boundaries of acceptable beliefs and practices, including which books were proper for worship and study, the recognition of these specific four Gospels as the normative ones for Christianity gradually occurred. Several criteria appear to have been instrumental in the church reaching a consensus about the canon. Among these criteria were (1) apostolic nature of the writing, (2) orthodoxy, (3) antiquity, and (4) widespread usage.

Apostolic Nature

The four New Testament Gospels were all assumed to have been written by an apostle (Matthew and John) or someone closely connected with an apostle (Luke and Mark). The claim of apostolicity was an attempt to ensure the accuracy of the traditions that the Gospels contained. In these Gospels, the church declared, were the reliable teachings and deeds of Jesus. Apostolicity imparted to these writings almost an eyewitness quality. These were the works from the earliest period of the church's history. The apostolic character of the writings was especially important once the original followers of Jesus had passed from the scene. They could no longer be consulted nor could they serve as guarantors of the tradition. Thus a writing's ability to claim some connection with the apostles was seen as a safeguard.

The claim of apostolic authorship, however, was not by itself decisive in determining canonical status. Several other works, as we have seen, also claimed apostolic authorship. The *Gospel of Peter*, for example, claims to have been written by Simon Peter, yet it was rejected by the church. Thus, the works chosen had to meet other criteria as well. We should note, also, that if the criterion of apostolicity were being enforced strictly today, then none of the four Gospels would likely be acceptable. As we have seen in chapter one, modern critical scholars seriously question the traditional claims of authorship of the Gospels. Many scholars would conclude that none of the Gospels can legitimately claim apostolic authorship.

Orthodoxy

One of the tasks facing the early Christian communities was the differentiation between acceptable belief and practices and unacceptable ones. The actions of Marcion to reject all Gospels other than Luke has often been cited as the major catalyst that forced the church to decide what works were acceptable. Although such an assessment of Marcion may overly emphasize his importance, his truncated canon likely was one factor in the church's move to demarcate its sacred writings. Other variant expressions of Christianity, such as Gnosticism and Montanism, also contributed to the need to decide which gospels contained reliable tradition. The application of this criterion is seen in the actions of the bishop Serapion in his rescinding permission for the church at Rhossus to continue reading from the *Gospel of Peter* in public worship. He rejected this work because he considered it a Docetic work. (Docetism was a belief—declared heretical by the church—that Jesus was not truly human; he only appeared to have a real body.)

As important as was the concern for correct doctrine in the development of the canon, the distinction between orthodoxy and heresy was not always an easy one to make in the early period of the Christian movement. A variety of Christian views and Christian groups coexisted, each vying for acceptance as the normative expression of the faith. Certainly from the standpoint of the later church, many of these views were heretical. In early Christianity, however, the labels "heresy" and "orthodoxy" are somewhat anachronistic. From a historical standpoint, one must say that "orthodoxy" is the belief that triumphs, while "heresy" is the belief that loses.

The diversity of early Christian beliefs is seen even in the four canonical Gospels. As the previous chapters have demonstrated, the authors of Matthew, Mark, Luke, and John did not see eye to eye in their understanding of Jesus of Nazareth. They each presented a different portrait of Jesus, a portrait determined by their own historical and sociological circumstances and their own theological interests. So even within the boundaries of orthodoxy, the church found room for diversity. The Jesus of John did not have to sound like the Jesus of Mark. Luke was allowed to tell the "good news" differently from Matthew. By restricting the canon to these four Gospels, however, the church said that there was a limit to that diversity. Matthew, Mark, Luke, and John—yes; the *Gospel of Peter*, the *Gospel of Thomas*, and the *Infancy Gospel of Thomas*—no. The author of the Muratorian Canon (a listing of canonical Christian writings that has been dated variously to the second century and the fourth century) commented on this diversity, yet unity, of the four New Testament Gospels when he wrote,

> And therefore, though various ideas are taught in the several books of the Gospels, yet it makes no difference to the faith of believers, since by one sovereign Spirit all things are declared in all of them concerning the Nativity, the Passion, the Resurrection, the conversation with his disciples

and his two comings, the first in lowliness and contempt, which has come to pass, the second glorious with royal power, which is to come.[18]

Antiquity

This criterion is related to the criterion of apostolicity. The church valued most highly those writings that came from the earliest period of the church because those were the works that were most closely connected with the apostles themselves and with the earliest Christian traditions. One should note that of all the gospels produced in the second century and later, none survived the scrutiny of the church and became a part of its official collection of scriptures, although for a while some were popular in certain areas. As with apostolicity, antiquity alone was not sufficient for a work to reach canonical status. Some ultimately rejected works, such as the *Gospel of Thomas* and the *Gospel of Peter*, possibly were written as early as or even earlier than the canonical Gospels.

Widespread Usage

Of all the criteria that affected the decisions about canonicity, widespread usage was probably the most important. No committee or church authority decided the question of canon. Granted, in later years various church councils or bishops made official pronouncements about the canon. But in reality, they were basically putting their stamp of approval on what had already become common practice. Thus the Gospels that survived and were popular were the ones that became the guideposts for the Christian church. Works that did not achieve widespread acceptance but were rather the favored writings of localized groups eventually lost out. Certainly the support of influential church leaders also enhanced a writing's status and helped it gain support and acceptance.

One could still ask, though, why these particular Gospels survived and others did not. Primarily, the writings that best met the needs of the churches for worship, teaching, proclamation, and guidance are the works that persisted and gained canonical status. They were widely used and accepted because they spoke to the needs of the churches. The church claimed that in these Gospels more than the others, the authentic traditions of Jesus could be found, traditions that the church cherished and to which it turned for guidance and support. In these documents, the Christian communities said, the words and deeds of Jesus most clearly continue to speak and address his followers.

The Gospels and the Historical Jesus

Our study began with a discussion of the nature of the canonical Gospels. We pointed out that the four Gospels are not historical accounts of the life of Jesus; rather they are stories about him, four different stories intended to present the individual Gospel writer's interpretation of the meaning and significance of Jesus of Nazareth. As interpretive, rather than strictly historical, accounts the Gospels present more of an impressionistic portrait of Jesus than a photograph of Jesus. The Gospel writers were not so much concerned to present the historical facts about Jesus as they were to present their understanding of the theological truth about Jesus.

Modern readers of the Gospel, however, are often not content with just a portrait of Jesus. They want to know the "facts" about Jesus. What did he do? Did he really perform miracles? Was he the product of a miraculous conception (the "virgin birth")? Was he really raised from the dead? What did he teach? Did he see himself as the Messiah? These and other questions comprise the search for the "historical Jesus." Scholars and laypersons throughout history have set off on this search for Jesus, hoping to peel back the layers of tradition and find the "flesh and blood" Jesus whose portraits hang in the galleries of the Gospels.

Unfortunately, other than the New Testament Gospels, our sources of information about the historical Jesus are almost non-existent. The Roman historian Tacitus, writing in the second century CE, mentions Jesus briefly, but the only information he provides is that Jesus had followers and was crucified by Pontius Pilate (*Annals* 15.44). Josephus, the Jewish historian of the first century CE, also mentions Jesus in two of his works, at least in the versions of those works as they now exist. The first text, likely genuine, identifies Jesus as the brother of James and as the one who was called the Messiah (*Jewish Antiquities* 20§200). Scholars have raised serious questions about the authenticity of the second of these texts of Josephus, suggesting that some references to Jesus are perhaps later Christian interpolations. In the portions of that text that a majority of scholars seem willing to accept as authentically by Josephus, he describes Jesus as a wise man who had followers, was a teacher, performed "startling deeds," was crucified by

Pilate, and continued to have followers (*Jewish Antiquities* 18§63-64). Later Jewish rabbinic writings occasionally mention Jesus, but they do not add much to what we have found already in Josephus.

The apocryphal gospels and other ancient Christian writings are another possible source of information about the historical Jesus. In the opinion of some scholars, a few of these works may indeed contain authentic historical traditions about Jesus, especially the *Gospel of Thomas*. Recently a group of North American biblical scholars called the Jesus Seminar has attempted to determine the historicity of the sayings of Jesus contained in the New Testament Gospels and the *Gospel of Thomas*. Their approach has been to consider each of these works, including the *Gospel of Thomas*, as on equal footing. Each contains a mixture of authentic materials plus embellished or created traditions. They have published the results of their study in a book entitled, *The Five Gospels: The Search for the Authentic Words of Jesus*. Not all New Testament scholars, however, are as certain as the Jesus Seminar about the reliability of noncanonical writings for information about the historical Jesus. Most scholars take a more cautious approach, restricting their search for Jesus information to the canonical Gospels.

If the main sources of information about Jesus, then, are the New Testament Gospels, and if those works are more impressionistic portraits than realistic photographs, how does one reconstruct the historical Jesus? At the outset, one important point needs to be emphasized. To claim that the Gospels are not historical writings in the modern sense of the term but are interpreted stories of Jesus does not mean that the Gospels are devoid of any historical information about Jesus of Nazareth. The Gospel writers certainly convey authentic information about Jesus and his social, political, and religious situation. The problem is that historical information is mixed with interpretations, embellishments, and additions to the story. The task of the scholar is to find a way to unravel the Gospel stories, to separate the threads of historical information from the nonhistorical traditions. Several criteria have been developed to help in this "unraveling" process. The most commonly used criteria are (1) dissimilarity, (2) multiple attestation, (3) embarrassment, (4) Palestinian environment, and (5) coherence.

Criterion of Dissimilarity

The criterion of dissimilarity looks for sayings or events in the life of Jesus that are dissimilar both to traditions from first-century Judaism and to practices or beliefs of the early church. The idea is that the dissimilar materials are more likely to be original to Jesus and not borrowed from Judaism or created by the church and subsequently read back into the life of Jesus. This criterion, then, looks for the ways in which Jesus stood out from his culture and from the church that revered him. An example of a tradition that is "doubly dissimilar" is Jesus' prohibition against fasting for his disciples (Mark 2:18-22). Fasting was a common act of religious devotion in first-century Judaism. The Christian church likewise called for fasting on occasion as a sign of piety. Thus this rejection of fasting by Jesus is rather striking and probably an authentic Jesus tradition.

An obvious problem with this criterion, however, is that what results from its use is a rather skewed picture of Jesus. Certainly Jesus was in many ways similar to the Judaism of his day. He was, after all, a devout Palestinian Jew himself. One would expect also to find traditions about Jesus that were similar to ones in the later church because the church understood itself as being shaped and informed by those traditions. To apply this rule strictly would be to cut off Jesus from both his surrounding culture and from his future influence. Thus the criterion of dissimilarity can help discern what is likely authentic (traditions that are dissimilar) but it cannot determine what traditions are not authentic (traditions that are similar may still be from Jesus).

The Criterion of Multiple Attestation

This criterion states that traditions that are found in more than one source—sources that are independent of one another—or in more than one form (parable, miracle story, controversy story) have a greater likelihood of being authentic. Thus a saying that is found in both Mark and Q or both Mark and John would be deemed to have a stronger argument for reliability than one found only in Mark. Jesus' prohibition against divorce, which is found in Mark 10:11 and in Q (Luke 16:18), is an example of a tradition that meets the criterion of multiple attestation. Again, one must note the weakness of using this criterion. A tradition could appear in more than one source and still not be authentic. Furthermore, that a tradition survives in only one source or only one form does not necessarily mean that the tradition is unreliable.

The Criterion of Embarrassment

This criterion is related to the criterion of dissimilarity. Sayings or activities that would have been an embarrassment to the early church are not likely to have been created by the church and thus have a greater chance of being authentic. The baptism of Jesus by John the Baptist is a good example. Jesus' baptism created theological problems for the church because it proclaimed that Jesus was sinless. Yet John's baptism was a baptism of repentance for sins. Why then did Jesus need to be baptized? The early church would not likely have created this story if it had not already been a part of the tradition.

The Criterion of Palestinian Environment

In using this criterion scholars look for traditions that are compatible with the Palestinian environment of Jesus' time. Sayings or activities that are out of place are deemed unlikely to be authentic. Mark 10:12 fails this criterion because it presents Jesus as referring to the practice of a woman divorcing her husband. Jewish divorce law did not permit a woman to divorce her husband. Roman law did, however. Thus this verse was likely a creation of Mark or someone earlier who was reflecting Roman legal traditions.

The Criterion of Coherence

The criterion of coherence is dependent on the prior use of some of the other criteria. The criterion of coherence says that a saying or deed has a good chance of being authentic if it is consistent with previously determined information about Jesus. Using this criterion a scholar asks, "Does this story or saying sound like what we already know about Jesus?" This criterion has often been used to argue for the authenticity of the story in John 7:53–8:11, the story of the woman caught in adultery. Even though this story was almost certainly not originally a part of the Gospel of John, a large number of New Testament scholars would consider it an authentic event from the life of Jesus because the story is consistent with the character and teachings of Jesus.

Attempts to discover the historical Jesus are studies in probability, that is, they are attempts to determine what events or sayings are most likely to have come from Jesus. Certainty can never be achieved in such a quest.

The best scholars can do is present the information that, based on their critical studies, seems to have the best chance of having originated with the historical Jesus. As one would suspect, scholars do not always agree on their views of the historical Jesus. As a result, a variety of "lives of Jesus" have been written over the years. Several excellent studies have been published recently, including works by John Dominic Crossan, Marcus Borg, Geza Vermes, E. P. Sanders, John P. Meier, N. T. Wright, and Raymond Brown.

Our task in this study has been to examine the presentation of Jesus by the Gospel writers, not to explore the questions and issues surrounding the quest for the historical Jesus nor to present a reconstruction of the life and teachings of Jesus based on historical inquiry. As important as are those pursuits, they are beyond the purview of this study. The student interested in pursuing those topics should consult some of the works listed in the bibliography.

The question "Who was Jesus of Nazareth?" is a question that people have been trying to answer for nearly two thousand years. The four Gospels in the New Testament represent some of the attempts of the early church to answer that question. By preserving all four Gospels—Matthew, Mark, Luke, and John—in its canon, the church gave witness to the idea that no one understanding of Jesus was sufficient. Each Gospel needed to be supplemented by the insights of the others. Yet in the midst of this diversity of Gospel presentations, the church proclaimed a unity, that is, the church said there is only one "gospel"—one message of "good news"—that is proclaimed in four different ways by the Gospel writers. This vision of one gospel in four different forms is seen in the titles that the church attached to the Gospels (the Gospel According to Matthew, the Gospel According to Mark, the Gospel According to Luke, the Gospel According to John). The titles of these works were likely first attached to them in the second century when they were brought together as a group. The church did not see these as four different "gospels" but one gospel in four versions ("according to").

In examining each of the Gospel writers' portrait of Jesus as we have done in this study, we have been faithful, then, to the understanding of the early church. We have sought four different portraits, each with its distinctive—and at times contrasting—understanding of Jesus of Nazareth. Yet as different as the four portraits are, they are still portraits of the same person. By recognizing and appreciating the similarities as well as the differences in the four Gospels, we have gained a better understanding of Jesus and the early church that preserved his memory.

Notes

❖

1. The Formation of the Four Gospels

1. Shaye J. D. Cohen, *From the Maccabees to the Mishnah* (Philadelphia: Westminster, 1987) 120.

2. Cf. John P. Meier, *A Marginal Jew: Rethinking the Historical Jesus*, vol. 1 (New York: Doubleday, 1991) 274: "Neither social expectations, government programs, nor demands of the marketplace created the conditions necessary for a high degree of literacy in the general population."

3. Eusebius, *Ecclesiastical History* 3.39.4, trans. Kirsopp Lake. Loeb Classical Library (Cambridge: Harvard University Press, 1980) 293.

4. Cited by Helmut Koester, *Ancient Christian Gospels: Their History and Development* (Philadelphia: Trinity Press International, 1990) 3-4.

5. James L. Bailey and Lyle D. Vander Broek, *Literary Forms in the New Testament: A Handbook* (Louisville: Westminster/John Knox, 1992) 91.

6. Charles H. Talbert, *What Is a Gospel? The Genre of the Canonical Gospels* (Philadelphia: Fortress, 1977), 17.

7. David E. Aune, *The New Testament in Its Literary Environment* (Philadelphia: Westminster, 1987) 17-76. See also David E. Aune, "Greco-Roman Biography," *Greco-Roman Literature and the New Testament*, ed. David E. Aune (Atlanta: Scholars Press, 1988) 107-26.

8. Thucydides, *History of the Peloponnesian War* 1.22.1, trans. Charles Forster Smith. Loeb Classical Library (New York: G. P. Putnam's Sons, 1928) 39.

9. Compare the information given in Luke 1:5, 36.

10. No copy of the Diatessaron has survived today. Scholars have partially reconstructed the text of Tatian's work by using quotations of and commentaries on the Diatessaron found in later works and by using translations of the Gospels that were apparently based on the Diatessaron. In addition to using the four canonical Gospels, Tatian seems to have used other sources for his harmony of the life of Jesus.

11. Raymond F. Collins, *Introduction to the New Testament* (Garden City, N.Y.: Doubleday & Co., 1983) 129.

12. William R. Farmer, *The Synoptic Problem: A Critical Analysis* (New York: Macmillan, 1964).

13. John S. Kloppenborg, *The Formation of Q: Trajectories in Ancient Wisdom Collections* (Philadelphia: Fortress Press, 1987) 92. Verses and parentheses are disputed by some scholars concerning their position in the order of Q (16:16) or their existence in Q (12:13-14, 16-21).

14. C. K. Barrett, *The Gospel According to St. John: An Introduction with Commentary and Notes on the Greek Text*, 2d ed., (Philadelphia: Westminster, 1978) 43.

15. Eusebius, *Ecclesiastical History* 3.39.15.

16. Eusebius, *Ecclesiastical History* 3.39.16.

17. Vernon K. Robbins, "By Land and by Sea: The We-Passages and Ancient Sea Voyages," *Perspectives on Luke-Acts*, ed. C. H. Talbert (Danville, Va.: National Association of Baptist Professors of Religion, 1978) 215-42.

18. Irenaeus, *Against Heresies* 3.1.1, in *The Ante-Nicene Fathers*, ed. Alexander Roberts and James Donaldson, vol. 1 (New York: Charles Scribner's Sons, 1899) 414.

2. The World of the Gospels

1. The name Septuagint, meaning "seventy," is derived from a tradition reported in the *Letter of Aristeas* that seventy or seventy-two Jewish scholars worked on the translation. The Roman numeral for seventy, LXX, is used as an abbreviation for the Septuagint.

2. Josephus, *Jewish Antiquities* 17§175-79; 17§193; *Jewish War* 1 659-69.

3. Philo, *Embassy to Gaius* 146-149, trans. F. H. Colson. Loeb Classical Library (Cambridge: Harvard University Press, 1962) 75-77.

4. Cited by Helmut Koester, *Ancient Christian Gospels: Their History and Development* (Philadelphia: Trinity Press International, 1990) 4-5.

5. Josephus, *Jewish Antiquities* 18§§81-84.

6. Tacitus, *Annals* 15.44, trans. John Jackson. Loeb Classical Library (Cambridge: Harvard University Press, 1937) 285.

7. S. Safrai, "Education and the Study of the Torah," S. Safrai and M. Stern, ed., *The Jewish People in the First Century*, vol. 2 (Philadelphia: Fortress, 1976) 946.

8. Meier, *A Marginal Jew*, 1:282.

9. S. Applebaum, "Economic Life in Palestine," S. Safrai and M. Stern, *The Jewish People in the First Century*, vol. 2 (Philadelphia: Fortress, 1976) 683.

10. Sean Freyne, *Galilee, Jesus, and the Gospels: Literary Approaches and Historical Investigations* (Philadelphia: Fortress, 1988) 153-55.

11. F. F. Bruce, "Travel and Communication (NT World)," *The Anchor Bible Dictionary* (New York: Doubleday, 1992) 6:650.

12. See Emil Schürer, *The History of the Jewish People in the Age of Jesus Christ (175 B.C.–A.D. 135)* English version rev. and ed. by Geza Vermes, Fergus Millar, and Matthew Black (Edinburgh: T & T Clark, 1979) 2:260-73, for a detailed discussion of these various offerings and taxes.

13. See John J. Rousseau and Rami Arav, "Tax and Tax Collectors," *Jesus and His World: An Archaeological and Cultural Dictionary* (Minneapolis: Fortress, 1995) 275-79; Richard A. Horsley, with John S. Hanson, *Bandits, Prophets, and Messiahs: Popular Movements at the Time of Jesus* (San Francisco: Harper & Row, 1985) 54-61.

14. See Horsley and Hanson, *Bandits, Prophets, and Messiahs* 58-61.

15. Freyne, *Galilee, Jesus, and the Gospels* 147.

16. S. Scott Bartchy, "Slavery (Greco-Roman)," *The Anchor Bible Dictionary* (New York: Doubleday, 1992) 6:66.

17. Carol Meyers, "Temple, Jerusalem," *The Anchor Bible Dictionary* (New York: Doubleday, 1992) 6:365.

18. S. Safrai, "The Temple," S. Safrai and M. Stern, *The Jewish People in the First Century* (Philadelphia: Fortress, 1976) 867.

19. Josephus, *Jewish War* 2§165; Acts 23:8; Matt 22:23.

3. The Gospel of Mark

1. See p. 36 for an example of Mark's geographical errors.

2. Elizabeth Struthers Malbon, "Narrative Criticism: How Does the Story Mean?" *Mark and Method: New Approaches in Biblical Studies*, ed. Janice Capel Anderson and Stephen D. Moore (Minneapolis: Fortress, 1992) 32.

3. Wilhelm Wrede, *The Messianic Secret*, trans. J. C. G. Greig (Greenwood, S.C.: Attic, 1971).

4. The quotation, which Mark introduces as being from "the prophet Isaiah," is actually a composite drawn from Exod 23:20; Mal 3:1; and Isa 40:3.

5. Elizabeth Struthers Malbon, *Narrative Space and Mythic Meaning in Mark* (San Francisco: Harper & Row, 1986) 72-75.

6. The location of Gerasa is unknown. The textual tradition reflects the uncertainty of location. Some manuscripts contain the wording "country of the Gerasenes," others have "country of the Gergesenes," while still others have "country of the Gadarenes." The presence of pigs and the statement

that the cured man spreads abroad in the Decapolis what Jesus has done indicate that the location is in non-Jewish territory.

7. Werner H. Kelber, *Mark's Story of Jesus* (Philadelphia: Fortress, 1979) 58.

8. This saying is found in one of the tractates of the Talmud, *Sukka* 51.2.

9. If the Gospel of Mark originally contained verses beyond verse 8, the additional verses must have been lost very early. Apparently the copies of Mark used by the authors of the Gospels of Matthew and Luke stopped at verse 8. Both of these Gospels follow the events of Mark rather closely up to verse 8, after which they have extremely divergent accounts.

4. The Gospel of Matthew

1. Jack Dean Kingsbury, *Matthew*. Proclamation Commentaries, 2d ed. (Philadelphia: Fortress, 1986) 96-107. See also Jack Dean Kingsbury, *Matthew as Story*, 2d ed. (Philadelphia: Fortress, 1988) 147-60.

2. See for example W. D. Davies, *The Setting of the Sermon on the Mount* (Cambridge: Cambridge University Press, 1963) 256-315.

3. Kingsbury, *Matthew as Story* 40-42.

4. Robert Gundry, *A Commentary on His Literary and Theological Art* (Grand Rapids: Eerdmans, 1982) 10-11. In a similar vein Graham N. Stanton, *The Gospels and Jesus* (New York: Oxford University Press, 1989) 62, writes, "While it is clear that the evangelist has taken great care over the composition of the five major discourses and of numerous shorter sections, he does not seem to have developed a broad overall structure as a way of underlining his main purposes."

5. See the *Thanksgiving Hymns*, the *Habakkuk Commentary*, and the *Psalms Commentary* for examples of harsh rhetoric against the opponents of the Qumran group.

6. Although Matthew claims that each section of the genealogy contains fourteen generations, the last grouping actually contains only thirteen. See Raymond E. Brown, *The Birth of the Messiah*, rev. ed. (Garden City, N.Y.: Doubleday & Co., 1993) 57-95 for a discussion of Matthew's genealogy. Brown believes that for the most part Matthew found the arrangement of the material into groups of fourteen in the sources he used.

7. Some scholars count ten miracle stories. The number nine is arrived at by considering the healing of the daughter of the synagogue leader and the healing of the woman with a hemorrhage as one story. Understanding them in this way seems consistent with Matthew's predilection for arranging items in groups of threes.

8. Kingsbury, *Matthew as Story* 79.

9. Ibid., 154.

10. John P. Meier, *Matthew*, New Testament Message 3 (Collegeville, Minn.: Michael Glazier, 1980) 198.

11. Robert H. Smith, *Matthew*. Augsburg Commentary on the New Testament (Minneapolis: Augsburg, 1989) 242.

12. Kingsbury, *Matthew as Story* 88.

13. Smith, *Matthew* 328.

5. The Gospel of Luke

1. If Paul were actually the author of all thirteen letters traditionally attributed to him, then Paul also would have written approximately one fourth of the New Testament. Only seven of those letters, however, are considered to be definitely from Paul.

2. Frederick W. Danker, *Luke*, Proclamation Commentaries 2d ed. (Philadelphia: Fortress, 1987) 2.

3. This outline is drawn from R. Alan Culpepper, "The Gospel of Luke," *The New Interpreter's Bible*, vol. 9 (Nashville: Abingdon, 1995) 7.

4. Luke Timothy Johnson, "Luke-Acts, Book of," *The Anchor Bible Dictionary* (New York: Doubleday, 1992) 4:412.

5. Johnson, "Luke-Acts" 410.

6. Charles H. Talbert, *Reading Luke: A Literary and Theological Commentary on the Third Gospel* (New York: Crossroad, 1984) 240.

7. Bruce J. Malina and Richard L. Rohrbaugh, *Social-Science Commentary on the Synoptic Gospels* (Minneapolis: Fortress, 1992) 296.

8. Culpepper, "Gospel of Luke" 24-25.

9. Talbert, *Reading Luke* 7-11.

10. O. C. Edwards, Jr., *Luke's Story of Jesus* (Philadelphia: Fortress, 1981) 18-19. The summary given here is a condensed version of that given by Edwards.

11. Malina and Rohrbaugh, *Social Science Commentary* 28-31.

12. Edwards, *Luke's Story of Jesus* 24.

13. Malina and Rohrbaugh, *Social Science Commentary* 296, explain, "Peasant houses normally had only one room (cf. Matt. 5:15, where one lamp gives light to all in the house), though sometimes a guest room would have been attached. The family usually occupied one end of the main room (often raised) and the animals the other. A manger was located in between. The manger would have been the normal place for peasant births, with the women of the house assisting."

14. Edwards, *Luke's Story of Jesus* 28.

15. See Culpepper, "Gospel of Luke" 95.

16. Culpepper, "Gospel of Luke" 354.

17. Malina and Rohrbaugh, *Social Science Commentary* 387-88.

18. For a good discussion of the idea of Jesus as a martyr in Luke, see Talbert, *Reading Luke* 212-18.

6. The Gospel of John

1. This collection of benedictions is normally called the Eighteen Benedictions because the Palestinian version contains eighteen separate benedictions. The Babylonian version, however, contains nineteen.

2. Irenaeus, *Against Heresies* 3.1.1, in *The Ante-Nicene Fathers*, ed. Alexander Roberts and James Donaldson, vol. 1 (New York: Charles Scribner's Sons, 1899) 414.

3. C. K. Barrett, *The Gospel According to St. John* 2d. ed. (Philadelphia: Westminster, 1978) 7.

4. Robert Kysar, "John, Gospel of," *The Anchor Bible Dictionary* (New York: Doubleday, 1992) 3:928.

5. G. R. Beasley-Murray, *John*. Word Biblical Commentary (Waco: Word Books, 1987) lxv-lxvi.

6. Robert Kysar, *John's Story of Jesus* (Philadelphia: Fortress, 1984) 65-66.

7. Kysar, *John's Story of Jesus* 79-80.

8. Raymond E. Brown, *The Gospel According to John XIII-XXI*, The Anchor Bible (Garden City, N.Y.: Doubleday & Co., 1970) 858.

9. Robert Kysar, *John's Story of Jesus*, 85.

10. R. Alan Culpepper, *Anatomy of the Fourth Gospel: A Study in Literary Design* (Philadelphia: Fortress, 1983) 136.

11. Gail R. O'Day, *The New Interpreter's Bible* vol. 9 (Nashville: Abingdon Press, 1995) 9:841.

12. See, for example, Brown, *Gospel According to John* 1077-78. Brown gives three principal reasons for this consensus: (1) A definite ending of the Gospel occurs in 20:30-31. (2) A beatitude appears in 20:29 for those who believe without having seen Jesus. A subsequent appearance story seems awkward. (3) The episode in chapter 21 does not fit very well following chapter 20. Why would the disciples not recognize Jesus if he had already appeared to them? Why would they be back in Galilee pursuing mundane tasks if they had already seen the risen Jesus and been commissioned by him?

7. The Other Gospels

1. John P. Meier, *A Marginal Jew: Rethinking the Historical Jesus*, vol. 1 (New York: Doubleday, 1991) 1:143-4.

2. Helmut Koester, *Ancient Christian Gospels: Their History and Development* (Philadelphia: Trinity Press International, 1990) 46.

3. Stephen J. Patterson, "Gospels, Apocryphal," *The Anchor Bible Dictionary* (New York: Doubleday, 1992) 2:1080.

4. Philipp Vielhauer and Georg Strecker, "Jewish Christian Gospels," *New Testament Apocrypha*, ed. Wilhelm Schneemelcher, English trans. ed. R. McL. Wilson, vol. 1, rev. ed. (Louisville: Westminster/John Knox, 1991) 172.

5. John Dominic Crossan, *The Cross that Spoke: The Origins of the Passion Narrative* (San Francisco: Harper & Row, 1988) xiii-xiv, 16-30.

6. "The Gospel of Peter," trans. Christian Maurer, *New Testament Apocrypha*, Schneemelcher and Wilson, 1:224-25.

7. "The Infancy Story of Thomas," trans. Oscar Cullmann, *New Testament Apocrypha*, Schneemelcher and Wilson, 1:444, 447.

8. "The Dialogue of the Savior," introd. Helmut Koester and Elaine H. Pagels, trans. Stephen Emmel, in *The Nag Hammadi Library*, ed. James M. Robinson, 3d ed. (San Francisco: Harper & Row, 1988) 244-55.

9. "The Apocryphon of James," trans. Francis E. Williams, in Robinson, *Nag Hammadi Library*, 29-37.

10. "The Gospel of Mary," intro. Karen L. King, trans. George W. MacRae, R. McL. Wilson, ed. Douglas M. Parrott, in Robinson, *Nag Hammadi Library*, 523-27.

11. Clement of Alexandria, *Stromateis* 3.92, in *Alexandrian Christianity*, trans. and ed. John Ernest Leonard Oulton and Henry Chadwick. The Library of Christian Classics (Philadelphia: Westminster, 1954), 83.

12. Meier, *A Marginal Jew* 1:138-139.

13. Ron Cameron, ed., *The Other Gospels: Non-Canonical Gospel Texts* (Philadelphia: Westminster, 1982) 24.

14. All quotations from the *Gospel of Thomas* are from "The Gospel of Thomas," intro. Helmut Koester, trans. Thomas O. Lambdin, in Robinson, *Nag Hammadi Library*, 124-38.

15. Raymond F. Collins, *Introduction to the New Testament* (Garden City, N.Y.: Doubleday, 1983) 20-21.

16. Harry Y. Gamble, "Canon, New Testament," *The Anchor Bible Dictionary* (New York: Doubleday, 1992) 1:855.

17. Irenaeus, *Against Heresies* 3.11.8, in *The Ante-Nicene Fathers*, ed. Alexander Roberts and James Donaldson, vol. 1 (New York: Charles Scribner's Sons, 1899), 414.

18. Quoted by Collins, *Introduction to the New Testament* 33.

Selected Bibliography

❖

For further study, students should consult, in addition to the works listed here, the many excellent articles on a variety of topics related to the Gospels and Jesus that are in the six-volume *Anchor Bible Dictionary*.

Chapter 1. The Formation of the Four Gospels

Aune, David E., ed. *Greco-Roman Literature and the New Testament*. Atlanta: Scholars Press, 1988.
———. *The New Testament in Its Literary Environment*. Philadelphia: Westminster, 1987.
Bailey, James L., and Lyle D. Vander Broek. *Literary Forms in the New Testament: A Handbook*. Louisville: Westminster/John Knox, 1992.
Burridge, R. A. *What Are the Gospels? A Comparison with Greco-Roman Biography*. Cambridge: Cambridge University Press, 1992.
Collins, Raymond F. *Introduction to the New Testament*. Garden City, N.Y.: Doubleday & Co., 1983.
Kelber, Werner H. *The Oral and the Written Gospel*. Philadelphia: Fortress, 1983.
Koester, Helmut. *Ancient Christian Gospels: Their History and Development*. Philadelphia: Trinity Press International, 1990.
Kloppenborg, John S. *The Formation of Q: Trajectories in Ancient Wisdom Collections*. Philadelphia: Fortress, 1987.
Talbert, Charles H. *What Is a Gospel? The Genre of the Canonical Gospels*. Philadelphia: Fortress, 1977.

Chapter 2. The World of the Gospels

Boring, M. Eugene, Klaus Berger, and Carsten Colpe. *Hellenistic Commentary to the New Testament*. Nashville: Abingdon, 1995.
Cohen, Shaye J. D. *From the Maccabees to the Mishnah*. Philadelphia: Westminster, 1987.
Ferguson, Everett. *Backgrounds of Early Christianity*. 2d ed. Grand Rapids: Eerdmans, 1993.
Freyne, Sean. *Galilee, Jesus, and the Gospels: Literary Approaches and Historical Investigations*. Philadelphia: Fortress, 1988.
———. *The World of the New Testament*. New Testament Message 2. Wilmington, Del.: Michael Glazier, 1980.

Horsley, Richard A. with John S. Hanson. *Bandits, Prophets, and Messiahs: Popular Movements at the Time of Jesus*. San Francisco: Harper & Row, 1985.

Koester, Helmut. *Introduction to the New Testament*. Vol. 1, *History, Culture, and Religion of the Hellenistic Age*. Philadelphia: Fortress, 1982.

Malina, Bruce J. *The New Testament World: Insights from Cultural Anthropology*. Atlanta: John Knox, 1981.

_____ and Richard L. Rohrbaugh. *Social-Science Commentary on the Synoptic Gospels*. Minneapolis: Fortress, 1992.

Murphy, Frederick J. *The Religious World of Jesus: An Introduction to Second Temple Palestinian Judaism*. Nashville: Abingdon, 1991.

Rousseau, John J., and Rami Arav. *Jesus and His World: An Archaeological and Cultural Dictionary*. Minneapolis: Fortress, 1995.

Safrai, S., and M. Stern, eds. *The Jewish People in the First Christian Century: Historical Geography, Political History, Social, Cultural and Religious Life and Institutions*. 2 vols. Philadelphia: Fortress, 1974 and 1976.

Schürer, Emil. *The History of the Jewish People in the Age of Jesus Christ (175 B.C.–A.D. 135)*. English version revised and edited by Geza Vermes, Fergus Millar, and Martin Goodman. 3 vols. Edinburgh: T & T Clark, 1973–1987.

Stambaugh, John E., and David L. Balch. *The New Testament in Its Social Environment*. Philadelphia: Westminster, 1986.

Chapter 3. The Gospel of Mark

Achtemeier, Paul J. *Mark*. Proclamation Commentaries. 2d ed. Philadelphia: Fortress, 1986.

Anderson, Janice Capel, and Stephen D. Moore. *Mark and Method: New Approaches in Biblical Studies*. Minneapolis: Fortress, 1992.

Collins, Adela Yarbro. *The Beginning of the Gospel: Probings of Mark in Context*. Minneapolis: Fortress, 1992.

Fowler, Robert M. *Let the Reader Understand: Reader-Response Criticism and the Gospel of Mark*. Minneapolis: Fortress, 1991.

Juel, Donald H. *A Master of Surprise: Mark Interpreted*. Minneapolis: Fortress, 1994.

Kelber, Werner H. *Mark's Story of Jesus*. Philadelphia: Fortress, 1979.

Matera, Frank J. *What Are They Saying about Mark?* New York: Paulist, 1987.

Perkins, Pheme. "The Gospel of Mark." *The New Interpreter's Bible*. Vol. 8. Nashville: Abingdon, 1995.

Rhoads, David, and Donald Michie. *Mark as Story: An Introduction to the Narrative of a Gospel*. Philadelphia: Fortress, 1982.

Chapter 4. The Gospel of Matthew

Boring, M. Eugene. "The Gospel of Matthew." *The New Interpreter's Bible*. Vol. 8. Nashville: Abingdon, 1995.

Edwards, Richard A. *Matthew's Story of Jesus*. Philadelphia: Fortress, 1985.

Kingsbury, Jack Dean. *Matthew*. Proclamation Commentaries. 2d ed. Philadelphia: Fortress, 1986.

————. *Matthew as Story*. 2d ed. Philadelphia: Fortress, 1988.

————. *Matthew: Structure, Christology, Kingdom*. Philadelphia: Fortress, 1975.

Meier, John P. *Matthew*. New Testament Message 3. Wilmington, Del.: Michael Glazier, 1980.

Overman, J. Andrew. *Matthew's Gospel and Formative Judaism: The Social World of the Matthean Community*. Minneapolis: Fortress, 1990.

Senior, Donald. *What Are They Saying about Matthew?* New York: Paulist, 1996.

Smith, Robert H. *Matthew*. Augsburg Commentary on the New Testament. Minneapolis: Augsburg, 1989.

Chapter 5. The Gospel of Luke

Culpepper, R. Alan. "The Gospel of Luke." *The New Interpreter's Bible*. Vol. 9. Nashville: Abingdon, 1995.

Danker, Frederick W. *Luke*. Proclamation Commentaries. 2d ed. Philadelphia: Fortress, 1987.

Edwards, O. C., Jr., *Luke's Story of Jesus*. Philadelphia: Fortress, 1981.

Fitzmyer, Joseph A. *The Gospel According to Luke*. The Anchor Bible. 2 vols. New York: Doubleday, 1981, 1985.

Powell, Mark Allan. *What Are They Saying about Luke?* New York: Paulist, 1989.

Talbert, Charles H. *Reading Luke: A Literary and Theological Commentary on the Third Gospel*. New York: Crossroad, 1982.

Tannehill, Robert C. *The Narrative Unity of Luke-Acts: A Literary Interpretation*. Vol. 1, *The Gospel According to Luke*. Philadelphia: Fortress, 1986.

Tiede, David L. *Luke*. Augsburg Commentary on the New Testament. Minneapolis: Augsburg, 1988.

Chapter 6. The Gospel of John

Brown, Raymond E. *The Community of the Beloved Disciple*. New York: Paulist, 1979.

————. *The Gospel According to John*. 2 vols. The Anchor Bible. Garden City, N.Y.: Doubleday & Co., 1966, 1970.

Culpepper, R. Alan. *Anatomy of the Fourth Gospel: A Study in Literary Design*. Philadelphia: Fortress, 1983.

Duke, Paul D. *Irony in the Fourth Gospel*. Atlanta: John Knox, 1985.

Kysar, Robert. *John, the Maverick Gospel*. Atlanta: John Knox, 1976.

————. *John's Story of Jesus*. Philadelphia: Fortress, 1984.

O'Day, Gail R. "The Gospel of John." *The New Interpreter's Bible*. Vol. 9. Nashville: Abingdon, 1995.

Sloyan, Gerard S. *What Are They Saying about John?*. New York: Paulist, 1991.

Smith, D. Moody. *John*. Proclamation Commentaries. 2d ed. Philadelphia: Fortress, 1986.

Chapter 7. The Other Gospels

Apocryphal Gospels

Cameron, Ron, ed. *The Other Gospels: Non-Canonical Gospel Texts*. Philadelphia: Westminster, 1982.

Cartlidge, David R., and David L. Dungan. *Documents for the Study of the Gospels*. Philadelphia: Fortress, 1980.

Crossan, John Dominic. *The Cross that Spoke: The Origins of the Passion Narrative*. San Francisco: Harper & Row, 1988.

———. *Four Other Gospels: Shadows on the Contours of Canon*. Minneapolis: Winston, 1985.

Funk, Robert W., Roy W. Hoover, and the Jesus Seminar. *The Five Gospels: The Search for the Authentic Words of Jesus*. New York: Polebridge, 1993.

Koester, Helmut. *Ancient Christian Gospels: Their History and Development*. Philadelphia: Trinity Press International, 1990.

Miller, Robert J., ed. *The Complete Gospels: Annotated Scholars Version*. Rev. ed. Sonoma, Calif.: Polebridge, 1994.

Robinson, James M., gen. ed. *The Nag Hammadi Library*. 3d. ed. San Francisco: Harper & Row, 1988.

Schneemelcher, Wilhelm, ed. *New Testament Apocrypha*. English trans. edited by R. McL. Wilson. Vol. 1, *Gospels and Related Writings*. Rev. ed. Louisville: Westminster/John Knox, 1991.

Canonization

von Campenhausen, Hans. *The Formation of the Christian Bible*. Philadelphia: Fortress, 1972.

Collins, Raymond F. *Introduction to the New Testament*. Garden City, N.Y.: Doubleday & Co., 1983.

Gamble, Harry Y. *The New Testament Canon: Its Making and Meaning*. Guides to Biblical Scholarship. Philadelphia: Fortress, 1985.

McDonald, Lee Martin. *The Formation of the Christian Biblical Canon*. Nashville: Abingdon, 1988. Rev. ed. Peabody, Mass.: Hendrickson Publishers, 1996.

Historical Jesus

Borg, Marcus. *Meeting Jesus Again for the First Time*. San Francisco: HarperSanFrancisco, 1994.

Brown, Raymond. *The Birth of the Messiah: A Commentary on the Infancy Narratives of Matthew and Luke*. Rev. ed. Garden City, N.Y.: Doubleday, 1993.

———. *The Death of the Messiah*. 2 vols. New York: Doubleday, 1994.

Crossan, John Dominic. *The Historical Jesus: The Life of a Mediterranean Jewish Peasant*. San Francisco: HarperSanFrancisco, 1991.

———. *Jesus: A Revolutionary Biography*. San Francisco: HarperSanFrancisco, 1994.

Meier, John P. *A Marginal Jew: Rethinking the Historical Jesus*. 2 Vols. New York: Doubleday, 1991, 1994.

Sanders, E. P. *The Historical Figure of Jesus*. London: Penguin, 1993.

———. *Jesus and Judaism*. Philadelphia: Fortress, 1985.

Theissen, Gerd. *The Shadow of the Galilean: The Quest of the Historical Jesus in Narrative Form*. Philadelphia: Fortress, 1987.

Vermes, Geza. *Jesus the Jew: A Historian's Reading of the Gospel.* 2d. ed. New York: Macmillan, 1983.

———. *Jesus and the World of Judaism.* Philadelphia: Fortress, 1984.

———. *The Religion of Jesus the Jew.* Minneapolis: Fortress, 1993.

Witherington, Ben, III. *The Jesus Quest: The Third Search for the Jew of Nazareth.* Downers Grove, Ill.: InterVarsity, 1995.

Wright, N. T. *Who Was Jesus?* Grand Rapids: Eerdmans, 1992.

Index

❖

Acts of Pilate, 223
agriculture of Palestine, 56
Agrippa I, 48-49, 51
Agrippa II, 49
Akiba, Rabbi, 50
Alexander the Great, 44-45
Alexandra Salome, 46
Antiochus IV Epiphanes, 46
Antipater, 47
apocalyptic thought, 70, 101-2, 138, 192
Apocryphon of James, 224-25
Applebaum, S., 56-57
Archelaus, 48
Aristeas, Letter of, 242n.1
Aristobulus II, 46
Atonement, Day of, 72
Augustine, 28
Augustus, 50-51
Aune, David, 21

Bailey, James L. and Lyle D. Vander Broek, 241n.5
Bar Kokhba, 50, 53
Barrett, C.K., 33-34, 184
Bartchy, S. Scott, 61
Beasley-Murray, G. R., 194
Beloved Disciple, 32, 41-42, 186, 211-13
"Benediction Against Heretics", 181
biography, ancient, 20-22
Borg, Marcus, 240
Brown, Raymond, 209, 240, 243n.6, 244n.12
Bruce, F. F., 242n.11

Caligula, 51
Cameron, Ron, 228
canonization, 230-35
Claudius, 51-52
Clement of Alexandria, 34, 226
Cohen, Shaye, 15, 55
Collins, Raymond F., 27, 245n.15
criteria for canonicity
    antiquity, 235

apostolic nature, 233
orthodoxy, 233-34
widespread usage, 235
criteria for historical authenticity
    coherence, 239
    dissimilarity, 237-38
    embarrassment, 239
    multiple attestation, 238
    Palestinian environment, 239
Cross Gospel, 219-20
Crossan, John Dominic, 219-20, 240
Culpepper, R. Alan, 154-55, 171, 243n.3, 244nn.15, 10
Cyrus of Persia, 44

Danker, Frederick W., 146
Davies, W. D., 243n.2
Dead Sea Scrolls, 68, 70, 112, 120, 182-83
Dialogue of the Savior, 217, 223-224, 226
Diaspora, 66
Diatessaron, 25, 231
Diodorus Siculus, 156
disciples
    in John, 186, 196, 205-8
    in Luke, 149, 155, 165-69, 170, 171, 175, 177-79
    in Mark, 82, 87-88, 94, 95, 97, 98-99, 101-6, 133-34, 165
    in Matthew, 113, 118, 126-28, 130-31, 132, 133-34, 136-37, 138, 140, 143, 165
divorce, 36, 54, 75, 136, 158, 239
Domitian, 53
Docetism, 234

education in the first century, 15, 54-56
Edwards, O. C., 157, 159, 160, 244
Egerton Papyrus 2, 220-21
Epiphanius, 215, 218
Epistula Apostolorum, 223
eschatology, 70, 112, 114, 170, 192
Essenes, 67-68
Eusebius, 18, 35, 37, 74, 231

Farmer, W. R., 28, 241
form criticism, 20
Four-Document Theory, 32
Freyne, Sean, 57, 242n.15

Gamble, Harry, 231-32
Gardner-Smith, P., 33
gematria, 121
Gentiles, 38, 40, 61-62, 72, 96, 109, 110, 126, 133, 145-46, 153, 160, 182
Gnosticism, 182, 194, 223, 225, 226, 229-30, 231, 233
"God-fearers," 61, 72
gospel genre, 18-25, 215-17
Gospel of the Ebionites, 215, 217-18
(Coptic) Gospel of the Egyptians, 217, 226
Gospel of the Hebrews, 218
Gospel of Mary, 19, 225-26
Gospel of the Nazoraeans, 218-19
Gospel of Nicodemus, 223
Gospel of Peter, 219-20, 231, 233, 234, 235
Gospel of Thomas, 16, 19, 216, 224, 226, 227-30, 234, 235, 236-37
Gospel of Truth, 217
Griesbach, J. J., 28
Griesbach hypothesis, 28
Gundry, Robert, 115

Hadrian, 53
Hanukkah (Feast of Dedication), 46, 72, 199, 202
Hellenization, 45-46, 58
Herod Antipas, 48-49, 131, 152, 166, 176
Herod the Great, 22, 47-48
Herodium, 49
Herodotus, 156
Hippolytus, 227
Holtzmann, H. J., 29
Horsley, Richard A. with John S. Hanson, 242nn.13, 14
Hyrcanus II, 46-47

Ignatius, 108
Infancy Gospel of Thomas, 19, 216, 221-22, 234
intercalation, 24, 79-80, 92, 94, 95, 100
Irenaeus, 41, 75, 183, 221, 232
irony, 24, 80, 100, 101, 104, 130, 140, 141, 152, 185, 196, 201, 204, 209
Isocrates, 20

Jamnia (Yavneh), 66, 110, 135, 181
Jesus
    conflict with religious leaders, 15, 82, 91-92, 100-104, 113, 129-31, 137, 141, 149-50, 163, 173-74, 199, 202, 204
    crucifixion, 104-5, 116, 141-42, 152, 155, 176-77, 187, 190-91, 210
    education and literacy, 14-15
    exorcisms, 91, 92, 94
    family, 92-93, 218
    healings, 81-82, 91, 92, 94, 96, 97, 99, 123, 126, 127, 132, 134, 163-66, 191, 199, 202
    historical Jesus, 34, 73, 124, 128, 130, 230, 235-240
    resurrection, 98, 105, 114, 115, 128, 142-43, 150, 165, 166, 169, 177-79, 190, 197, 203-4, 211, 220, 224, 229, 234
Jesus Seminar, 236-37
John the Baptist, 89, 122, 127, 129, 131, 150, 155, 157-59, 161, 171, 183, 191, 195-96, 198, 199, 218, 219, 239
John Hyrcanus II, 46
John, Gospel of
    authorship, 41-43
    characteristics, 184-88
    date of writing, 180-81
    intended readers, 181-82
    major themes, 189-93
    outline, 193
    place of writing, 182-83
    reading guide, 194-213
    structure, 188
John Mark, 35-37
Johnson, Luke Timothy, 148, 150
Josephus, 64, 67, 156, 236
Judas Maccabeus, 46, 72
Justin Martyr, 231

Kelber, Werner, 100
kingdom of God, 90, 93, 104, 108, 109, 124, 127, 128-30, 135, 136, 138, 150, 169, 170-71, 172, 174, 184, 185, 191
Kingsbury, Jack Dean, 108-9, 134, 243nn.3, 9, 12
Kloppenborg, John, 31
Koester, Helmut, 215, 241n.4
Kysar, Robert, 180, 192, 209, 244nn.6, 9

Lachmann, Karl, 29
language of Palestine, 45, 55-56
levirate marriage, 54
L traditions, 32, 147
Levites, 59
"Little Apocalypse", 101-2
logos (Word), 182, 186, 190, 194-95
Luke, Gospel of
    authorship, 39-40, 42-43
    characteristics, 146-51
    date of writing, 144-45
    intended readers, 145
    major themes, 151-56
    outline, 156
    place of writing, 145
    reading guide, 156-79

structure, 150-51
M traditions, 32
Machaerus, 49
Malbon, Elizabeth Struthers, 78, 242n.5
Malina, Bruce J. and Richard L. Rohrbaugh, 244nn.7, 11, 13, 17
Marcion, 25, 231-33
Mark, Gospel of
    authorship, 35-36, 42-43
    characteristics, 76-83
    date of writing, 73-74
    intended readers, 76
    major themes, 83-88
    outline, 88
    place of writing, 75-76
    reading guide, 89-106
    structure, 82
Markan priority, 29-32, 108
marriage customs, 53-54
Masada, 47, 49, 68
Matthew, Gospel of
    authorship, 37-39, 42-43
    characteristics, 111-15
    date of writing, 107-8
    intended readers, 108-10, 112, 113, 119-20
    major themes, 115-120
    outline, 120
    place of writing, 110
    reading guide, 121-43
    structure, 114
Meier, John P., 215, 228, 240, 241n.2, 242n.8, 243n.10
Messiah, 70, 84-86, 89, 98, 100, 104, 112, 116, 117, 119, 121, 123, 126, 129, 133, 140, 148, 152, 159-60, 165, 172, 174, 175-76, 178, 189, 195-96, 198, 201, 203, 212, 236
messianic secret, 86-87, 186, 189, 196
Meyers, Carol, 242n.17
Montanism, 231, 233
Muratorian Canon, 234

Nag Hammadi, 223, 224, 225, 226, 227
Nebuchadrezzar, 44
Nero, 52, 74, 75
Nerva, 53
Nicephorus, 218
noncanonical gospels, 19, 214-40

O'Day, Gail R., 211
"oral law," 67
oral traditions, 13-18, 27, 34, 214, 220, 224
Origen, 226

Papias, 18, 35, 37-38, 74, 75

Papyrus Oxyrhynchus 840, 223
parables, 93-94, 128, 130-31, 135, 137, 139, 140, 153, 154, 166-67, 169-70, 171-72, 173, 184, 224, 228
Passover, Feast of, 71, 103, 139-40, 174-75, 176, 182, 188, 195, 199, 200, 206, 218
Patterson, Stephen, 215-16
Paul the apostle, 13, 17, 35, 39-40, 145, 183
Pentecost, Feast of, 71
Pharisees, 67, 113, 122, 124, 125, 127, 129-30, 132, 133, 136, 137-38, 142, 149, 163, 164, 168, 170, 173, 181, 186, 202, 205
Philip, 48
Philo, 50-51, 67, 156, 194
Philostratus, 20
Pilate, Pontius, 79, 104, 141-42, 152, 176, 209-10, 219-20, 236
Platonism, 182
Pliny the Elder, 67
Polybius, 156
Pompey, 46
Priene inscription, 18, 51
priesthood, 59-60, 68
priority of Mark, 29-30
proselytes, 61, 72
Protevangelium of James, 19, 222-23
Ptolemy, 45
Purim, 72
purity laws, 72

Quelle (Q), 16, 30-32, 37, 111, 124, 145, 147, 149, 157, 226-27, 228, 230, 235, 238
Qumran, 68, 70, 112, 120, 182-83

rabbi, 60, 140, 145, 189, 196
redaction criticism, 20, 76
righteousness, 113, 118, 122-25, 130, 136, 139
Robbins, Vernon, 40
Rosh ha-Shanah, 72
Rousseau, John J. and Rami Arav, 242n.13

sacrificial system, 58, 63, 71
Sadducees, 67, 122, 129, 133, 137, 174, 186
Safrai, S., 54-55, 242n.18
Samaritan, 68-69, 128, 154, 167, 170, 185, 198
Sanders, E. P., 240
Sanhedrin, 64, 66, 67, 175
Satan (the devil), 82, 90, 91-92, 94, 101, 123, 127, 161, 167-68, 174, 186
Schürer, Emil, 242n.12
scribes, 38, 60, 93, 101, 102, 108, 124, 138, 140, 145, 149, 174, 175, 186
Secret Gospel of Mark, 223
Seleucus, 45
Septuagint, 40, 148

Serapion, 231, 233-34
Sermon on the Mount, 29, 107, 109, 124-26, 138, 164
Sicarii, 68
"signs source," 187-88
slaves, 60-61
Smith, Robert H., 243nn.11, 13
son of Abraham, 121
Son of David, 85, 112, 116, 117-18, 121, 133, 137, 174
Son of God, 84-85, 86-87, 89, 104, 112, 116-17, 122, 123, 126, 132, 133, 134, 140-42, 148, 151-52, 158, 161-62, 165, 167, 175-76, 189, 196, 199, 203, 212
Son of Man, 85-86, 87, 104, 112, 118, 138-39, 148, 152, 165, 168, 170, 174, 176, 189, 197
source criticism, 20, 76
Stanton, Graham N., 243n.4
Stoicism, 182, 194
Streeter, B. H., 32
Suetonius, 20, 52
suffering, 87, 97-98, 125, 136, 150
synagogue, 14, 66, 71, 108, 113, 119, 127, 131, 163, 181-82, 183, 187
Synoptic Problem, 26-32

Tabernacles ("Booths"), Feast of, 71, 199, 201-2
Tacitus, 52, 236
Talbert, Charles, 20, 151, 156
Tatian, 25, 231
taxes, 58, 134-35, 137, 173, 176

Temple, Jerusalem, 14, 46, 47, 49-50, 51, 56-59, 62, 63-66, 67, 68, 71, 72, 74, 79-80, 100-102, 104, 108, 110, 134, 137, 141-42, 150, 153, 155, 157, 158, 160, 172-74, 179, 188, 197, 204, 208, 219, 221, 222
Thucydides, 21, 156
Tiberius, 51, 161
Titus (emperor), 52, 74, 102
Trajan, 53
transportation and travel, 57-58
Two-Gospel Hypothesis, 28
Two-Source Theory, 31-32

Unleavened Bread, Feast of, 71

Vermes, Geza, 240
Vespasian, 52

Weisse, Hermann, 29
"we-sections" in Acts, 39-40
women, status of, 62, 154-55, 226
worship in Judaism, 79
Wrede, Wilhelm, 86
Wright, N. T., 240

Xenophon, 20

Zealots, 68